Dictionary of Cliché

The Wordsworth
Dictionary of Cliché
—

Terry & David Freedman

Wordsworth Reference

This edition published 1996 by Wordsworth Editions Ltd
Cumberland House, Crib Street, Ware, Hertfordshire SG12 9ET

ISBN 1 85326 369 9

Typeset by Antony Gray
Printed and bound in Great Britain by
Mackays of Chatham plc, Chatham, Kent

INTRODUCTION

Clich s, like individual words, are the currency of everyday speech, but their function is frequently misunderstood. They are often frowned upon as trite, over-used expressions which must be avoided at all costs. Indeed, in literary prose, or wherever an original, sharp concept needs to be put into words, clich s have little place. They belong, instead, to informal language and social intercourse. Ready-made vehicles for easy communication, they draw on the experiences and history which we all share.

Some clich s are from old proverbs, many were once lively images which conveyed meaning with novelty and precision, such as **straitlaced**. Who now thinks of ladies squeezed into tight corsets when they use that expression? Large numbers of clich s have become an essential part of the language, but their origins have been forgotten, as in the case of **to leave someone in the lurch**. Our love of catchy rhymes is reflected in such pairs as **eager beaver**. Some expressions, like **a Parthian shot**, have been changed through time into more comprehensible images — thus **a parting shot** has taken the place of the earlier expression.

This dictionary aims to list some of the vast number of clich s in the English language and to provide wherever possible an account of their origins, highlighting past activities and objects which we might never have heard of otherwise, such as the game of jinks which is the source of high jinks, or the bitts on a ship s deck which gave rise to the phrase to the bitter end. We have included many current clich s, such as surfing the internet and road rage, but whether they will survive as long as those handed down from Chaucer and Shakespeare it is impossible to tell.

The entries are arranged in alphabetical order according to the key word, which is not always the first word but the one which seems most likely to suggest itself to the user. Cross references are contained within the text.

We would like to thank Peter Barlow for his valuable help in tracing the origins of the more elusive clich s.

Terry & David Freedman

A

Abandon   Abandon hope, all ye who enter here
An ironical warning to those who are about to encounter an unpleasant place or situation. The words are a translation of those inscribed over the entrance to hell in Dante s *Inferno*, the first part of the *Divine Comedy* (*c.*1300).

ABC   As easy as ABC
Rudimentary or straightforward. Children learn the alphabet from an ABC book.

Abject   Abject terror
A despicable display of fear. The expression has become common in the twentieth century.

Abject   An abject apology
An apology which is too grovelling and is therefore often used ironically, though it was probably sincere when first noted at the ended of the nineteenth century.

About   To go about face
To change one s decision or opinion. Used as a military command in the USA, it came to be used figuratively around 1900.

Above   Open and above board
In the open. Without concealment or deceit. This phrase probably comes from card-playing etiquette where it is essential to keep your hands above the table (or board). Otherwise a player might use underhand tactics and conceal or swap cards under the table in order to trick other players.

Absence   Absence makes the heart grow fonder
Separation intensifies love. This sentiment was first expressed in an anonymous sixteenth century poem and again was the last line of a song, *The Isle of Beauty* by T. H. Bayly (1797—1839); it became very common by the end of the nineteenth century.

Accidents   A chapter of accidents   see **Chapter**

Accidents Accidents will happen

Even the most careful people suffer misfortunes. This is popularly offered as a consolation to someone after a mishap.

Accounting Creative accounting

Clever management of accounts so as to exploit all possible chances of profit without actually breaking the law. The 1968 film *The Producers* introduced the term.

Accuracy Pinpoint accuracy see Pinpoint

Ace To be within an ace of something

To be close to danger, mishap or success. To be on the verge of something. The lowest throw of the die is the single pip. If you throw two dice and get a single pip on each, you are within an ace of having the lowest throw.

Achilles Achilles' heel

A person s weak spot. In Greek mythology, the mother of Achilles dipped her baby son in the River Styx so that the magic water would make him invulnerable in battle, but as she held him by the heel that part of his body was not protected. He died after being struck by an arrow in his heel.

Aching An aching void

Nostalgia or yearning. The poet William Cowper originated the phrase in his *Olney Hymns* (1779), reminiscing about happy hours in the past:

> They have left an aching void,
> The world can never fill.

Acid The acid test

The ultimate proof of whether someone or something is genuine. The original acid test for gold was to apply nitric acid to the metal. False gold reacted with the metal, but real gold stayed intact.

Acquaintance A nodding acquaintance

Someone you know perhaps only to greet (or nod to). It can also be used to refer to a slight knowledge of a subject (especially literary).

Across Across the board

Affecting everyone equally, regardless of rank. This comes from horse-racing terminology in the USA, where a bet covering all winning possibilities is described as betting across the board. In the 1950s, it began to be used of pay increases and other changes affecting various types of people.

Act   A hard act to follow

Difficult to equal. A stage act may be so good that the following act will struggle to compete. It is often used to refer to a person implying that they have unique talents or qualities.

Act   Act your age!

Behave sensibly! In 1932, the journal *American Speech* indicated that Be your age had become a common saying.

Act   To get in on the act

To intrude on another person s conversation or activity. The expression, Everybody wants to get into the act , which refers to rivalry between actors, became one of the trade marks of the American comedian Jimmy Durante in the 1930s.

Actions   Actions speak louder than words

What people say is less important than what they actually do. Similar proverbs exist in many cultures. This form has been common in English since the nineteenth century.

Adam   Not to know someone from Adam

To be completely unacquainted with someone. Possibly Adam is named because, as the first man, he is the most remote from us and all we know is his name.

Adams   Sweet Fanny Adams   see Sweet

Add   To add fuel to the flames

Make a bad situation worse. This was a common saying in Latin and it also appears in John Milton s *Samson Agonistes* (1671): who knows how he may report thy words by adding fuel to the flame?

Add   To add insult to injury

To heap humiliation on someone after they have already been hurt. The words appear to be from a Latin writer, Phaedrus, who refers to Aesop s fable of the bald man who swatted a fly, missed and smacked himself on the head. The fly saw this as adding insult to injury .

Advocate   The devil's advocate

Someone taking a critical stance whether or not it is their genuine opinion. From the title of Advocatus Diaboli (Devil s Advocate), the person appointed (in the Roman Catholic Church) to oppose the

claims of a candidate for canonisation. The supporter is called Advocatus
Dei (God s Advocate).

Affluent   The affluent society

Those prosperous Western societies after World War II whose people
could rely on social services, a high standard of living and plentiful
supplies of goods. On this theme the economist J. K. Galbraith
published *The Affluent Society* (1958), fixing the concept in the public
mind.

Afraid   To be afraid of your own shadow

Extremely timid. The image has a long history from ancient Greek to
the writings of Sir Thomas More in the sixteenth century.

After   A man (or woman) after my own heart

With similar tastes and attitudes to yourself. In the Bible, in the first
Book of Samuel (13:14), Samuel told Saul that having offended God he
was to be supplanted: The Lord hath sought him a man after his own
heart.

Aga   An Aga saga

A tale, often one dramatised on TV, which deals with romance and
intrigue set in middle-class homes in country villages. The slow-
burning Aga cooker, used instead of the more modern gas or electric
cooker, symbolises the self-conscious return of some wealthier people
to so-called natural ways of living.

Against   Against the grain   see Grain

Agog   To be all agog

Waiting for something to happen. Old French *en gogues* meant
 mirthful , so presumably it came to signify a state of happy anticipation
or curiosity when it came into use in English.

Air   Hot air   see Hot

Air   To walk on air

To be extremely happy. In *Memories and Portraits* (1887) Robert Louis
Stevenson writes: I went home that morning walking upon air.

Airs   To put on airs and graces

To assume an affected manner, an appearance or tone of superiority.
The expression was in use in the seventeenth century, sometimes in a
slightly different form, as in Joseph Addison s travel account of Italy
(1704) when he mentions the airs they give themselves .

Alarm   A false alarm   see **False**

Alas   Alas poor Yorick
A lament for a dead person or scheme. This quotation from Shakespeare s *Hamlet* (Act v, Sc. 1) is often used ironically, but it was originally Hamlet s sad remark on finding the skull of his old friend the court jester in the graveyard.

Alec   A smart Alec   see **Smart**

Alive   Alive and kicking
Active or flourishing. The metaphor is from fish selling, when the freshest fish for sale were those just caught and still moving.

All   All and sundry
All, both collectively and individually. It was in common use from about 1830. Sir Walter Scott uses it in *Old Mortality* (1816).

All   All due respect   see **Respect**

All   All hell broke loose   see **Hell**

All   All in a day's work
Such problems or hardships are routine in human affairs. A common consoling remark in the twentieth century, used as early as 1820 by Sir Walter Scott in *The Monastery*.

All   All my eye   see **Eye**

All   All systems go   see **Systems**

All   All things considered
When everything has been taken into account. This is a cautious formula often used before or after one has assessed a situation.

All   All things to all men
Changing your attitude to suit your company in order to please everybody and avoid controversy. In the Bible in his first epistle to the Corinthians (9 : 20), St Paul wrote: I am made all things to all men, that I might by all means save some.

All   All thumbs   see **Thumbs**

All   All to the good
It will turn out to be an advantage in the end. Current by the end of the nineteenth century, this was originally a commercial term for net profit in accounting.

All   It's all Greek to me   see Greek

All   It's all over bar the shouting   see Shouting

All   To all intents and purposes   see Intents

All   To be all ears
To listen very attentively. In *Comus* John Milton writes: I was all ear, and took in strains that might create a soul under the ribs of death.

All   To be all eyes
To be looking very attentively.

All   To be all there
To be in full possession of your senses. The negative version, he [or she] is not all there , is more common.

All-out   All-out war   see War

All-time   An all-time high (or low)
A success (or failure) never previously achieved. Originally applied to the value of certain currencies in world markets, the phrase is now used in a variety of situations from indicating someone s popularity to assessing a sports team s success rate.

Alley   A blind alley   see Blind

Almighty   The almighty dollar   see Dollar

Alphabet   Alphabet soup
A large number of books and documents, or simply titles and names, especially of organisations known by their initials. The allusion is to a tinned soup fed to children which contains letters of the alphabet made of pasta. An American politician of the 1920s, Alfred E. Smith, used the words to sneer at the government agencies with new names which proliferated under President Roosevelt.

Also   An also ran
Someone who is unsuccessful or unimportant. This is a description used in reporting horse-racing results describing any horse which fails to gain one of the first three places in a race.

Altogether   In the altogether
Naked. A euphemism for altogether naked , dating from the end of the nineteenth century.

American   The American dream
The ideals of democracy, liberty and progress that inspired the founding of the United States. Ronald Reagan is often cited as an example of the American dream, having risen from poverty to the presidency. The phrase was coined by J. T. Adams in *The Epic of America* (1931).

American   The American way
A fair, tolerant method of running society for and by hard-working individuals. The term is meant to sum up the ideals of American society.

Amok   To run amok   see Run

Amused   We are not amused
The situation is nothing to laugh at. This remark was attributed to Queen Victoria by Caroline Holland in her *Notebooks of a Spinster Lady* (1919). An equerry was said to have told an improper story and was thus reproved. Some say that the remark was addressed to Lord Palmerston and others doubt whether it ever happened at all.

Anal   Anal retentive
Excessively orderly, mean, or narrow-minded. In psychoanalysis, it describes a stage of psychosexual development in which the child s interest is fixed on the anal region.

Ancestral   Ancestral home
The place or house inhabited by your forebears. The phrase conjures up a grand residence, but is often used ironically to refer to one s birthplace or parents house.

Ancient   Ancient history
Something which happened long ago and is of no interest or relevance now. This is used as a dismissive remark.

And   And how!
That is certainly the case! The words are used for emphasis and seem similar in use to Italian *e come* and French *et comment*.

And   And so to bed
That is the end of today s events. This closing remark was often used by Samuel Pepys in his diary, kept from 1660—69.

Angel   To sing/dance/speak/cook like an angel

To perform a task superbly well. The comparison of human excellence with angelic qualities has long been common.

Angry   Angry young man

A young protester against establishment values and policies. This was the title of the autobiography of the social philosopher Leslie Paul in 1951 and was used to describe the rebellious heroes of works by many writers of the 1950s, particularly Jimmy Porter in John Osborne s *Look Back in Anger* (1956).

Annie   Little orphan Annie   see Orphan

Annus   Annus   horribilis

A horrible year, a year of disasters. In a speech made in 1992, referring to the recent scandals and misfortunes which had struck the Royal family, Queen Elizabeth II used this phrase to sum up the previous twelve months, quoting from a letter sent to her by a sympathetic correspondent. It is based on the much older *annus mirabilis*, describing 1666, year of marvels, or calamities such as the great fire of London.

Another   But that's another story

Something which is not relevant to the present discussion. This formula comes from fairy tales which sometimes tantalise the reader by mentioning an unresolved part of the plot and end by telling the reader that it belongs to another, future, story.

Ants   Ants in your pants

Restless. The vivid image of crawling biting insects conveys jumpiness, but the phrase probably owes its popularity to its rhyme.

Apple   A rotten apple   see Rotten

Apple   An apple a day keeps the doctor away

Apples are good for the health. This saying appeared in John Ray s proverb collection of 1670 and has been common in different versions.

Apple cart   To upset the apple cart

To ruin everything. To mess up careful plans. The idea of upsetting the cart was used in Roman times with the same meaning, but the qualifiying apple was added in the nineteenth century.

Apple   To be the apple of someone's eye

Beloved, specially favoured by someone. A figurative use of the round, delicious fruit for the pupil of the eye. The image appears in many parts of the Bible.

Apple-pie   In apple-pie order

Perfectly tidy. The French expression *nappe pli e* is the probable origin of this expression in English.

Apron   To be tied to your mother's apron strings

To be unhealthily under the influence or protection of a mother or wife or some other woman. In English law, Apron-string tenure referred to a husband's claim to property passed on by his wife's family. The historian Thomas Babington Macaulay wrote of William of Orange hating to be tied to the apron strings of even the best of wives .

Arguably   Arguably the best / worst

I claim that something is the best (or worst) of its kind. Whereas arguably originally meant that the matter was open to discussion, it is used in the late twentieth century to begin an assertion.

Ark   Out of the Ark

Extremely old-fashioned. A rather contemptuous description, implying that something is so old that it originated in Noah s ark.

Arm   To keep someone at arm's length

Not to allow someone to become too friendly or familiar.

Armchair   An armchair critic / general / traveller

A self-proclaimed expert in the field without any practical experience.

Armed   Armed to the teeth

Over-supplied with weapons. The phrase yarmed to the teth occurs in the fourteenth century *Libeaus Disconus* and in a speech of Richard Cobden in 1849, protesting against overspending on armaments.

Arms   To be up in arms

To react angrily to someone or something. The allusion is to a soldier or an army springing to fight, all weapons ready.

Arms   To greet with open arms

To welcome someone or something.

Art   To get something down to a fine art

To perfect something. To become highly skilled at something. This phrase has been extended from the obvious reference to a handicraft, to a sarcastic use when, for example a person is always late, you might say that their poor time-keeping is so well practised that they have made an art of it.

Arty   Arty crafty

Having a showy or pretentious interest in artistic products and hand-crafted goods. This is now also the title of an arts and crafts magazine in the UK.

Ashes   To rise from the ashes

To be renewed, repaired or rebuilt after a calamity. The phoenix was a legendary bird which was believed to set fire to itself and then resurrect itself from the ashes every five hundred years.

Asking   Asking for trouble

Doing something which will obviously cause problems.

Aunt   An Aunt Sally

Someone set up as the object of disapproval or insults. Traditionally, Aunt Sally was the name of a wooden female head set up as a target for fairground games.

Auspicious   On this auspicious occasion

On this happy, or important occasion. Once a favourite opening for speeches, this phrase was so overworked that it has become a humorous example of a trite phrase.

Avoid   To avoid someone or something like the plague

To keep away from someone or something at all costs. The plague is a powerful and often-used symbol of danger. Thomas More wrote of St Augustine that he avoided school like the plague .

Away   Away with the fairies   see Fairies

Awkward   The awkward squad

Difficult or uncooperative people. Originally this was a military term used to refer to new and untrained recruits, but was used in its extended meaning by the eighteenth century. Robert Burns is said to have used the term in his dying words, to refer to his literary opponents.

AWOL [ay-wol]   To go AWOL

To leave work or duties without permission. This acronym for absent without leave was originally a military usage, but is now used in other situations.

Axe   To have an axe to grind

Having a selfish motive which is usually disguised. As a child, the eighteenth-century Benjamin Franklin was laboriously sharpening an axe for a man who pretended to be interested in how the grinder worked. When his axe was sharpened to his satisfaction, he jeered at Franklin for being gullible.

B

Babe   A babe in arms
A young inexperienced person. This patronising remark is often made to mock the person in question.

Babes   Out of the mouths of babes
Children sometimes show surprising wisdom and insight. This concept occurs in several parts of the Bible, for example in Psalm 8: Out of the mouths of babes and sucklings thou hast ordained strength.

Baby   Baby snatching
Going out with a girl- or boy-friend much younger than yourself. This twentieth-century expression uses a 1930s slang term.

Baby   To be left holding the baby
To be abandoned by everyone and left to take responsibility or blame alone. The older eighteenth-century expression was to be left holding the bag .

Baby   To throw out the baby with the bath water
To reform or remedy something so drastically that the good, essential elements are got rid of together with the bad. A popular saying in the twentieth century.

Back   Back to basics   see Basics

Back   Back to the drawing board   see Drawing Board

Back   Back to square one   see Square one

Back   The back of beyond
Far from civilisation.

Back   To get someone off your back
To free yourself from an interfering or nagging person. Ronald Reagan, as Governor of California (1966—74), popularised the slogan Let s get the government off our backs.

Back   To get someone's back up
To annoy someone. The allusion is to the way a cat arches its back when it is angry.

Back   To have your back against the wall

In extreme danger or hardship, with no obvious way of escape. The phrase was in use in the sixteenth century. During World War I Sir Douglas Haig urged his troops to stand firm with our backs to the wall, each one of us must fight to the end .

Back   To take a back seat

To accept an inferior or less active role than someone else. The seat behind the driver has been considered inferior since coaching days.

Backhanded   A backhanded compliment

Praise which is expressed in such a way that it is clearly more of a criticism. The back of the hand is traditionally associated with scorn or disapproval, the front of the hand is used to pat in a congratulatory gesture.

Backhander   A backhander

A bribe. The image is of a person secretly passing money in his closed hand to someone behind him.

Backseat   A backseat driver

A person who gives unasked-for advice to the person in charge. The description was, and mostly still is, applied to interfering car passengers.

Backwards   To bend over backwards see **Bend**

Bacon   To bring home the bacon

To earn or win something of value, to succeed. This may come from a game common at old country fairs where contestants pursued a greased pig which was awarded to the winner. Alternatively, it could have arisen from the prize of the Dunmow flitch, a side of bacon awarded to a married person who could prove that his or her marriage was harmonious.

Bacon   To save your bacon

To avoid punishment or trouble, to come out unscathed. In this case, bacon is a corruption of an Old English word baec meaning back or body .

Bad   A bad patch   see Patch

Bad   To be bad news   see News

Bad   To be in someone's bad (black) books   see Books

Bad   To turn up like a bad penny

To return, unwanted and a nuisance to everybody. In the past, a bad coin was one made of inferior metal or containing less than its face value. Such coins seemed to occur with undue frequency, like an unwelcome person.

Bag   A bag of tricks

All one s resources. In the past, travelling entertainers carried the props necessary for their acts. In one of his fables, La Fontaine (1694) tells of a fox who carried a sac des ruses .

Bag   Bag and baggage

The entire belongings of a person departing or departed from a place, usually for ever. As a military term in the past it meant the complete possessions of an army which, in honourable retreat, would go without leaving anything behind for the enemy.

Bag   It's in the bag

Almost sure of success. The expression refers to the bag or amount of quarry taken by a hunter or a group of hunters.

Baker   A baker's dozen

Thirteen. Following an act of parliament in 1266, bakers were obliged to make loaves of a precise weight. To protect themselves bakers began to add an extra loaf to each dozen sold.

Bale   To bale (or bail) someone out

To help someone out of a predicament. This is an extension of the legal term for releasing or obtaining the release of someone from custody by putting down money or some other security. The verb is from Old French, meaning to hand over .

Ball game   It's a whole new ball game

A completely changed situation. The expression originated in the USA in the 1970s, ball game referring to baseball, but also to any game played with a ball. New rules would change the nature of a ball game.

Ball   On the ball

Very efficient, alert. This refers to the game of baseball where a pitcher who puts spin or speed on the ball tends to strike out more batters.

Ball   The ball is in your court

It is up to you to do something. The term is from various sports, indicating that it is the turn of the player addressed.

Ball   To keep the ball rolling

To keep an activity going. Though this seems to be a reference to ball games in general, a much earlier use of the expression probably refers to the movement of the planets.

Band wagon   To jump on the band wagon

To join or give support to a political party, or a person or movement which seems to be assured of success. The traditional band wagon in parades in the USA was the brightly coloured vehicle which carried the band at the front of the procession.

Bank   To cry all the way to the bank

Celebrate a big financial gain which other people consider to be undeserved. In his autobiography (1973), the pianist Liberace popularised the expression when he used it as a retort to critics who thought his sentimental style of playing did not merit the success it had with the public. Another version is, To laugh all the way to the bank.

Baptism   A baptism of fire

A painful initiation. In France it was traditionally used to describe a soldier s first experience of battle. It may originally have come from the experience of those martyrs who wished to embrace Christianity formally, but were burnt at the stake before they could be baptised by a priest; those martyred by other violent methods were said to have undergone a baptism of blood.

Bare-faced   A bare-faced lie   see Lie

Bargained   To get more than you bargained for   see More

Bark   Someone's bark is worse than his bite

A person is not as fierce or disagreeable as his or her manner suggests. This proverbial expression is at least three centuries old.

Bark   To bark up the wrong tree

To be following the wrong line of enquiry. In early nineteenth-century America, racoon hunters trained packs of dogs to pursue the racoons hiding in the trees at night. Occasionally the barking dogs were on the wrong scent beneath the wrong tree.

Barking   Barking mad

Crazy, angry. The verb to bark was used in the past not only of dogs but also of any loud harsh noise, such as a rumbling stomach. Probably the phrase refers to the furious cries and raucous noises that often accompany insanity.

Barrel   A barrel of laughs

Very funny. This is frequently used sarcastically to indicate someone or something not at all funny, possibly from circus acts involving monkeys or clowns performing tricks with a barrel. However, as early as Chaucer, English writers used barrel as a general term for a great many .

Barrel   To have someone over a barrel

To have someone in your power. The origin may be in an old method of reviving a person who had nearly drowned. The victim was placed over a barrel which was rocked back and forth in an attempt to empty the lungs of water.

Barrel   To scrape the barrel

To be obliged to use your last and weakest resources. Before modern methods of food preservation were discovered household supplies were kept for months in barrels and the quality of the food at the bottom of the container was often scarcely edible.

Basics   Back to basics

A return to the supposed traditional standards of good practice and behaviour in society, often lamented as lost when the older generation view the innovations brought in by the young. Schools in the nineteenth century often advertised that they taught the basics, meaning reading, writing and arithmetic. British prime minister John Major used this clich as part of a political campaign in the early 1990s.

Bat   Like a bat out of hell

Very quickly. Bats being nocturnal and sinister-looking have traditionally been connected with witchcraft, hell and death. The popular image of the creature was of an evil shape swooping rapidly down on human victims from out of its evil lair. The phrase was used as the title of a bestselling rock album in the 1980s by Meatloaf.

Bath water   To throw out the baby with the bath water   see Baby

Batten   To batten down the hatches

Take defensive or preventive action. As a nautical term from the early nineteenth century, it meant the precautions taken on a ship before a storm. These included making fast doors and hatches and any movable parts.

Battle   A battle royal

A fierce fight or contest. In cockfighting, the term described a contest in which several birds fought until the survivor was declared the winner.

Battle   A ding-dong battle

An argument, fight or controversy which involves rapid ferocious exchanges. It has been suggested that the regular chime of a clock has been evoked here, but ding dong may also refer to the clanging of metal armour.

Battle   A pitched battle   see Pitched

Battle   Half the battle

Something that contributes significantly to a satisfactory result. In military history, it has often been observed that successful generals have half-won their battles before they started because of their excellent preparation and planning.

Battle   A losing battle   see Losing

Be   Be that as it may

Nevertheless. This phrase from the late nineteenth century is often used to introduce an argument.

Be-all   The be-all and end-all

The most important factor, the ultimate purpose. Shakespeare, who may have originated it, used the expression in *Macbeth* (Act 1, Sc. 6) where Macbeth contemplates the murder of King Duncan: that but this blow might be the be-all and the end-all here .

Beam   On your beam ends

At the end of your resources, desperate. This is a nautical term for a ship which has keeled over through an angle of 90¡ on to its beam or side. In this situation it is about to founder and is therefore unlikely to be able to finish the voyage.

Beans   Full of beans

High-spirited and energetic. Beans were once a staple food for the poor, therefore a well-fed person might be full of beans and ready to undertake demanding tasks with relish.

Beans   Not worth a row (or hill) of beans

Worthless. For centuries beans, compared with meat, have been considered a low-cost food. In *Troilius and Cressida* (1380), Chaucer wrote: Swich arguments ne been nat worth a bene. A hill of beans describes the American method of planting in mounds, rather than rows.

Beans   To spill the beans

To confess. To let out some information. To reveal something.

Bear   To bear the brunt

Suffer the worst pain or shock of an attack or mishap. The brunt, as used by John Lydgate in the *Chronicle of Troy* (1430), meant the main force of the enemy attack.

Beard   To beard the lion in his den

To confront your opponent or a wrongdoer fearlessly face to face. In the Bible (Samuel 1 17:35), David pursued a lion which had stolen one of his lambs. When the lion prepared to attack him: I caught him by his beard, and smote him, and slew him.

Beat   To beat about the bush

To approach a topic or activity in a roundabout way. Shooting parties employ someone to beat the undergrowth to startle the birds out of the bushes so that the hunters can eventually fire at them directly.

Beat   To beat someone hollow

To defeat someone completely. For centuries hollow has carried this meaning of completely and its origin is in dispute, though it has been suggested that it is connected with wholly.

Beat   To beat the living daylights out of someone

To punish someone with physical violence. It has been suggested that daylights means eyes in boxing slang, but it is more probable that the phrase is a corruption of an older threat to beat the liver and lights out of someone, the lights being the lungs.

Beaten   Off the beaten track

Remote. Away from civilisation. Straying from the norm. The beaten track is the one used by everyone, so that it is well worn and easy to use.

Beauty   Beauty sleep   see Sleep

Beaver   An eager beaver   see Eager

Bed   A bed of roses

A comfortable, beautiful situation. The phrase has been in use since at least the sixteenth century and is usually used in the negative to warn, for example, that life is not a bed of roses.

Bed   And so to bed   see And

Bed   To get out on the wrong side of the bed

To start the day feeling disgruntled. The idea stems from ancient Rome where it was regarded as unlucky to put the left foot down first. If you did so, you could expect the day to go badly.

Bee   To have a bee in your bonnet

To be obsessed with something. As early as the seventeenth century, Robert Herrick connected a bee in the bonnet with insanity in the *Mad Maid s Song*: . . . the bee which bore my love away. I ll seek him in your bonnet brave.

Beeline   To make a beeline for someone or something

To go straight to someone or something. It is commonly supposed that bees always move in a straight line towards their hive.

Beg   To beg, borrow or steal

To get something in any way possible. The phrase is at least seven centuries old and appears in Chaucer s *Canterbury Tales* in The Tale of the Man of Law : Thou most for indigence or stele, or begge, or borwe thy despence.

Beggar   To beggar description

Impossible to express in words. Shakespeare says of Cleopatra s beauty: It beggar d all description (*Antony and Cleopatra*, Act ii, Sc. 2).

Bell   Clear as a bell

Very clear. This phrase alludes to the resonance of a bell rung over large distances and has been in use for at least three hundred years.

Bell   That rings a bell   see Ring

Belt   To have something under your belt

A success that you can congratulate yourself on. Probably the reference is to food digested in your stomach.

Belt   To hit below the belt   see Hit

Bend   To bend over backwards

To go to a lot of trouble and personal sacrifice to help someone else. The image has been in constant use during the twentieth century.

Beneath   Beneath contempt

Utterly despicable. Originally beneath was an effective superlative, but over-use in this case has weakened it.

Benefit   To give someone the benefit of the doubt
To assume someone is innocent or that they are telling the truth if there is any uncertainty whatsoever. The law is based on the premise that a person is innocent until proved guilty, so that a verdict of not guilty must be passed in a court of law if there is any doubt.

Berth   To give someone a wide berth
Take care to avoid someone or something. In nautical language, this was an injunction to sailing ships to keep a suitable distance between themselves and other ships, especially those riding at anchor and liable to swing round.

Beside   To be beside yourself
To behave in an uncharacteristic or abnormal way through shock or some other deep emotion. In the Bible in Acts 26: 24, St Paul is addressed thus: Paul, thou art beside thyself; much learning makes thee mad.

Best   To make the best of a bad job   see Job

Bet   You can bet your boots
You can be very sure of something. Boots were held to be the most prized possession of American cowboys and gold miners. If they gambled on their boots, they were very confident of not losing.

Better   To have seen better days
It is worn out or shabby.

Better   Your better half
Husband or wife. Once, in ancient Rome and in Elizabethan England, an affectionate description of a beloved friend or spouse, now it is always jocular.

Between   Between the devil and the deep blue sea
A choice of two evils. In the days of sailing ships, a sailor applying pitch to caulk the seams of the vessel had to lower himself below the jutting plank (known as the devil) at the water line in order to plug any gaps between it and the hull. He could not easily get back on board and was dangerously close to the sea.

Between   Between you me and the gatepost
In confidence. A common opening remark before an item of gossip. Presumably the gatepost and bedpost, like the proverbial doorpost, were thought of as silent witnesses.

Beyond   Beyond the pale   see **Pale**

Big   Big brother is watching you

A sinister authority is spying on you. This is from George Orwell s *Nineteen Eighty-Four* (1949), a view of the future in which a dictatorship headed by Big Brother rules all aspects of human life. His portrait with the caption Big Brother is watching you was on display everywhere.

Big   Big deal   see **Deal**

Big   To open your big mouth   see **Mouth**

Big-wig   To be a big-wig

A very important person. When wigs were worn in the past, longer ornate ones signified high status, just as today the judge s wig is a symbol of his office.

Bike   On your bike!

Go away, or stir yourself to travel in order to seek work. The latter meaning has overtaken the former since the late 1980s when Tory minister Norman Tebbit suggested that the unemployed should go to other towns, just as his own father had cycled around in search of work.

Bill   Bill and coo

To whisper loving remarks to a girl- or boy-friend. The reference is to the characteristic noise of doves which symbolise loving, peaceful couples.

Bird's   A bird's eye view

An overall view of something. Originally this indicated one type of perspective achieved by drawing something as if seen from above, as a bird might view it.

Birds   Birds of a feather flock together

People of similar tastes and attitudes (often with the implication that these are undesirable) associate with each other. The proverb arose from the obvious fact that birds of the same species are seen together. By the time John Bunyan wrote *The Life and Death of Mr Badman* (1680) the first four words of the proverb formed a common phrase: They were birds of a feather, well met for wickedness.

Birds   The birds and the bees

Human sexual behaviour as explained to children by parents and teachers. This euphemism is an ironical reference to the traditional indirect method of teaching children about sex by allusion to the mating habits of insects and birds.

Birds   To kill two birds with one stone see **Kill**

Bit   A bit on the side

A sexual partner or sexual activity indulged in secretly by a married person with someone other than the spouse, As used in twentieth-century Britain, it always implies a superficial, temporary relationship.

Bit   To get the bit between your teeth

To be obstinate, to rebel. When a horse grasps the bit or metal mouthpiece in its teeth, its master can no longer control it with the bridle.

Bite   To bite the bullet

Prepare to suffer hardship bravely. Before anaesthetics made operations bearable, wounded soldiers were given a lead bullet to grip between their teeth to brace themselves for the surgeon s knife. Another possible reference is to the Indian Uprising in 1857, sparked off when both devout Muslim and Hindu soldiers rebelled against having to grip cartridges between their teeth before inserting them into their rifles. The problem was that the cartridges were greased with lard, and pig meat was forbidden to Muslims and all meat to Hindus.

Bite   To bite the dust

To be defeated, killed or finished. The image, from the description of a fighting man falling dead from his horse, was sometimes used in literature, but became common in early twentieth-century cowboy and Indian films.

Bite   To bite off more than you can chew

To take on more than you can accomplish, to be too ambitious. The image of putting too much in your mouth dates from the Middle Ages.

Bites   Two bites of the cherry see **Cherry**

Bitten   Once bitten, twice shy

After having a bad experience, you approach similar situations with greater caution. This is an old proverb which alludes to the way that animals as well as humans learn to be wary through experience.

Bitter   A bitter pill see **Pill**

Bitter   To fight to the bitter end see **End**

Black   A black hole see **Hole**

Black   Not as black as you are painted
Not as bad as you are said to be.

Black   The black sheep of the family   see **Sheep**

Black   To swear black is white
To lie blatantly.

Black   The pot calling the kettle black   see **Pot**

Blank   A blank cheque   see **Cheque**

Blank   To draw a blank   see **Draw**

Blanket   A wet blanket
Someone who spoils other people s fun. The image is from the damp
cloth used to smother flames when fire breaks out.

Bleed   To bleed someone white
To extract as much money from someone as possible. The reference
may be to money being the vital element (i.e. blood) of commerce.

Bleeds   My heart bleeds for you   see **Heart**

Blind   A blind alley
A street without an exit at one end, or a situation without hope. The
figurative meaning has been in use since the sixteenth century.

Blind   A blind spot
An area in a person s understanding where he or she is lacking in
judgement or perception. The metaphorical usage comes from the
physical blind spot, which is not sensitive to light, situated on the retina
where the optic nerve enters the eye.

Blind   Blind drunk
Extremely intoxicated. The concept of being too drunk to see anything
is at least as old as the verse of Jeremy Taylor, who says of a drunk
(1622): He s bewitch t . . . or blinde.

Blind   To turn a blind eye   see **Eye**

Bliss   Unalloyed bliss
Pure pleasure. The phrase dates from the nineteenth century and
compares pure happiness with pure metal unmixed with other
substances.

Blonde   A dumb blonde   see **Dumb**

Blood   Bad blood

Hatred between individuals or rival groups. In the Middle Ages, the blood was associated with strong emotions such as anger and irascibility. To breed bad blood was to incite people to enmity and aggression.

Blood   Fresh (or new) blood

A new, usually younger, member of a concern who will bring innovation and improvements.

Blood   In cold blood

Done deliberately, not in the heat of passion.

Blood   Like getting blood out of a stone

Almost impossible. This is a nineteenth-century expression much used by Charles Dickens.

Blood   To make your blood boil

To make you angry. This comes from the association of blood with the passions, especially anger, since the Middle Ages.

Blow   Blow by blow

In step by step detail. This originally described the typical delivery of American sports commentators broadcasting commentaries on boxing matches. They gave graphic descriptions of every blow.

Blow   To blow a raspberry

To make a noise conveying derision by blowing through the lips with the tongue slightly protruding. The expression comes from rhyming slang for fart , which is raspberry tart , hence raspberry.

Blow   To blow hot and cold

To be indecisive, to waver. The expression comes from a fable of Aesop which tells of a satyr and a man dining together on a cold day. When the man used his breath to warm his hands and then to cool his soup, the satyr objected, taking it as a sign of hypocrisy and indecision.

Blow   To blow the whistle on someone

To inform against someone who is doing wrong. In the nineteenth century, it simply meant to call an end to an activity, but has come to imply performing a public-spirited action by helping to stop an injustice.

Blue   A blue-chip company

A commercial company of high standing, financially sound and increasingly good prospects. The term is from gambling where a blue chip has the highest value.

Blue   A bolt from the blue   see **Out of the blue**

Blue   Blue blood

Aristocratic. This is a translation of Spanish *sangre azul,* used for those Spaniards who had not intermarried with the dark-skinned Moors. Their blood was called blue because the blue veins were conspicuous under their fair skin.

Blue   Once in a blue moon   see **Once**

Blue   Out of the blue

A sudden unexpected, sometimes catastrophic, event. Thunder or lightning from a calm blue sky conveys the unexpectedness of a disaster. Describing the terror of the French Revolution (1837), Thomas Carlyle wrote of arrests sudden really as a bolt out of the blue .

Blue   The blue-rinse brigade

An uncomplimentary description of older women, especially when they act as a group. One way of enhancing grey hair is to give it a blue tint. The use of brigade suggests that a group of active middle-aged women is intimidating.

Blue   True blue   see **True**

Bluff   To call someone's bluff

To uncover a deception, or to challenge someone s threat or dubious claims. The expression comes from poker where players bet as to which player has the best hand. Sometimes players bluff or deliberately stake on a bad hand so as to tempt the other player to throw up his cards and forfeit his stake.

Blushing   The blushing bride

The shy bride. The hackneyed description of the young inexperienced girl on her wedding day belongs to the newspapers and magazines of the start of the twentieth century.

Board   Above board   see **Above**

Board   Across the board   see **Across**

Board   To go by the board

To go for ever, to be got rid of for good. Here, board means the ship s side from which rubbish is thrown.

Boat   Don't rock the boat

Do not upset a peaceful situation. A lively image from boating, where a quiet sail can turn to disaster if someone moves clumsily on a small craft. The popular song *Sit Down, You re Rockin the Boat* (1950) fixed the words in the language.

Boat   To be in the same boat

To be in the same (usually difficult) situation. Many cultures share this image of people together in a vessel all vulnerable to the same dangers.

Boat   To miss the boat

To fail to seize an opportunity.

Bobtail   Ragtag and bobtail   see Rag

Bodice   Bodice ripper

A romantic modern novel with much titillating detail of pursuit and seduction. The bodice was a short tight-fitting laced garment worn over a blouse or dress and figures in seduction scenes in eighteenth-century novels.

Body   To keep body and soul together

To manage to feed, clothe and provide yourself with shelter.

Bolt   To shoot your bolt

To try your utmost, to use up all your resources. In the Middle Ages, the bolt was a type of arrow used with the crossbow. An archer who had used up his bolts was left defenceless.

Bombshell   To drop a bombshell

To give sudden and astounding news. The expression arose in World War I from the shock following a bomb.

Bone   A bone of contention

The cause of a quarrel. The image of dogs fighting over a bone has frequently been transferred to human disputes and appeared in John Heywood s *Proverbs* (1562).

Bone   To have a bone to pick with someone   see Pick

Bone   Too near the bone   see **Near**

Bones   I feel it in my bones   see **Feel**

Bones   To make no bones about it
To come straight to the point, to act without fuss or scruples. The word bones is an old term for dice. Some players try to coax the dice into giving a high score, other make no bones and simply throw and accept the outcome.

Bonnet   To have a bee in your bonnet   see **Bee**

Book   A closed book
Not easily accessible or understood.

Book   An open book
Easily understood.

Book   To go by the book
To act according to the rules. The book is often used to symbolise the ultimate authority in various situations.

Book   To read someone like a book
To perceive the motivation and attitudes of a person, to judge their character. In *Romeo and Juliet* (Act 1, Sc. 3), Shakespeare wrote: Read o er the volume of young Paris face.

Books   A turn-up for the books
A sudden reversal of fortune, unexpected luck. This is from accounting where a sudden rise in income is a turn up in the cash book — especially in racecourse betting when the bookie makes a profit.

Books   To be in someone's bad (black) books
To be out of favour. The original expression referred to black books and meant literally a book which contained a list of disgraced persons, such as was kept by some Oxford colleges in the eighteenth century.

Books   To cook the books   see **Cook**

Boon   A boon companion
A good, cheerful friend. Boon, from French *bon* or good, implies a companion in jollity and possibly drinking. The phrase is used almost exclusively of a man.

Boots   You can bet your boots   see **Bet**

Born   I was not born yesterday

I am not a fool. The retort, used to squash someone who tries to treat the speaker as innocent or gullible, has been in use since the early nineteenth century.

Borrow   To beg borrow or steal   see Beg

Borrowed   Borrowed plumes

Airs and graces, a fine show with no real merit. The allusion is to the fable of the jay which dressed up in peacock s feathers.

Bottle   To bottle up your feelings

To suppress any display of emotion. The implication is that such strict control is psychologically harmful.

Bottom   Bottom drawer

Goods or money set aside in preparation for marriage by a young woman. In the past, it was the custom to store up linen and clothes in the deep bottom drawer of a clothes chest.

Bottom   The bottom line

The final result or the most important element. In accounting, the bottom line of a financial statement shows the final balance or income. In the twentieth century it has come to mean the crux of the matter in hand or the ultimate consequence of an event.

Bottom   To bottom out

To reach the lowest point. The image is from shipping when a boat reaches its lowest point in the water.

Bow   To have two strings to your bow

To have more than one option. To have two ways of doing something. This derives from the tradition of an archer carrying a spare string for his bow. It appeared during the fifteenth century.

Boy   The old boy network   see Network

Boys   Boys will be boys

Children, especially boys, will naturally behave with a degree of immaturity. There is a similar saying in Latin and it was common in the nineteenth century. Nowadays it is used less as an excuse for children than as an ironical comment on the childish or wild behaviour of some adult men.

Brain   The brain drain
The late twentieth-century emigration of scientists and technologists to the USA from Britain for better pay and working conditions.

Brain   To have something on the brain
To be obsessed with something.

Brains   To pick someone's brains   see **Pick**

Brains   To rack your brains   see **Rack**

Brass   To get down to brass tacks
Concentrate on the essential details of the matter. Possibly the image comes from the fact that shops selling material by the yard measured it precisely by unrolling the stuff on a counter which had brass tacks embedded in it to indicate a yard s length.

Brass   Top brass
Those in authority, the directors. The term is from the army where high-ranking officers were referred to as brass hats or top brass because they wore gold-coloured insignia on their hats.

Bread   To know which side your bread is buttered on
To be aware of what is advantageous for you.

Bread   To take the bread out of someone's mouth
To deprive someone of their basic needs. As in most of the expressions referring to bread, it symbolises the necessities of life.

Breadline   On the breadline
Living at subsistence level. The line is the queue of poor people waiting for charity handouts of bread or soup from government or charitable organisations.

Break   Make or break   see **Make**

Break   To break the ice
To open conversation in an awkward situation or to make a start on something difficult or unpleasant.

Breath   To waste your breath
To speak when nobody is listening to you.

Bricks   To come down like a ton of bricks
To scold someone fiercely.

Bridge   Water under the bridge   see **Water**

Bright-eyed and bushy-tailed
Lively, healthy and energetic. The image is from descriptions of the squirrel, possibly from children s stories in the early twentieth century. It is a rather arch, jocular comment on a person s general condition and spirits.

Bring   To bring the house down
To evoke enthusiastic applause for a performance. Victorian music-hall performers might comment on a feeble response from the audience by saying sarcastically that their applause was so loud it would bring the house down.

Broad   It is as broad as it is long
It is all the same.

Broad   To have broad shoulders   see **Shoulders**

Brooms   New brooms sweep clean
Newcomers to a situation or job tend to make changes.

Brownie   To win Brownie points
Earn praise or rewards. The junior Girl Guides, or Brownies, can earn an award after accumulating a certain number of points for proven skills. In a wider context it came to be used jokingly and usually negatively, as in You won t win any Brownie points for that!

Buck   The buck stops here
I accept ultimate responsibility. In 1949, USA president Harry Truman is said to have had these words posted up in his office. See also **To pass the Buck.**

Buck   To pass the buck
To evade responsibility by shifting the onus on to someone else. The expression comes from the game of poker as played in the nineteenth century when a piece of buckshot would be passed round to remind players who was next to deal.

Bull   A bull in a china shop
A person who behaves clumsily or tactlessly. The image of such a large animal in such a vulnerable shop is vivid. Possibly it was inspired by Aesop s fable of the ass in a potter s shop. It has been suggested that the image of a bull instead of an ass was suggested by a British cartoonist who was satirising the British (represented by the figure of John Bull) dealing very clumsily with the China trade.

Bull   A red rag to a bull   see **Red**

Bull   To take the bull by the horns
To confront a problem without hesitation. It has been suggested that matadors grasp the bull s horns in order to wrestle it to the ground. Alternatively, the origin of the image may be in the farming practice of taking hold of a tethered bull by its horns.

Bum's   To give someone the bum's rush
To throw somebody out or ostracise them. In 1920s America, bums, or undesirable customers, were physically ejected from clubs and bars by rough doorkeepers.

Bureaucrats   Faceless bureaucrats
Anonymous civil servants who are suspected of running the country behind the scenes while elected representatives come and go. This phrase is often invoked by those who fear the European Union.

Burn   Go for the burn!
Exercise until it hurts This advice was made famous by actress Jane Fonda in the 1980s when she advocated and practised a vigorous and demanding exercise routine.

Burn   Burn the midnight oil
Study or work late into the night. The reference is to oil lamps in use before the days of electric light.

Burn   To burn your boats (or bridges)
To start on a course of action leaving oneself no way of turning back. This arises from the old military custom of destroying a bridge or boats used to gain access to enemy territory.

Burning   The burning question   see **Question**

Bury   To bury the hatchet
To make peace. The custom of North American Indians tribes was to bury a symbolic weapon to ratify a peace treaty.

Bush   To beat about the bush   see **Beat**

Bushel   To hide your light under a bushel   see **Hide**

Business   Mind your own business   see **Mind**

Butter   Butter would not melt in his or her mouth
He or she is too angelic-seeming to be credible. This proverbial saying appeared in John Heywood s collection (1546).

Butterfingers   To be a butterfingers
Clumsy.

Buzz   A buzz word   see Word

Buzz   To get a buzz out of doing something
To be stimulated. The expression was originally American slang for the pleasant sensation experienced when taking drugs, but now extended to that obtained from any source.

Bygones   Let bygones be bygones
Agree to forget past grievances and quarrels. The word bygone meaning a happening in the past is rarely used as a noun outside this phrase.

C

Cain   To raise Cain
To have a fit of anger, to cause a fuss. This is a reference to the Bible story of Cain who killed his brother Abel in furious jealousy.

Cake   A piece of cake
Something achieved with very little effort. In the nineteenth century, Southern American black people held a traditional contest for the best-dressed couple. The contestants simply had to walk slowly round the prize cake until it was cut and awarded to those judged to be winners.

Cake   To sell like hot cakes   see Hot

Cake   You can't have your cake and eat it
You can t retain a thing and use it up. You can t have it both ways. The proverb suggests that difficult choices have to be made.

Calf   To kill the fatted calf   see Kill

Call   The call of nature
A need to go to the toilet. This is one of numerous euphemisms in use for the need to urinate and defecate, terms which are not socially acceptable.

Call   The call of the wild
The appeal of natural surroundings far from civilisation. The expression became common with the publication of Jack London s *Call of the Wild* (1903) based on his experiences in the Canadian wilderness.

Call   To call a spade a spade   see Spade

Call   To call it quits   see Quits

Call   To call someone's bluff   see Bluff

Call   To call your soul your own   see Soul

Calm   The calm before the storm
The deceptively peaceful phase before the onset of trouble, such as war. Folklore has it that violent tempests often come unexpectedly after a period of still weather.

Can To open up a whole new can of worms

A complicated problem, the extent of which is not obvious until you start to look into it. The expression may come from fishing where the mass of wriggling, tangled bait is kept in a closed container; it may also refer to the unpleasant shock of opening canned food and finding it contaminated.

Candle Not to be fit to hold a candle to someone see Hold

Candle The game is not worth the candle see Game

Cannon A loose cannon

A grave threat. Serious danger. On sailing ships, cannon were attached to the deck on mounts. If a cannon came loose from its mount it could roll across the deck and fire inward on to its own ship.

Cap Cap in hand

In the humiliating position of having to beg for something. Doffing the cap before a superior is an old tradition, holding it out for money is the mark of the beggar.

Cap If the cap fits, wear it

If a criticism or a situation applies to you, recognise and accept it. This is an allusion to the fact that hats come in different sizes. The original expression referred to a dunce s or fool s cap.

Cap To put your thinking cap on

Consider carefully before you come to a decision. This arises from the legal tradition whereby a judge puts on an official cap before passing the death sentence.

Captain A captain of industry

The director or owner of a large industry. The expression has been in use since the 1920s and suggests that running a big company is like being in control of a ship. The expression was first used by Thomas Carlyle in *Past and Present* (1843).

Carbuncle A monstrous carbuncle see Monstrous

Cards To lay your cards on the table

To show that you are being completely frank. In many card games the players have to turn their cards face up so that the other players can see what they have.

Cart   To put the cart before the horse
To reverse the natural or proper order of things. This expression is found in medieval texts and in many other cultures.

Carte   To give someone *carte blanche*
To confer absolute freedom of action on another person. The French words mean white, or blank, paper , that is, a paper empty apart from a signature so that the recipient can write his or her own terms. Its main use was military, in order to obtain unconditional surrender, but it is now purely figurative, meaning to let someone do as he or she likes.

Cash   Cash-flow problems
Shortage of money. Commercially, cash flow refers to statements showing where income is from and how it is disposed of, but in common ironical usage it means that a person s income is not sufficient to cover any debts.

Cast-iron   A cast-iron alibi (or case)
So strong that it cannot be challenged. Iron heated with a large amount of carbon is extremely strong and has to be cast or poured into a mould to be shaped and cannot easily be broken.

Caste   To lose caste
To lose your social position. Hindu society is divided into hereditary castes and the word has come to be used of other societies to mean social class or rank.

Castles   Castles in the air (or in Spain)
Unrealisable dreams of wealth, romance or adventure. The proverbial expression describes dreamers as building castles in the air. Building castles in Spain is a translation of the equivalent French saying.

Cat   A cat fight
A quarrel between two women. This twentieth-century term implies that women, like cats, will disagree in a shrill, ferocious manner.

Cat   A fat cat   see Fat

Cat   Not enough room to swing a cat in
A very small space. The cat o nine tails was the notorious whip used to keep discipline in the navy in the past. In the limited room on a ship space had to be found to operate the cat effectively.

Cat   To let the cat out of the bag
To reveal a secret unintentionally. Piglets were taken to medieval markets in sacks and swindlers sometimes substituted a cat for the

piglet once the buyer had paid. If the cat escaped the dealer would inadvertently reveal his deception.

Cat   To play cat and mouse with someone
To toy with a helpless victim in the way that cats play with mice before killing them.

Cat   When the cat's away
When the person in authority is absent his or her charges will take advantage. The full version, which appears in sixteenth-century proverb collections, is When the cat s away, the mice will play.

Catch   Catch 22
A situation in which a kind of mad logic prevails, defying any solution. The phrase was invented by Joseph Heller for the title of his novel (1961) about US fliers in World War II. Captain Yossarian tries to get out of flying missions on the grounds that he is mentally ill and the doctor confirms that according to regulations, he must ground any bombardier who is crazy. However, the catch is that anyone who wants to get out of flying missions is definitely not crazy.

Catch   To catch someone red-handed   see Red-handed

Catch   To catch someone with his trousers down
To surprise someone in a shameful or compromising situation. This derives from two possible embarrassments, being found while urinating or while having sex.

Caught   To be caught napping   see Napping

Ceremony   To stand on ceremony
To keep strictly to the rules of behaviour and rank. The expression is usually used in the negative to encourage someone to behave in a relaxed way and to drop formalities.

Chalice   To hand someone the poisoned chalice
To make an offer which is apparently a gift or an asset but which is in reality a burden or severely damaging to the recipient. There are many stories of poison disguised as a refreshing drink, such as that which killed Gertrude in Shakespeare s *Hamlet*.

Chalk   At the chalk face
In the school classroom. A twentieth-century expression (echoing the mining term at the coal face) meaning the real situation, with all its problems, which pupils and teachers experience, rather than the theoretical one discussed by academics.

Chalk   By a long chalk

By a big margin. Games in pubs and clubs were traditionally scored by means of chalk marks on a board where the winner was easily identified by the length of his chalked scores.

Chalk   Chalk and talk

The traditional way of teaching, featuring teacher, blackboard and pupils in rows rather than more modern methods. There is an implied criticism of tradition in this phrase which came into use in the 1960s.

Chalk   The difference between chalk and cheese

The lack of similarity between two people or things despite a superficial resemblance. In the Middle Ages one test of sanity was to see if the patient could taste the difference between chalk and cheese.

Champ   To champ at the bit

To show impatience to go into action. At the start of a race horses may chew at the bit, the metal mouthpiece which controls them. The expression has been used metaphorically for the last hundred years.

Chance   Chance is (or would be) a fine thing

There is no possibility of doing what has been suggested. If it were possible, it would be very acceptable.

Chance   Not the ghost of a chance   see Ghost

Change   A change of heart

An altered attitude, usually more favourable, to someone or something.

Change   A change of scene

The beneficial effect of moving to a new environment. This has been a well-worn expression in the twentieth century.

Change   A sea change

A transformation. Shakespeare introduced the phrase in Ariel s song in *The Tempest* (Act 1, Sc. 2). The spirit sings of the transformed body of Ferdinand s father who was thought to have perished at sea. The poetry of the phrase has caught people s fancy in the late twentieth century.

Change   The leopard cannot change its spots

A person is not likely to undergo a radical change of character. This observation is found in the Bible (Jeremiah 13: 23): Can the Ethiopian change his skin, or the leopard his spots?

Change   To change your tune

Reverse your previous opinion or standpoint on a certain issue.

Referring to opinions and attitudes as songs or tunes goes back to the Middle Ages.

Chapter   A chapter of accidents
A series of mishaps which relate to one episode or period, just as connected matters in a book come under one chapter heading.

Chapter   To quote chapter and verse
To support a belief or assertion with precise evidence from an authoritative source. In the Western world, quotations from chapters of the Bible as the ultimate authority have been used to confirm or disprove ideas.

Charmed   A charmed life
An unusual ability to come out unscathed from trouble or danger. Shakespeare was probably the first to use the phrase in *Macbeth* (Act v, Sc. 3) when Macbeth defied Macduff to harm him: I bear a charmed life , using charmed in the sense of magical .

Chattering   The chattering classes
Gossiping and opinionated intellectuals. This is a fairly new phrase which seems to have been started in the quality British newspapers in the 1990s to describe the people who subscribe to common current beliefs and prejudices.

Cheek   Cheek by jowl
Very close together, as jowl means the same as cheek. In use since the sixteenth century, it appears in Shakespeare s *A Midsummer Night s Dream*.

Cheek   To turn the other cheek
To face up to insult or provocation with humble response. In the Bible, Jesus tells his followers: unto him that smiteth thee on the one cheek offer also the other (Luke 6 : 29).

Cheek   Tongue in cheek   see Tongue

Cheese   Cheese-paring
Stinginess, trying to be too economical. In the past, a whole cheese would be bought and used over a period. An old folktale recounts how a man chose his bride from three sisters by testing to see which one cut cheese sensibly, neither cheese-paring to the point of scraping the rind, nor chopping wasteful large slices.

Cheesed   Cheesed off

Bored, discontented. Possibly Charles Dickens invented it, as it appears in *The Old Curiosity Shop* (Chapter 50) where Dick Swiveller is asked, How is the cream of the clerkship? and replies Turning rather sour, I m afraid, almost to cheeseness.

Cheque   A blank cheque

Free licence to do what you see fit. If you give someone a signed bank cheque and leave the amount section blank, you are allowing them to fill it in themselves for as much as they like.

Chequered   A chequered career

A life of mingled good and bad fortune and achievement — an alternating pattern, like the black and white squares on a draughts or chess board.

Cherry   Life's a bowl of cherries   see Life

Cherry   Two bites of the cherry

Two chances to take advantage of something good

Cheshire cat   To grin like a Cheshire cat

To give a broad smile. The ancient reference to the grinning cats of Cheshire appears in Lewis Carroll s *Alice in Wonderland* where the Duchess tells Alice that the cat is grinning because: It s a Cheshire cat.

Chest   To get something off your chest

To relieve your feelings by confessing or by speaking frankly about something formerly repressed. See also **Clean breast**.

Chicken   No spring chicken

No longer young.

Chicken   To run round like a headless chicken   see **Headless**

Chickens   Don't count your chickens

Do not be too optimistic about some future prospect until you have definite proof. The full proverbial expression is the warning, Don t count your chickens before they hatch.

Child   A child of his (or her) time

The product of a certain culture or time. It has long been thought that different ages bring forth people with characteristics typical of their environment. The expression goes back to the Old Testament. Michael Tippet (*b*.1905) composed his oratorio A *Child of Our Time* in 1941.

Child   A child of nature

An unsophisticated person reared in country surroundings. For the poet Wordsworth (1770—1850) this was a very positive quality and he addressed a poem of praise to a girl who was disapproved of because she walked in the countryside, beginning, Dear child of nature . The term has also sometimes been used to refer to an illegitimate child.

Child   Child's play

Extremely easy. The phrase is used in medieval literature, possibly first by Chaucer (1340—1400) in *The Merchant s Tale:* it is no childes play to take a wyf .

Chin   To take it on the chin

To accept unpalatable facts or hard news without flinching. The expression comes from boxing.

China   A bull in a china shop   see Bull

China   Not for all the tea in China

Never. Not at any price. This phrase seems to have originated in Australia in the late nineteenth century and then spread to the rest of the tea-drinking world.

Chip   A chip off the old block

A child bearing a strong resemblance in appearance or character to one of his or her parents. The comparison of the child to a small off-cut from a large piece of wood or stone is found in ancient Greek literature and more recently in a seventeenth-century collection of proverbs by John Ray (1670).

Chips   When the chips are down

The crucial point. In betting games such as poker chips represent money and the exciting moment is when the players have placed their chips in the pot and committed their bets.

Chitchat   Idle chitchat   see Idle

Chock-a-block   To be chock-a-block

Full to capacity, very crowded. This is derived from the nautical block and tackle in which two blocks are brought close together when the ropes are pulled as tight as possible.

Choice   Hobson's choice   see Hobson

Chop   To chop and change

To have no steady system or idea. The original phrase to chap (to sell) and change (barter) , referred to a type of selling and bartering done in the past by rule of thumb, without fixed rates and therefore precarious.

Chump   Off your chump
Mad, deranged or foolish. Chump is a late-nineteenth-century slang word for head .

Circles   To go round in circles
To indulge in pointless, repetitive activity.

Clanger   To drop a clanger
To be guilty of an embarrassingly bad mistake, or indiscreet remark or action, which has such an impact that it is like letting fall a piece of heavy clanging or ringing metal. It appeared only in the twentieth century in this sense.

Clap   Clap trap
Nonsense or insincerity. Traditionally in the theatre this was the name of any device or stratagem which encouraged or trapped the audience into applauding.

Clapham   The man on the Clapham omnibus
The average reasonable person. The man in the street . This term was first used by Lord Bowen in 1903 in a court case, saying we must ask ourselves what the man on the Clapham omnibus would think .

Clappers   To go like the clappers
To be very busy, to be engaged in fruitful, energetic activity. The allusion is to the clappers of a bell. The expression is often used to denote speed of travel.

Clay   Feet of clay   see Feet

Clean   A clean bill of health
Confirmation of fitness or efficiency or honesty after some kind of investigation. In the nineteenth century it was literally a bill or certificate signed by the port authorities when a ship was setting sail to state that there were no infectious diseases in the port of origin and therefore the ship should be allowed to enter the port of destination. In the twentieth century it is used for any guarantee of the acceptability of someone or something.

Clean   To make a clean breast of it
To make a full confession. There are a number of terms which imply that guilt or conflict is felt to lie on the breast or chest (see Chest). In Shakespeare s *Macbeth* (Act v, Sc. 3), Macbeth himself begs the doctor

to help Lady Macbeth who is tormented by guilt: Cleanse the stuffed bosom of that perilous stuff.

Clean   To make a clean sweep

Start afresh by getting rid of old material, habits and methods. This is typically the first action of a new person in charge and can be traced to the proverb New brooms sweep clean.

Clean   To show a clean pair of heels

To escape trouble quickly. A lively picture of a departing person which has lost its edge through over-use.

Cleaners   Take someone to the cleaners

To deprive someone of their money or assets. Like the older expression to clean someone out , this originated in the gambling world, when someone lost everything. The advent of commercial dry-cleaning inspired the more drastic image of the loser being not only cleaned out, but dry-cleaned out.

Clear   Clear as a bell   see Bell

Clear   To clear the air

Remove doubt, suspicion or confusion and start afresh. Like many well-used phrases, this comes from a weather observation that a storm dispels a stifling atmosphere.

Clear   To clear the decks

Get ready for action. Before a naval battle, the crew of a sailing ship used to remove all unnecessary objects and fasten down the rest.

Cleft   To be in a cleft stick

To be caught between two embarrassing or unpleasant possibilities. In Shakespeare s *The Tempest* the witch Sycorax torments Ariel by trapping him in a cleft pine tree.

Cliff   A cliff-hanger

A situation in which the important result is very much in doubt until the last minute. In the early days of the cinema, many serial films ended each instalment with the main character left in a perilous plight, hanging by the fingernails from a cliff edge or under the wheels of a train.

Climb   To climb the walls

To vent your frustration and anger in some furious activity. In the Bible, the Book of Joel (2 : 7) speaks of those who shall climb the wall like men of war .

Clip   To clip someone's wings

To restrain a person who is too ambitious, exuberant or self-important. The metaphor, used for centuries, comes from the practice of snipping the wings of domestic fowl so that they cannot escape.

Cloak   Cloak and dagger

Underhand, sinister, bloody. Traditionally the theatrical dress of a spy or assassin was a cloak to conceal his sword or dagger. The seventeenth-century Spanish dramas of fighting and intrigue were actually called *comedias de capa y espada*, cloak-and-sword or -dagger plays.

Clock   To beat the clock

To finish something despite lack of time. In most cultures the idea of time hurrying by too quickly is a common one.

Clock   To put back the clock

Revert to the customs or conditions of a former time. The comparison is with moving of the hands of a clock to set it at an earlier hour.

Clockwork   To run like clockwork

To function with precision. In modern times there are more precise mechanisms than that of a clock, but this expression remains in the language from an age when the functioning of a clock was a byword for regularity.

Close   A close shave   see Shave

Closed   A closed book   see Book

Closet   To come out of the closet

Openly reveal one s homosexuality. This is essentially a modern usage because the practice of homosexuality was against the law until well into the twentieth century. The use of closet , as in closet politician , to describe a person who pursues an activity in secret or only in theory is at least three centuries old.

Cloud   Cloud cuckoo land

An absurdly impractical scheme or fantasy world. The drama *The Birds* by Aristophanes (414 BC) is an escapist fantasy in which the birds build an ideal city in the sky, called Nephelokokkygia in Greek, meaning cloud-cuckoo land .

Cloud   Every cloud has a silver lining   see Every

Cloud   To be on cloud nine

In a state of high excitement and happiness. The expression is from meteorology in the USA, where the weather bureau used the term cloud nine for a cloud capable of reaching heights of thirty to forty thousand feet.

Cloud   To be under a cloud
In disrepute, suspected of ill deeds.

Clover   To be in clover
To be in a favourable, comfortable situation. On a dairy farm cattle thrive in pastures of clover, which is also an important source of nitrogen for the soil.

Coals   To haul someone over the coals
To scold someone for an offence. Before Jews were banished from medieval England they were frequently required to lend large sums of money to the king with little security for themselves. If they refused they were dragged over burning coals until they agreed.

Coast   The coast is clear
There are no obstacles or enemies to spoil one s plans. This has been in use at least since the eighteenth century when Samuel Johnson included it in his dictionary. Naval expeditions and smugglers alike would have had to be sure that the coasts were free of danger before setting out.

Cock   A cock-and-bull story
A complicated and unbelievable story or excuse. The reference is to fables in which animals, amongst other incredible feats, were able to converse with each other. In Bentley s Boyle lecture (1692) he states cocks and bulls might discourse .

Cock   To be cock-a-hoop
Excited, triumphant. Possibly the reference is to when the cock or tap was removed from the hooped beer barrel at celebrations in the past so that beer could flow freely.

Cockles   To warm the cockles of your heart
To give pleasure or satisfaction. The cockles are the *cochlea cordis* or ventricles of the heart which is supposed to be the seat of the emotions.

Coin   To coin a phrase
To invent a new expression. It is often also used when the expression is not new but one about which the speaker is self-conscious or ironical.

Cold   Cold comfort
A description of sympathy or advice which offers no real consolation at all. Shakespeare used the phrase in *The Tempest* and *Taming of the Shrew*.

Cold   Cold turkey

A method of giving up an addiction, especially to drugs, which is simply to stop the habit without any special help or treatment. It derives from to talk cold turkey meaning to hold a frank discussion, presumably from the plain appearance of a meal of cold turkey as opposed to the bird served hot with its festive trimmings.

Cold   To do something in cold blood

To perform a calculated action which arouses horror or fear in others without showing any sign of emotion. The medieval notion was that the temperature of the blood governed emotions.

Cold   To give someone the cold shoulder

To snub someone. The cold shoulder is the leftover meat, given in rich houses in the past to the inferior or unwelcome guest who was not considered worthy of a specially cooked meal.

Cold   To throw cold water on something

To discourage, or scorn someone s ideas. The image of cold water to dampen enthusiasm was used in ancient Rome and appears in William Scarborough s collection of Chinese proverbs (1875).

Colours   To be shown up in your true colours

To have one s true character (probably unworthy) revealed. A ship signals its national identity by flying a certain flag, but some ships involved in crime are found to be using a false flag or colours to conceal their activities.

Colours   To come out (or pass) with flying colours

To achieve a great success. The image is from the days of sailing ships returning from a successful sea battle flying their flags, known as colours.

Colours   To go under false colours

To conceal your real intentions or attitudes. See also **To be shown up in your true colours.**

Comb   To go through something with a fine-tooth comb   see **Fine**

Comforts   Creature comforts   see **Creature**

Company   Two's company, three's a crowd

The relationship of a couple is spoilt by the presence of a third person.

Compliment   A backhanded compliment   see **Backhanded**

Compliments   To fish for compliments   see **Fish**

Conclusion   A foregone conclusion   see **Foregone**

Contempt   Beneath contempt   see **Beneath**

Cook   To cook someone's goose

To spoil someone s plans. The phrase was established in the nineteenth century. According to Henry Mayhew in *London Labour and the London Poor*, a popular street chant against Catholics was: If they come here we ll cook their goose.

Cook   To cook the books

To falsify accounts. Cooking has provided numerous expressions like this which suggest a mixing of ingredients to suit the needs of the cook.

Cooks   Too many cooks spoil the broth

More people working on a simple task will tend to interfere rather than help. This is an old proverb.

Corner   To turn the corner

To recover from a crisis.

Corns   To tread on someone's corns

To offend someone by a tactless remark or manoeuvre. Corns have always been an unglamorous but significant feature of popular sayings and beliefs.

Cost   To cost an arm and a leg (or a fortune, or a packet)

Something for which too high a price is paid or asked. The powerful idea of sacrificing a limb or a fortune to buy something is losing its force through repetition.

Couch   A couch potato

Someone who spends an excessive amount of time inert on the sofa in front of the television set. This reflects the current anxiety that, because of television, too few people exercise their minds and bodies and so become like vegetables.

Country   God's own country   see **God**

Courage   Dutch courage   see **Dutch**

Coventry   To send someone to Coventry

To make someone feel they are in disgrace by ignoring them. Edward Hyde, Earl of Clarendon, who was adviser to King Charles I, mentions in his *History of the Great Rebellion* (1702) that Royalist prisoners were sent to isolation and ignominy in Coventry which was a Parliamentary town.

Cow   A sacred cow

An institution, cause or idea that must not be criticised because it is dear to those in authority. The idea comes from the Hindu religion in which cows are sacred animals.

Cows   Till the cows come home

Going on for a very long time. The old saying till the cow come home was current in the sixteenth century.

Cracked   Not all it is cracked up to be

Not living up to its reputation. The verb crack up means to eulogise or praise something .

Cracks   To paper over the cracks   see Paper

Cradle   Cradle snatching

Taking a romantic or sexual partner who is much younger than oneself. In the past this described the crime of child kidnapping, but has come to be used ironically.

Cramp   To cramp someone's style

To prevent someone from displaying their abilities or talents or from doing what they want. Charles Lamb (1775—1834) used the words to describe the numbness in his hands which made writing difficult, but in the twentieth century they came to be used figuratively.

Creature   Creature comforts

Material things like good food and accommodation which make life pleasant. It has been a commonplace since the seventeenth century. In *Nicholas Nickleby*, Charles Dickens played on the other meaning of creature , that is alcoholic spirits, to pun that Mr Squeers, the sadistic schoolmaster, had been seeking forgetfulness in creature comforts , which turned out to be brandy and water.

Credibility   A credibility gap

The difference between what is claimed and the actual truth of the matter. This dates from an article in the *Washington Post* (13 May 1965) challenging the US government s claim that the USA was not escalating military action in Vietnam.

Cricket   It's not cricket

Not done in a fair and sportsmanlike way. In England since the nineteenth century cricket has been considered synonymous with good sporting behaviour.

Crocodile   Crocodile tears

Pretended sorrow or sympathy. One of the myths about crocodiles, especially amongst Europeans who had never seen one, was that they wept as they ate their victims. Sir John Mandeville, a great fantasist of the fourteenth century, wrote in an account of his voyages of how crocodiles slay men and they eten hem weping .

Croesus   Rich as Croesus

Wealthy. King Croesus was ruler of Lydia from 560—54 BC and famous for his wealth and his patronage of Greek writers such as Aesop.

Cropper   To come a cropper

To fail completely. An earlier saying, to fall neck and crop , comes from Scandinavian *nakk* meaning the top of a hill and Anglo-Saxon *cropp* meaning the head of a plant, so that falling neck and crop is a headlong crash, or cropper.

Cross   Don't cross bridges before you come to them

Do not worry about mishaps until they actually occur. The saying appears in sixteenth-century collections of proverbs.

Cross   To cross swords

To quarrel or fight.

Cross   To have a cross to bear

To have a great sorrow or hardship in your life. The implication is that the suffering has virtue and will have a good result just as Christ s carrying of the cross benefited mankind.

Crow   As the crow flies

By the most direct route. Crows are said to fly straight to their destination.

Crowning   Crowning glory

The most wonderful or beautiful element. This trite phrase is often applied to women s hair.

Crumb   A crumb of comfort

A small consolation.

Crunch   To come to the crunch

To reach the culminating point. It has been suggested that the crunch is the sound made by a machine or engine about to grind to a halt.

Cry In full cry
At the height of an activity, protest or demonstration. The term is from hunting when the hounds are signalling that they have the scent of the fox.

Cry To cry all the way to the bank see Bank

Cry To cry for the moon
To long for something you cannot have.

Cry To cry over spilt milk
To waste time lamenting something in the past which cannot be remedied.

Cry To cry wolf
To raise a false alarm. An ancient fable tells of a shepherd boy who, as a joke, called on villagers to help him fend off a wolf from his flock. Having been tricked several times, they failed to respond when a wolf did attack and the boy genuinely needed help.

Crystal Crystal clear
Transparent or obvious. As a poetic image clear as crystal has been in vogue since biblical times, as in the Book of Revelations where Jerusalem is described as having the glory of God . . . clear as crystal . It has also long been used as a synonym for something self-evident.

Crystal To look into the crystal ball
To try to predict the future. The practice of gazing into a glass globe was held to be a method by which those so-gifted could make out the shape of events to come.

Cuff Off the cuff
Impromptu. This is from the habit of speakers scribbling brief notes for their speeches on their starched cuffs in the days when such garments were common.

Cup of tea Not my cup of tea
Not to my taste. In the nineteenth century the expression was positive and described someone or something very agreeable to the speaker as just my cup of tea . In the twentieth century it has been more often negative.

Curry To curry favour
To gain an advantage by flattery. The original expression referred to currying or grooming Favel, the magical but fickle horse in a medieval story.

Curtains   It is curtains for someone

Disaster or failure is imminent for someone. On Death Row in some American state prisons criminals about to be executed have a curtain drawn round their cell.

Cut   Cut and dried

Clearly defined, routine, already decided. Probably the term originated in the timber industry where logs are cut then laid out to dry or season before use.

Cut   To be cut to the quick

Profoundly hurt. The quick is an old term for the flesh below the skin which might be reached by the cut of a whip or the sting of a hornet. The phrase has been in use since the seventeenth century. The word quick is still in use to describe the tender flesh of the finger-nail bed.

Cut   To cut corners

To do a job carelessly or skimp on materials. When a vehicle takes the short route round a curve, it is at the expense of safety.

Cut   To cut no ice

To have no effect at all. The expression is recorded in American magazines in the late nineteenth century and perhaps comes from skating terminology or from the use of icebreakers.

Cutting   At the cutting edge

In the forefront of new developments. The allusion is to the sharp blade of a knife or tool. The term has been used in science and technology since the 1950s to describe innovative research and has spread into everyday life to the extent that it is the title of a British television programme.

D

Daggers To look daggers
To stare with hatred and hostility. This is at least four centuries old, sometimes taking the form to speak daggers as in Shakespeare s *Hamlet*. Hamlet says of his mother, I will speak daggers to her.

Daisy Fresh as a daisy
Clean, pure, energetic, ready for action. The name of the flower means the day s eye because it opens with the morning sun.

Damn To damn with faint praise
To pay such feeble compliments that you actually disclose contempt. From *The Epistle to Dr Arbuthnot* by Alexander Pope (1735).

Damocles The sword of Damocles
Imminent danger. According to Greek legend King Dionyseus demonstrated the burden of being king to Damocles by suspending a sword above him by a thread.

Dance To dance attendance
To be ready to obey someone s every wish. From an ancient wedding custom by which the bride had to dance with every guest.

Dander To get your dander up
To goad or enrage. The English dialect word dander means rage , but probably the expression was taken to America by Dutch colonists using the word *donder* meaning thunder or rage .

Darby Darby and Joan
An affectionate elderly couple, originally characters in an eighteenth century ballad by Henry Woodfall.

Dark A dark horse
A person who proves unexpectedly to be successful. Originally a racing term referring to a horse whose ancestry was unknown.

Darken Never darken my door again
Go away and never return. The idea of darkening someone s door simply means to cross someone s threshold and has been in use since the late eighteenth century but became a clich with the advent of

Victorian melodrama which often featured a young girl who was driven out of the family home.

Darkest   The darkest hour before the dawn
The worst point before the resolution of a crisis. The expression existed in Latin.

Day   All in a day's work
Part of everyday life, just routine.

Day   Day in day out
All day long and every day. The implication is always negative, the repetition stressing the idea of tedium.

Day   Day of reckoning
The point at which you have to account for your actions. According to the Bible, the day of judgement (or reckoning) will be when Jesus Christ pronounces God s sentence on all of humankind.

Days   Someone's days are numbered
Someone s useful life is about to end. Probably derived from the Book of Daniel in the Old Testament. Daniel predicts Belshazzar s fate from the handwriting on the wall: God hath numbered thy kingdom.

Days   The good old days
The past fondly remembered. Throughout human history there has been a tendency to idealise the past.

Dead   A dead duck
A loser. Someone of no further consequence.

Dead   A dead heat
A race in which two or more competitors tie for first place. In many sports a heat means a race.

Dead   A dead letter
Something which is no longer valid or important. The term is used for a letter which the post office cannot deliver due to an incorrect address or an untraceable person. It also refers to a law or regulation which is no longer upheld.

Dead   A dead weight
A person who encumbers without assisting, referring to the weight of a lifeless body that is difficult to lift.

Dead   Dead as a door-nail
Completely lifeless. A door-nail probably refers to the stud on which the knocker strikes, suggesting that after being hit on the head so often, it must have no life left in it whatsoever.

Dead   Dead men's shoes
The position left available by someone s retirement or death. This is often used as waiting for dead men s shoes .

Dead   Dead set against something
To be absolutely opposed to doing something.

Dead   Dead to the world
Asleep. Unresponsive to any outside stimulus as if dead.

Dead   To flog a dead horse   see **Flog**

Deaf   Deaf as a post
Physically unable to hear, or completely unresponsive. The simile was used in the sixteenth century by J. Palsgrave and has been common ever since; a post being a good example of something that cannot hear.

Deal   Big deal!
An ironical exclamation used to show that you are not impressed by something. Originally it would have been a description of a successful business contract or a good bargain. Also used dismissively, as in, It s no big deal.

Deal   To wheel and deal
To act as a free agent, especially to advance your own interests in business or politics.

Dear   A Dear John letter
A letter from a girl to her soldier boy-friend or husband to say that she loves someone else. It has been in use at least since World War I.

Death   At death's door
Seriously ill or on the point of dying. The notion of dying as passing into another room was common in the Middle Ages.

Death   Death warmed up
Looking weak and ill.

Death   In at the death
Present at the climax. This is from hunting where the participants like to be present when the animal is finished off.

Deep   To go off the deep end

To give full vent to angry feelings without restraint. The image is of a swimmer leaping into deep water.

Deliver   To deliver the goods

To be absolutely reliable, to obtain or achieve something on time or where required. This echoes advertisements by shop owners in the nineteenth century that they could bring goods direct to the house.

Demon   The demon drink

Alcohol, a term once serious, now ironical. It dates from the days of the temperance movement in nineteenth-century America and was possibly invented by T. S. Arthur who wrote about slaves to the demon rum .

Den   A den of thieves

A place or a group of people connected with criminal activities. The term originated from the Bible in the New Testament where Jesus accused the money lenders of making the Temple into a den of thieves .

Denmark   There is something rotten in the state of Denmark

Used ironically to indicate that something is suspicious, perhaps with reference to a government or organisation. In *Hamlet* the young prince uses these words when he suspects his uncle of murdering his father.

Dependency   The dependency culture

This is sometimes used to describe modern British society which is seen to lean too heavily on state support as opposed to individual effort.

Deserts   To get your just deserts

To be treated as you deserve. The implication here is usually that you deserve punishment. The word desert is little used apart from this expression.

Devil   Better the devil you know

Trust the person or thing you are familiar with rather than risking the unknown.

Devil   Between the devil and the deep blue sea   see Between

Devil   Give the devil his due!

Give credit even to a bad person if they deserve it.

Devil   The devil incarnate

The embodiment of evil. The expression was in use in the fourteenth century when it was commonly believed that the Devil could take possession of someone s body.

Devil   The devil to pay

Serious consequences. The term appeared in the fourteenth century and refers to stories of pacts with the Devil to obtain wealth or beauty, the victims suffering severely for this folly afterwards.

Devil   To go to the devil

To degenerate morally and spiritually. In the seventeenth century the expression was used jokingly to refer to the Devil Tavern, London, which was frequented by lawyers and writers.

Devil   Why should the devil have all the good tunes?

Why not make good causes appeal to popular taste? Charles Wesley made this observation in 1740 with reference to his adaptation of popular songs for hymn tunes.

Diamond   A rough diamond

A person unrefined in manner who is talented or worthy of esteem.

Dice   No dice

Nothing doing, useless, worthless. The term is from games with dice where a throw of the dice is declared invalid.

Dictates   According to the dictates of conscience

Going by what you believe to be right. The expression was used by Archbishop Bramhall in 1656: contrarie to the dictate of his conscience .

Die   Never say die

Do not give up. Charles Dickens used the expression in *Pickwick Papers*.

Die   The die is cast

The decision is irrevocable. The dice have been thrown already. This is a translation of Julius Caesar s words when he crossed the Rubicon to seize power in Italy in 49 BC, meaning that he could not turn back at that point.

Die   To die in harness

To remain active to the end. This analogy with a working horse is at least as old as Shakespeare. Before the battle with Macduff, Macbeth says: At least we ll die with harness on our back.

Die   To die laughing

To laugh uproariously.

Dig   To dig yourself into a hole

To put yourself into an inextricable situation. An older related term is in a hole from early twentieth-century slang.

Ding-dong   A ding-dong battle

A fierce struggle, either verbal or physical. This onomatopoeic expression alludes to a rapid exchange of blows like the action of a striking clock or bell.

Dirt   Dirt cheap

At a very low price. The phrase appeared in *Blackwell s Magazine* in 1821.

Dirty   A dirty dog

A dishonest or contemptible person. The appeal of the alliteration probably explains the frequent use of this as dogs are not particularly dirty animals.

Dirty   A dirty old man

A salacious man, considered too old and undesirable for sex. It is often used of an old man lusting after young women. This became a clich in the twentieth century.

Dirty   To wash your dirty linen in public

To make intimate or private matters public.

Discontent   A winter of discontent

A time of trouble. It was used to describe an era of industrial action in Britain in the 1970s. It comes from Shakespeare s *Richard III*: Now is the winter of our discontent made glorious summer by this sun of York.

Distance   Distance lends enchantment

Things seem to look better from further away. This is an old concept expressed by Thomas Campbell in his poem *Pleasures of Hope* (1799): tis distance lends enchantment to the view .

Ditch   A last-ditch effort

A final desperate struggle. This comes from trench warfare where the final trench or ditch is where the last chance of defence lies.

Divide   To divide and rule

To get the upper hand by causing your opponents to quarrel amongst themselves. The principle is as old as the Roman emperors. In Bishop Hall s *Meditations* (1605) he stated: for a prince . . . a sure axiom, divide and rule .

Do   Do as I say, not as I do

Follow my instruction but not my actions. The concept is medieval. In the *Decameron* (1350), Boccaccio says, Do as we say and not as we do.

Do   Do or die

Act immediately, even if it is painful, in order to get the result you require. Sir Walter Scott writing in 1809 suggested that this common expression was once the motto of a Scottish family.

Do   To do your own thing

To follow your own choice of career; to work for yourself.

Does   It does my heart good   see Heart

Dog   A dirty dog   see Dirty

Dog   A dog in the manger

Someone who prevents another person from using something even though he or she has no interest in it personally. Aesop s fable tells of a dog lying in a manger full of hay. An ox tries to eat the hay but the dog prevents him although he has no use for the hay.

Dog   A dog's life

A poor quality of life. Erasmus commented in 1542 that people called it (life) a miserable life or a dog s life .

Dog   Dog eat dog

A situation of merciless competition. This derives from an older saying: Dog does not eat dog. The implication being that if dogs did such an unnatural thing the rivalry would be fierce.

Dog   In the dog-house

To be in disgrace like a dog sent to its kennel. In J. M. Barrie s *Peter Pan*, Mr Darling had to do penance in the dog kennel.

Dogs   Let sleeping dogs lie

Where there is potential for danger or trouble do not encourage or aggravate the situation. This is a traditional proverb.

Dogs   The dogs of war

The bloodshed and destruction caused by war. This image is from *Julius Caesar*: Cry havoc and let slip the dogs of war.

Dogs   To go to the dogs

To deteriorate or become dilapidated.

Doldrums   In the doldrums

To be depressed or in a bad mood. Sailors used the term for a region where ships were often becalmed.

Dollar   The almighty dollar

The power of money. Sometimes, more specifically, the power of the first world economy. In 1837 Washington Irving wrote of the almighty dollar, that object of universal devotion .

Don't   Don't let the grass grow under your feet

Do not allow opportunities to go unrealised. A proverbial expression.

Don't   Don't look a gift horse in the mouth

Do not criticise something which is given to you as a gift. This is an ancient saying which appears in many languages and comes from the practice of assessing the age and state of health of a horse by examining its teeth before purchasing.

Done   Done to a turn

Perfectly finished like a piece of meat roasted evenly by turning on a spit over a fire.

Done   Done to death

Over-used, overstated to the point where people are tired of something.

Donkey   For donkey's years

A long time. Donkeys are said to have a long life and it is rare to see a dead one.

Doorstep   Never darken my door again   see Darken

Dose   To give someone a dose of his or her own medicine

To treat someone the way that they have treated you or others. The expression seems to date from the early nineteenth century.

Dot   On the dot

Exactly at a given time. Punctual or precise.

Dot   To dot the i's and cross the t's

To be meticulous in every detail. Traditional teaching of handwriting insisted on careful attention to the letters i and t to which the dot and the bar have to be added after the word is written.

Double   A double bind

An unresolvable dilemma.

Double   A double-edged sword

A situation with two options, both equally troublesome or dangerous. It can also be used of an argument which harms the person expressing it as well as the victim. Dryden mentioned the Delphic sword which cuts on either side in *The Hind and the Panther*.

Double   A double whammy

Used to describe a situation (for example in politics) where the consequences are bad on two counts. It was brought into use from the world of boxing where a man known as Evil Eye Finkel would be paid to put a curse (a whammy) on a boxer and paid more to put a double curse on him so that the boxer would lose.

Double   Double Dutch

Incomprehensible or nonsensical speech. The Dutch were singled out as foreigners to be ridiculed because of the traditional seafaring rivalry between the English and the Dutch.

Double   Double-think

The ability to hold two conflicting views at the same time. George Orwell invented the concept in *Nineteen Eighty-Four* (1949) in his portrayal of a tyrannical regime in the future.

Doubt   To give someone the benefit of the doubt

To assume that someone is probably right or telling the truth even if you are not convinced.

Down   Down and out

To be poor and homeless. This probably originated from boxing where the defeated man is knocked down and therefore goes out of the contest.

Down   Down at heel

Shabby. Worn-down heels signal lack of money for repairs. The expression was common in the eighteenth century.

Down   Down in the dumps

Depressed. In the sixteenth century, the dump was a mournful tune or a slow dance. Another possible connection is the Dutch word *dompig*, meaning dull .

Down   Down In the mouth

Gloomy. Dispirited. This comes from the downturned shape of the mouth when a person looks disheartened.

Down   Down memory lane   see Memory

Down   Down the drain

Wasted. This allusion to water got rid of through a drainpipe was current at the end of the nineteenth century.

Down   Down to earth
Practical. Unpretentious.

Downhill   To go downhill
To do badly, to degenerate.

Draw   To draw a blank
To fail to find or understand something. Blank was the term for a lottery ticket that did not bring a prize.

Draw   To draw the line at something
To indicate the point at which you can no longer tolerate a certain type of behaviour. The line refers to property boundaries. The figurative sense was used in the nineteenth century in England.

Draw   To draw the short straw   see **Straw**

Drawer   Top drawer
Upper class. Traditionally the top drawers of a chest were reserved for the more valuable items.

Drawing board   Back to the drawing board
To be forced to return to the initial stages of a venture. First used by architects, now applied to various types of project.

Dream   The American dream   see **American**

Dressed   Dressed to kill
Looking your best, perhaps for courting. In a letter, John Keats wrote one chap was dressed to kill for the King .

Dressed   Dressed up to the nines
Smartly or elegantly clothed. It has been suggested that this is a corruption of an older form thyne eyne , that is, dressed up to your eyes.

Drink   The demon drink   see **Demon**

Drink   To drink like a fish
To drink or have the capacity to drink large quantities of alcohol.

Drive   To drive someone up the wall
To annoy someone intensely. See also **Climb the walls**.

Driven   Pure as the driven snow   see **Snow**

Driver   A backseat driver   see **Back**

Drop   A drop in the ocean
A minute amount, not worth considering.

Drop   At the drop of a hat
At short notice or promptly. At sporting events the starter of a race sometimes used a swift downward motion of his hat to start a race or a game.

Drop   To drop a bombshell   see Bombshell

Drowned   A drowned rat
A bedraggled person. A lively image of a wet disgusting creature.

Drum   To drum something into someone's head
To make a person understand by regular insistent repetition.

Drummed   To be drummed out of the Brownies
To be excluded from a certain group or activity. A soldier who committed an offence might be dismissed from his regiment to a drum roll. This is a jocular expression in which the Brownies or junior Girl Guides are substituted for the army.

Drunk   Blind drunk   see Blind

Drunk   Punch drunk   see Punch

Dry   A dry run
A rehearsal or practice in simulated conditions. This is a military term for firing practice which is conducted without live ammunition.

Dry   Dry as dust
Boring. Sir Walter Scott perpetuated this common image by addressing some of the prefaces of his novels to Dr Jonas Dryasdust.

Duck   A lame duck
An ineffectual person who cannot function socially or in the workplace. The original lame duck was said to have been a London stockbroker in Exchange Alley, home of the stock market in the eighteenth century, who lost all his money and waddled out of the Alley .

Duck   A sitting duck
An easy target. A duck sitting on the bank is not hard for a hunter to hit. The expression was used figuratively by the beginning of the twentieth century.

Duckling   An ugly duckling
A person or a project which seems doomed to failure or unpopularity,

but which turns out to be very successful in the end. Hans Anderson made the phrase famous with his story of the cygnet reared in a family of ducklings and despised for its odd appearance until it grew into a beautiful swan.

Ducks   To play ducks and drakes
To squander money. The traditional name for the game of skimming stones across a pond just to make a pleasant splash is Ducks and Drakes .

Dudgeon   In high dudgeon
Resentment or indignation. The Welsh *dygen* meaning ill feeling gave rise to this expression.

Dull   Dull as ditchwater
Boring or dreary. The murky waters of roadside ditches were a familiar sight in the past. Charles Dickens used the phrase in *Our Mutual Friend*.

Dumb   A dumb blonde
A pretty but stupid woman. Early Hollywood films spread the concept of the beautiful woman without personality or intelligence.

Dumb   Dumb insolence
Showing scorn and defiance by a refusal to speak or by your attitude.

Dumps   Down in the dumps   see Down

Dutch   A Dutch uncle
A person who gives unwelcome and unsolicited advice. This negative characteristic attributed to the Dutch is in keeping with the seventeenth-century propaganda spread by sailors who regarded the Dutch as rivals.

Dutch   Dutch courage
False bravery inspired by alcohol. As in most of the images of the Dutch which date from the seventeenth century this is also pejorative.

Dutch   To go Dutch
To share the costs of an outing or treat equally. The implication that the Dutch are ungenerous derives, like the above expressions, from rivalry between Dutch and English sailors.

Dyed   Dyed in the wool
Through and through. In the textile industry, wool dyed before being woven is more thoroughly impregnated with colour than that dyed as finished cloth. The phrase is used to describe people with fixed and often bigoted views.

E

Eager   An eager beaver
Someone dedicated to work or certain aims. The allusion is to the legendary industriousness of the beaver. The appeal of the rhyme probably kept the phrase in use.

Eagle   An eagle eye
A close watch. As the quintessential bird of prey, the eagle is known for its sharp eyes. John Keats speaks of: stout Cortez . . . with eagle eyes .

Ear   In one ear and out the other
To go unheard or unheeded. The phrase has a long history of use by complaining schoolteachers.

Ear   To keep your ear to the ground
To be alert to what is going on around you. The allusion is to the hunter who bends to listen for vibrations of the earth to track his prey.

Ear   To play it by ear   see Play

Early   An early bird
A person who arrives before everyone else and therefore gains advantage.The original proverb which appears in William Camden s *Book of Proverbs* (1605) says that the early bird catches the worm . Nowadays it is often simply a jocular comment on a person s punctuality.

Early   Early to bed, early to rise
If you go to bed early you will be able to get up in the morning. The virtues of early rising are advocated in the rest of this traditional rhyme which states that it makes a man healthy, wealthy and wise .

Earner   A nice little earner   see Nice

Ears   Lend me your ears
Listen carefully. These are the words of Mark Antony in Shakespeare s *Julius Caesar* at the funeral oration. Nowadays the words are often used in a jocular fashion.

Ears   Wet behind the ears

Immature and inexperienced. When a calf is born, the last place to dry is the hollow behind its ears.

Earth   An earth mother

A woman who relishes her fertility and glories in child-rearing. The term is often used ironically now, but in the past was simply the name given to goddesses of fertility.

Earth   The four corners of the earth

The farthest limits of the world. The expression comes from the Book of Isaiah in the Bible: And gather together the dispersed of Judah from the four corners of the earth.

Earth   To run someone or something to earth

To trace someone or something. In fox hunting the fox is pursued by the hounds to its earth, the hole where it lives.

Easier   Easier said than done

It is much easier to talk about something than actually do it.

Easy   Easy as ABC   see ABC

Easy   Easy come, easy go

Whatever is gained too easily is also quickly lost. This sentiment appears in ancient Chinese proverbs and in English medieval texts. Chaucer has a similar saying in *The Pardoner s Tale*: As lightly it cometh, so wol we spende.

Easy   Easy pickings

Easy gains.

Easy   On Easy Street

In comfortable circumstances.

Eat   To eat humble pie

To behave or be forced to behave with humility. At medieval feasts the higher ranking guests ate venison while the lower classes were obliged to make do with umbles or entrails and offal baked in a pie.

Eat   To eat out of someone's hand

To be docile and obedient like a tamed animal taking food from a human. The expression became common in the early twentieth century.

Eat   To eat someone out of house and home

To consume more than your fair share. This concept appears in ancient Latin and Greek writings and in later English texts. In Shakespeare s *Henry IV*, Mistress Quickly says of Falstaff: He hath eaten me out of house and home.

Eat   To eat your hat

To perform the absurd feat of consuming your hat. This promise is usually offered as a guarantee of the truth of something you have said.

Eat   To eat your heart out

To worry or pine. This is a common idea in many cultures and appears in British writing from the sixteenth century onwards. Nowadays it tends to be a light-hearted taunt: Eat your heart out, Mr X! when you have just demonstrated that someone s talent is superior to his.

Eat   To eat your words

To be obliged to take back something you have said. In the sixteenth century John Calvin used the expression in a tract: God eateth not his word.

Eating   The proof of the pudding is in the eating   see **Proof**

Economical   Economical with the truth

Lying. The modern fashion for using this euphemism comes from the testimony of Sir Robert Armstrong, the British Cabinet Secretary, when he was being questioned in an Australian court in 1986 over the British government s attempts to prevent publication of a book about MI5. He applied the description to a letter he had written. However, previous users of the phrase include Samuel Pepys, Mark Twain and Arnold Bennett.

Edge   To push someone over the edge

To drive someone to the limit of psychological endurance, to make them mad or desperate. This is linked to the notion of despair being like an abyss which the sufferer eventually tumbles into.

Egg   Nest egg   see **Nest**

Egg   To come away with egg on your face

To have made a fool of yourself. This expression, common in twentieth-century America, may have come from the practice of pelting poor theatrical performers or political speakers with eggs.

Elbow   Elbow grease
Hard physical effort.This seventeenth-century expression is said to have originated when a lazy apprentice was given a strong hint to put his arms to work more vigorously by being sent to a shop to buy some elbow grease.

Elbow   Elbow room
Enough space This sixteenth-century expression has been in use ever since. In Shakespeare s *King John*, the king speaks of his soul having freedom to leave his body: Now my soul hath elbow room.

Elbow   More power to your elbow!
Carry on! I wish you success. This expression of encouragement is connected with the idea of using the elbow to work vigorously. See also **Elbow grease.**

Element   To be in your element
To be in the situation which suits you best. The allusion is to the medieval idea that the universe was composed of four substances, earth, air, fire and water. Each living creature had its proper element.

Elephant   A white elephant
A possession which is useless and burdensome. A king of Siam was said to be in the habit of giving a white elephant to those courtiers he was about to eliminate.

Eleventh   At the eleventh hour
At the last minute. The phrase comes from the Bible from a parable in Matthew (20 : 9) where some labourers who were hired very late, at the eleventh hour, were paid the same as those who had started early.

Eloquent   An eloquent silence
A deliberate failure to speak which indicates a person s attitude better than words. The Roman poet Ovid referred to this in his *Artis Amatoriae*: Often there is eloquence in a silent look.

Embarrassment   An embarrassment of riches
Too much of a good thing. This is a translation of the title of an eighteenth-century French comedy by the Abb d Allainval. It was performed in English in London.

Empty   Empty vessels
Stupid prattling people. This comes from the proverb, Empty vessels make the most sound — vessels meaning pots or jars.

Encyclopaedia A walking encyclopaedia
A very knowledgeable person.

End It is not the end of the world
What has happened is not a disaster. This reassurance dates from the nineteenth century and was used by Bernard Shaw in *Major Barbara*.

End To be at the end of your tether
To be unable to tolerate further hardship. The image is of a tethered animal which can graze no further than the rope allows him. It was already a clich by the seventeenth century.

End To fight to the bitter end
To struggle on to the finish despite difficulties. The last link of a cable on a ship is the bitt end, that is, the part secured to a bitt, which is a bollard fixed to the deck.

End To keep your end up
To put up a creditable performance. In this case your end is your share or part of an operation which you ensure is up to standard.

Ends To make ends meet
To live within your income and be able to pay debts.

Enemy Public enemy number one
A person who is a serious threat to society. This was first used of the American gangster John Dillinger, shot by the police in 1934.

Enemy The enemy within
A person or group who harms his own family, country or social group. This is probably connected with the idea of the enemy within the gate .

Enfant An enfant terrible
An unpredictable person who says or does embarrassing things and harms his own group. This is a translation of a French term for a wilful child.

English The Queen's English
English as it should be spoken. The term seems to have been in use at least since the reign of Queen Elizabeth I. As the idea of what is or is not acceptable English has changed frequently and cannot be easily defined, people tend to use the term to define their own preferred variety.

Englishman   An Englishman's home is his castle

A person is safe inside his own home. This is a legal concept whereby, for example, bailiffs cannot force an entry into someone s house to seize their goods.

Enough   Enough to make someone turn in his or her grave

A shocking event or circumstance which would offend a person now dead. James Payne in *Lost Sir Massingberd* says: This holiday-making and mixture of high and low here are enough to make Sir Massingberd turn in his grave.

Enough   To give someone enough rope to hang themselves see Rope

Enter   To enter the lists

To compete or enter into a struggle. The list or lists was the barrier round the jousting area in medieval tournaments; to enter was to signal that you were ready to compete.

Envy   Green with envy   see Green

Errand   An errand of mercy

Going somewhere to help someone. A common expression since the nineteenth century.

Eternal   An eternal triangle

Three lovers, either two men in love with the same woman, or two women in love with the same man. The situation is so called because the situation is familiar throughout human history. It seems to have originated in a book review which appeared in the *London Daily Chronicle* in 1907.

Eternal   Eternal truths

Ideas which have endured throughout human history. John Locke wrote in his *Journal* (1681) of *eternae veritates* or eternal truths. It is sometimes used ironically of principles which a certain group or person believe to be fundamental but others may not.

Even   The even (or noiseless) tenor of their way

A tranquil way of life. In his *Elegy Written in a Country Churchyard* (1750) Thomas Gray reflects on the peaceful life of the villagers: They kept the noiseless tenor of their way.

Every   Every cloud has a silver lining

There is room for optimism even in the worst situations. John Milton probably initiated the idea in *Comus* (1634): A sable cloud turns forth its silver lining.

Every   Every dog will have his day

Even the most despised or humble person will have their revenge. This was a Macedonian proverb which originated in a comment on the death of the Greek playwright Euripides. The great writer was on a visit to the king of Macedonia when he was killed by a pack of dogs which had been set upon him by a jealous rival.

Every   Every inch

An admirable example of his or her kind. Every inch a man appears in Thomas Dekker s *The Shoemaker s Holiday* (1600) and in Shakespeare s *King Lear*. When the blind Earl of Gloucester recognises the voice of the king and asks: Is t not the king? , King Lear answers: Ay, every inch a king.

Every   Every man for himself

Look after your own interests first. The fuller version is, Every man for himself and the devil take the hindmost. Having begun as sound advice to stand on your own feet, this seems to have acquired a more unpleasant meaning in modern times. In the *Knight s Tale*, Chaucer warns: Ech man for himself, ther is non other. Nowadays it is rather an encouragement to be selfish.

Every   Every man has his price

Everybody can be bribed. Although an older maxim existed, it was Sir Robert Walpole who fixed the phrase in the public mind when he made a parliamentary speech condemning certain corrupt politicians: All those men have their price.

Every   Every man Jack

Everyone, without exception. Jack means fellow or ordinary man . For at least four centuries this phrase has been used for emphasis when something applies to every single person.

Everything   Everything but the kitchen sink

Absolutely everything, even useless, unnecessary items. The phrase became common during World War II. An article in the *Wall Street Journal* (1958) speaks of the military services who want everything in a weapon but the kitchen sink .

Evil   An evil empire

A regime of aggression and terror. The science fiction film and book of *Star Wars* by George Lucas (1977) made famous the adventures of Luke Skywalker and his struggle against the evil Galactic Empire ruled by the tyrant Darth Vader. In 1983 President Reagan described the

Soviet Union as the Evil Empire against which all Americans must struggle, and since then the phrase has been used for various oppressive power groups.

Evil   The evil eye
The power to harm people just by looking at them. Many cultures believed and still believe in such magic, but nowadays the expression is often an ironical comment on people who always seem to bring bad luck on the others around them.

Evil   To fall on evil days
To suffer hardship after being in comfortable circumstances.

Ewe   A little ewe lamb
A single prized possession or beloved person. A story in the Bible in the Book of Samuel tells of a poor man deprived of his pet ewe lamb.

Ex   Ex cathedra
With absolute authority. Meaning from the chair or throne this Latin phrase is used by the Catholic Church to indicate when the Pope is speaking in his capacity as infallible head of the Church. It is often used ironically to characterise dogmatic, pompous pronouncements by ordinary individuals.

Exception   The exception that proves the rule
Making an exception of certain things shows that a law or rule does obtain and that it applies to the remaining things.

Explore   To explore every avenue
To investigate all possibilities. This metaphor became common in the early twentieth century.

Eye   A jaundiced eye
Seeing everything as bad or faulty. In the past it was believed that the disease of jaundice not only coloured the skin and eyes yellow, but that the sufferer saw everything as yellow, as John Webster says in his play The White Devils (1612): They that have the yellow jaundice think all objects they look upon to be yellow.

Eye   Able to be seen with half an eye
Extremely obvious.

Eye   All my eye
Nonsense. This is usually considered to be part of the expression, All my eye and Betty Martin , although all my eye , meaning rubbish is

older. The name Betty Martin is said to be an interpretation by British sailors of Latin prayers to St Martin, which they heard in European churches: O mihi, beate Martine , meaning Grant me, blessed St Martin . . .

Eye   An eye for an eye
Retaliation. Biblical in origin, the words occur in Exodus where Moses expounds to the people the system of punishment against those who break God s commandments.

Eye   An eye opener
A circumstance that reveals the truth about someone or something.

Eye   An eye to the main chance
Looking out for your own interests. At least four centuries old, this saying is cited by Samuel Butler in *Hudibras:* have a care o th main chance .

Eye   In the public eye
Well known in society, famous.

Eye   In the twinkling of an eye
Quickly. In the Bible these are the words of St Paul (1 Corinthians) speaking of the day of judgement.

Eye   In your mind's eye   see Mind

Eye   To keep your eye on someone
To watch someone carefully.

Eye   To turn a blind eye
To pretend not to see something. This is a reference to the naval commander Horatio Nelson who chose to disregard orders in order to engage the enemy at the Battle of Copenhagen (1803). To avoid seeing the signal to turn back his ships, he put the telescope to his blind eye.

Eyes   To be up to your eyes in something
To be overwhelmed with work.

Eyes   To have eyes in the back of your head
To be very observant. The expression appeared in Latin literature and was quoted by Erasmus in a collection of traditional sayings.

Eyes   To shut your eyes to something
To pretend not to see what you do not wish to see.

F

Face   To change the face of something
To transform something.

Face   To face the music
To accept the consequences of your actions. Theatrical in origin, this image is from the situation of the actor who must face the orchestra pit and accept the audience s reaction, whether favourable or not.

Face   To keep a straight face
To refrain from laughing. A twentieth-century expression.

Face   To lose face
To be humiliated. This translation of a Chinese phrase came into English in the nineteenth century. See also **Face   To save face**

Face   To put on a brave face
To act more confidently than you actually feel. This may refer to the habit amongst many peoples of applying war paint to go into battle.

Face   To put your face on
To apply make up. A rather coy expression used by some women.

Face   To save face
To redeem your dignity. The concept of losing and saving face is regarded as Chinese and Japanese as their society lays emphasis on the importance of one s public image. See also **Face   To lose face.**

Faceless   Faceless bureaucrats
Government officials who are not accountable to the people of a country because they are not identified by name.

Fact   The fact of the matter is . . .
The truth is as follows. This is a common opening to untruthful or evasive remarks and dates, as such, from the nineteenth century.

Fair and square
Honest. Both words mean the same, but rhyme has a powerful appeal and the expression has been current for three centuries.

Fair   Fair game
A legitimate object of attack. The allusion is to hunting, where certain animals and birds have been regarded as appropriate victims of the chase, whereas it is forbidden to hunt others such as swans.

Fair   Fair to middling
Reasonably good.

Fair   The fair sex
Women. A patronising term which is usually disliked by modern women. The eighteenth-century essayists, Joseph Addison and Richard Steele, introduced it as a translation of the French *le beau sexe*.

Fairies   Away with the fairies
Impractical or unworldly. There are numerous folktales of humans being bewitched by fairies.

Fair weather   A fair-weather friend
Someone who remains loyal only as long as you are well and prosperous. Alexander Pope in 1736 played on two possible meanings when he complained in a letter of fair-weather friends of the summer who left him for London when the summer was over.

Fall   Fall head over heels
To be overwhelmed (often by love). The expression originally referred also to a physical somersault as well as an emotional one and began as hele ouer hed . Head over heels is a later form.

Fall   To fall between two stools
To fail as a result of indecision when there are two possibilities. This may be a translation of a French proverb which speaks of being seated between *deux chaises*, meaning two chairs . However, a similar saying was known in medieval England and in 1536 a collection of proverbs included this version: Between two stolis, the ars goth to grwnd.

Fall   To fall by the wayside
To fail to complete a worthy activity. This biblical expression appears in the Gospel of St Matthew 13, in the parable of the sower, some of whose seeds fell by the wayside and failed to germinate. The seeds represent the word of God.

Fall   To fall for it
To be deceived or captivated. In the early twentieth century, the latter sense was more common, as in Louis J. Vance s *Cynthia* (1911): There s only one sensible thing . . . I can see you falling for it.

Nowadays, the sense of being fooled is more prevalent.

Fall   To fall from grace
To lose favour. In the Bible (Galatians 5 : 4) St Paul says that those who lose faith in God are fallen from grace , meaning that they will suffer eternal damnation.

Fall   To fall on deaf ears
To get no response. This usually refers to unheeded advice or warnings and has been in use since the fifteenth century.

Fall   To fall on stony ground
To fail to flourish. Like to fall by the wayside , this expression comes from the parable of the sower in the New Testament, Matthew 13. The seeds that fell on stony ground germinated but eventually failed because they had no deepness of earth .

Fall   To fall on your feet
To be lucky in the face of numerous dangers and pitfalls. The comparison is with the well-known ability of the cat to land on its feet after a fall or a leap. In 1678 John Ray s proverb collection included the following: He s like a cat; fling him which way you will, he ll light on his legs.

False   A false alarm
An unfulfilled warning. In traditional military strategy the false alarm kept the enemy in a state of fear and the term still refers sometimes to a deliberate attempt to frighten a person. The term is also used for a predicted disaster which failed to materialise.

False   A false scent
A clue or line of inquiry which leads to nothing. The image is from hunting where the hounds follow a mistaken trail that takes them away from the fox.

False   To go under false colours   see Colours

False   To strike a false note
To say or do something inappropriate. The image is from playing an instrument where the wrong note ruins the harmony.

Far   A far cry
A long way or a big gap. The expression is probably military in origin, the army s distance from the enemy being measured in terms of shouting.

Far   Far be it from me

I would certainly not do the thing I am about to mention. This tends to be a hypocritical way of disclaiming something which you actually are about to do. An early record of this opening remark is in John Wycliff s translation of Genesis (44 : 17): *Fer be it fro me that thus I do.*

Far   Far from the madding crowd

A peaceful situation, away from noise and competition. This quotation is from Thomas Gray s *Elegy in a Country Churchyard* (1750): Far from the madding crowd s ignoble strife refers to the tranquil lives of the humble villagers. Thomas Hardy used the words for the title of one of his novels (1874).

Fast   Fast and loose

To trifle with someone, especially with their love. This probably comes from the game of Fast and Loose played at traditional country fairs in the past. A belt would be unrolled with the loop at the edge of a table and the customer had to try to catch the loop in a stick, but the stall holder usually managed to make it impossible to win.

Fast   The fast lane (or track)

An exciting, competitive activity probably leading to rapid success. This twentieth-century phrase referred originally to fast railway routes, but more often now alludes to the so-called fast lane of motorways.

Fat   A fat cat

A rich person. The term has a negative implication, hinting that the person has become lazy and smug.

Fat   The fat's in the fire

A disaster is about to happen and it is too late to stop it. The expression was mentioned in John Heywood s proverb collection of 1546 and has been used ever since. It evokes an image of cooking fat spilling on to the flames with which we are all familiar.

Fate   A fate worse than death

Seduction or rape. Originating in the seventeenth century, this term acquired a comic tone in Victorian times, probably because it had been over-used in melodrama.

Father   A father figure

A person looked up to for guidance, though not actually the father. The term comes from the psychological theories of Sigmund Freud (1856—1939) about the importance of the father in a child s early development.

Fatted   To kill the fatted calf   see Kill

Fear   Without fear or favour
Impartially. Since the nineteenth century the term has been much in use by legislators and politicians hoping to convey their responsible and fair attitude.

Feather   A feather in one's cap
An achievement. Many cultures have had the custom of awarding a feather in a warrior s headgear to mark the enemies he has killed.

Feather   Feather-brained
Superficial or stupid. This term refers to the light soft quality of feathers.

Feather   To feather your nest
To look after your own interests. A sixteenth-century expression alluding to a bird s instinctive urge to make a soft nest for its young.

Fed   Fed up to the back teeth
Extremely disgruntled.

Feel   I feel it in my bones
I have a premonition about something. In Shakespeare s *Timon of Athens*, the Third Lord, speaking of Timon s madness, says: I feel it upon my bones.

Feel   The feel-good factor
It is not enough for people to have their lives improved. They must actually be made to feel better off. In business and politics since the 1980s this has been increasingly recognised as a fundamental principle and is often cited by policy makers to be taken into account as well as financial and technological factors.

Feel   To feel the pinch
To suffer or be deprived. Pinch has long been used to mean stress, need or poverty. In Shakespeare s *King Lear* the king speaks of necessity s sharp pinch .

Feelers   To put out feelers
To approach people cautiously to find out their views on something. The allusion is to insects using their sensitive antennae to probe their surroundings.

Feet   Feet of clay
A serious flaw in the character of a person of high status. This biblical

expression is from the Book of Daniel (2 : 33) where the prophet Daniel interprets the dream of King Nebuchadnezzar in which the king saw a splendid figure made of gold, silver and brass, but with feet of iron and clay. In the king s dream the feet were smashed, which Daniel explained as meaning the break-up of the empire.

Feet   To vote with your feet   see Vote

Feisty   A feisty woman

Tough, courageous, cheerful. The word feisty comes from a dialect word for small dog and means frisky . In the late twentieth century it has come to be used excessively to describe outspoken modern women.

Fell   At one fell swoop

In one swift, often violent, operation. The phrase was invented by Shakespeare in *Macbeth*, where Macduff learns that Macbeth has murdered his wife and children like a kite swooping down on defenceless chickens: What! all my pretty chickens and their dam, at one fell swoop?

Fence   On the fence

Neutral.

Festive   The festive board

The table laden with food for a celebration.

Fettle   In fine fettle

In good health or spirits. The word fettle meaning health or spirits is no longer used outside this phrase. It is connected with a dialect word to fettle , meaning to arrange or put into good order.

Few   Few and far between

Infrequent. This is a quotation from Thomas Campbell s poem *The Pleasures of Hope* (1799) where he describes his hours of bliss as being like angel visits, few and far between .

Fiddle   To fiddle while Rome burns

To waste your time on trifles or show complete indifference while a disaster is happening. The Roman historian Suetonius tells how in AD 64 the Emperor Nero instigated the burning of Rome, then sat watching the spectacle from a high tower and played his lyre.

Fiddle   To play second fiddle

To take a subordinate role in an activity.

Field   To have a field day

To take the opportunity to indulge your special needs and interests without restraints. Traditionally a field day was an open day for the army when manoeuvres and lavish displays of skill and weaponry were put on for the public.

Fight   To fight tooth and nail

To fight hard using all possible means. The concept is contained in the Latin proverb *dentibus et unguibus*, with teeth and nails . In the sixteenth century Ninian Winger wrote in his tracts of contending with tuith and naill .

Figment   A figment of the imagination

An imaginary event. The phrase has been popular since the early nineteenth century. As figment itself means a fantastic notion the last three words are superfluous.

Figure   To cut a sorry figure

To give a bad impression.

Fill   To fill the bill

To serve the purpose. It was the practice in nineteenth-century American theatres to display posters with the names of the main stars, then to add minor attractions later to fill out the bill or list of attractions.

Filthy   Filthy lucre

Money. This biblical phrase is St Paul s term for money gained dishonestly. In Timothy (3 : 5) he lists the qualities needed in a bishop: not given to wine, no striker, not greedy of filthy lucre .

Find   To find it in your heart

To be willing to do something which may be difficult or need careful consideration. It appears in Thomas More s *Utopia* and in the King James Bible. Nowadays it has an ironical or pompous flavour.

Fine   A fine kettle of fish

A mess. This refers to a Scottish border custom of setting up a picnic, complete with fish kettle (a container for cooking fish), by a salmon river so that the catch could be cooked on the spot. Presumably these were hectic noisy affairs which soon became connected with confusion.

Fine   To go through something with a fine-tooth comb

To investigate with minute care. The fine-tooth comb for removing head lice dates from the nineteenth century, as does this expression. See also **Nit picking**, which has a more negative meaning.

Finger A finger in every pie

Involved in numerous activities, often in a meddlesome way. This metaphor from the child who tastes the newly cooked pies was in use in the sixteenth century. In Shakespeare s *Henry VIII* the Duke of Buckingham says of Cardinal Wolsey: No man s pie is freed from his ambitious fingers.

Finger My fingers itch

I am eager to do something.

Finger To have something at your fingertips

To be completely familiar with something. The source may be the translation of a similar Latin saying: To know something as well as your fingers and nails.

Finger To point the finger

To make an accusation.

Fingers Keep your fingers crossed!

Hope for success! Behind this injunction is the ancient superstition that forming the shape of the crucifix with your fingers would ward off ill fortune.

Finishing The finishing touch

The last step towards the completion of your creation. The phrase has been in use since the eighteenth century and comes from painting where the artist is romantically thought to add the last careful stroke of the brush to achieve perfection.

Fire A baptism of fire see **Baptism**

Fire To be under fire

To be attacked, either physically or verbally.

Fire To go through fire and water

To face great hardship or to test your endurance for somebody or for a cause. The allusion is to the Anglo-Saxon practice of making suspected criminals undergo an ordeal which if they survived unscathed would prove their innocence. The ordeal by fire might entail walking blindfold over hot metal. Those undergoing the ordeal by water were thrown into water to sink or swim.

Fire To play with fire

To meddle with matters that may lead to serious trouble.

First   First and foremost

Most important. This phrase first appeared in print in a fifteenth-century work by William Caxton. The second word is redundant as it means the same as the first, but this is the sort of weighty phrase which appeals to public speakers.

First   In the first flush of youth

Young and enthusiastic.

First   Of the first magnitude

Of the highest quality. The brightness of stars is graded according to magnitude, the first magnitude describing the most brilliant. From the seventeenth century onwards the term has been used to refer to human stars in their field. In *Love for Love* (1695), the playwright William Congreve used it in a derogatory manner: Thou liar of the first magnitude.

First   Of the first water

The best quality. Diamonds used to be graded for colour or lustre by classifying them as of the first or second water. The concept was transferred to people, as in Sir Walter Scott s *Journal* (1826), where he calls someone a swindler of the first water .

First   When someone or something first saw the light

When someone was born, or when someone understood something for the first time. This has been a biographer s favourite phrase since the Middle Ages.

Fish   A fine kettle of fish   see Fine

Fish   A fish out of water

A person who is away from his normal environment and therefore uneasy. The fourth century St Athanasius is said to have originated this image which is meaningful to anybody who has seen a fish struggling on dry land.

Fish   Neither fish, flesh nor fowl

Belonging to no definite category. Of no use to anyone. The original saying, which appears in John Heywood s *Proverbs* (1546), referred to the classification of foods as eaten by different groups. Fish was food for monks, meat for the people and fowl for the poor.

Fish   To fish for compliments

To try to obtain praise by putting leading questions or remarks as bait to the other person.

Fish To fish in troubled waters

To look for personal advantage in a time of calamity or political unrest. This comes from the notion that fishing is best when storms have made the water turbulent.

Fish To have other fish to fry

To have more important matters to see to. This expression is at least three centuries old and appears in John Evelyn s *Memoirs* (1660).

Fit Fit as a fiddle

In excellent health. Various suggestions have been made for this comparison. Possibly the original expression was as fit as a fiddler , in the sense that he had nimble fingers. It may, however, refer to the good fit of the fiddle or railing round the edge of nautical furniture which serves to prevent breakages when the ship meets stormy weather.

Fit To have a fit

To get very angry.

Fits By fits and starts

Intermittently. Illustrating two bursts of activity. The phrase, which sometimes appears in reverse order, is about four centuries old and is found in the writing of Bishop John Wilkins (1640) on the motion of the earth: always equal and like itself; not by fits and starts .

Fittest The survival of the fittest

The success of the strongest of a species. The phrase was first used by Herbert Spencer (1864) to summarise Charles Darwin s theories of natural selection. Since then the phrase has almost invariably been attributed to Darwin himself.

Flash A flash in the pan

A temporary success. Charles James defines this military term in his dictionary of 1810: An explosion of gunpowder without any completion beyond the touch hole. The old flintlock musket had a pan where gunpowder was inserted and ignited by sparks from a flint in order to set off the charge which propelled the bullet. If the powder ignited but then failed to set off the charge this was called a flash in the pan .

Flat As flat as a pancake

Extremely flat. The comparison is ancient and appears in Thomas Middleton s play *The Roaring Girl* (1611): Beat all your feathers as flat down as pancakes.

Flat   In a flat spin
In a panic, out of control. In the early days of flying this term described the situation where the longitudinal axis of the aircraft inclined downward at an angle of less than 45¡ so that the plane went out of control. In modern aerial warfare, however, this can be used as a manoeuvre performed at low level as an evasive action.

Flat   To go flat out
At top speed, fully extended. This is probably from flat racing, where the race is run on level ground with no obstacles to speed such as hurdles.

Flattery   Flattery will get you nowhere
It is no use trying to win someone over with excessive praise. In modern times this is a jocular reply to a compliment, but serious condemnation of flattery is frequent in Shakespeare, as in *Richard II* where the king complains: He does me double wrong that wounds me with flatteries of his tongue.

Flea   To have a flea in your ear
Aggrieved at having been scolded. The original expression seems to have meant simply upset or irritated, as a person might be if he had an insect crawling round his ear. In *Euphues* (1579) John Lyly describes a certain Philautus who stood as though he had a flea in his ear .

Flesh   Flesh and blood
A living person or a member of your family. The phrase originates in the Bible in Matthew (16 : 17) where Jesus asks his disciples who people say he is and Simon Peter replies that he is the son of the living God. Jesus answers: Blessed art thou, Simon Barjona, for flesh and blood hath not revealed it to thee, but my Father which is in heaven.

Flesh   The way of all flesh
Death. This is probably biblical in origin, from Joshua (24 : 13): this day I am going the way of all earth . In medieval writings this had become to goe the way of all flesh .

Flies   There are no flies on him (or her)
He (or she) is alert, functioning well and not easily cheated. Flies cannot settle easily on moving animals. *The Detroit Free Press* (1888) offered an explanation of this farming image: There ain t no flies on him signifies that he is . . . wide awake. Another version of the phrase was recorded in 1836 in a British publication: Don t let the flies stick to your heels.

Fling To have a fling

To indulge in a bout of impulsive, wild, enjoyable behaviour. This may have been invented by W. S. Gilbert in his lyrics for the *Pirates of Penzance* (1879): Peers must be peers and youth must have its fling.

Flip To flip your lid

To lose your self-control. Though the phrase dates from the mid-twentieth century the notion of keeping your temper under a tight lid is much older, as in Martin Mahoney s *A Chronicle of the Fermors* (1873): the lid was constantly getting off her temper .

Flog To flog a dead horse

To try to revive a long-lost cause. The Victorian politician John Bright has been credited with using this vivid image to describe the attempts of Lord John Russell to encourage a second reform of parliament in the 1860s.

Floodgates To open the floodgates

To instigate something which will set off violent emotions or activity. The floodgate in a dam is the door which releases pent-up water during a flood.

Flotsam Flotsam and jetsam

Rubbish, or numbers of poor, wandering people of low status. The terms originally referred to wreckage items floating on the sea (flotsam) and things thrown from ships (jetsam) to lighten the load.

Flow To go with the flow

To allow your own feelings to dictate what you do, not to resist. The reference is to the current of a stream.

Flower Flower power

The philosophy of love and peace, as against aggressive competition. This was the hippy slogan of the 1960s proclaimed by mostly young people using the flower as a symbol of the anti-war movement.

Fly A fly in the ointment

A drawback. This is a biblical saying from Ecclesiastes (10 : 1): Dead flies cause the ointment of the apothecary to send forth a stinking savour: so doth a little folly him that is in reputation for wisdom and honour.

Fly A fly-by-night

An unreliable person who settles briefly to some activity, then departs creating problems for the people left behind. In the eighteenth century the term was used for a witches who were thought to come and go on broomsticks in the dark, then later as a term of abuse for a woman.

Fly   Fly on the wall
Secret observation of someone s activities, eavesdropping. This comes from the common remark: I wish I were a fly on the wall , when speculating about another person s private activities or reactions. This phrase often describes the type of television programme begun in the 1970s in which a real family s daily life is televised.

Fly   To fly in the face of something
To challenge, to insist on doing something despite overwhelming odds. The reference seems to be to a bird, when attacked, flying in the face of a much stronger enemy to try to intimidate it.

Fly   To fly off the handle
To lose your temper. The image is of a hammer head coming off its handle.

Fly   To fly the nest
To leave home.

Flying   To pass with flying colours   see Colours

Foam   To foam at the mouth
To show rage. This brings to mind a picture of a rabid or ferocious dog, but it may also refer to the image of people possessed by devils who were said to foam at the mouth in frenzy.

Fogey   An old fogey   see Old

Follow   To follow in the footsteps of someone
To imitate or be guided by someone s example. This expression was common in the sixteenth century and appears in the *Complaynt of Scotlande* (1549): follou the futsteppis of your predecessours in vertu .

Follow   To follow suit
To do the same as someone else.

Follow   To follow your nose   see Nose

Food   Food for thought
A stimulating idea. Something to contemplate. The idea that the mind, like the body, needs nourishment is an old one. In *Tales of Paraguay* (1825), the poet Robert Southey wrote of a lively tale . . . fraught with food for thought .

Fool   A fool and his money are soon parted

A stupid person is easily tricked out of his money. This was a common saying in the sixteenth century.

Fool   A fool's paradise

The delusion that all is well when it is not. The concept dates from the Middle Ages. It appears in the *Paston Letters* (1462): I wold not be in a folis paradyce.

Fool   Fool's gold

Something which is not what it appears to be. This name was given to several minerals, including iron pyrite, of a brassy, yellowish colour which miners sometimes mistook for gold.

Fool   No fool like an old fool   see No

Foot   One foot in the grave

Very old or infirm.

Foot   To put your foot down   see Put

Foot   To put your foot in it

To make a gaffe. The reference is to stepping inadvertently into dirt or mess as you walk along the street.

Footloose   Footloose and fancy free

Not engaged or romantically linked to anybody. Footloose is an American term for at liberty and fancy free is an archaic English phrase with the same meaning.

For   For better or for worse

Under all circumstances, good or bad. These words, now extended to other situations, are part of the marriage ceremony in the *Book of Common Prayer*. The bride and groom promise to cleave to each other for better or for worse, for richer, for poorer .

For   For crying out loud!

This exclamation of annoyance is a euphemism, probably for For Christ s sake!

For   For good and all

Conclusively. This phrase with its emphasis on finality appears as early as the sixteenth-century *Parliament of Birds*.

For   For the birds
To be ignored, worthless. This twentieth-century phrase perhaps implies that only someone with the small brain of a bird would value the thing in question.

For   For the life of me
Not even to save my own life. The phrase was current in the early eighteenth century and sometimes appeared in the form for my life as in Oliver Goldsmith s *Vicar of Wakefield* (1766): Nor could I for my life see that the creation of the world had anything to do with what I was talking about.

For   For what it's worth
If it is of any use to you. This is common as an opening remark before giving advice, but has itself become almost meaningless.

Forbidden   Forbidden fruit
Something taboo or out of bounds. The allusion is to the biblical story of Adam and Eve in Genesis, where Eve disobeyed God s command not to eat the fruit of a certain tree.

Foregone   A foregone conclusion
Already decided, not open to further argument. Shakespeare seems to have invented the phrase in *Othello*, where Iago talks of Cassio dreaming about Desdemona.

Forewarned   Forewarned is forearmed
If you know about something in advance you can prepare yourself. This translates a Latin motto: *Praemintus praemunitus*, and has been current in English since the sixteenth century.

Forlorn   A forlorn hope
A project that is unlikely to succeed. This is a misunderstanding of a Dutch phrase *verloren hoop*, meaning the lost troop , which refers to the small, unlucky band of soldiers sent to spearhead an attack and therefore very much at risk.

Fort   To hold the fort   see Hold

Fortunes   The fortunes of war
The way the battle works out, for good or ill. In 1484 William Caxton wrote of a town being taken by fortune of warre .

Forty   Forty winks

A short nap. It is easy to connect the closing of an eye in a wink with the meaning of a brief sleep, but harder to explain the number forty. Possibly it is favoured because it is a frequently used number in the Bible.

Fouling   To foul the nest

To spoil your own surroundings or situation. The old proverb says: It is an ill bird that fouls its own nest, a common sentiment in many languages and one frequently used in the former USSR of dissident writers.

Fraught   Fraught with danger

Full of peril. The phrase has been long used and retains the archaic word fraught meaning loaded with .

Frazzle   Worn to a frazzle

Exhausted. A frazzle is a little-used word for a frayed end or fringe.

French   To take French leave

To do something or leave without asking permission. Because of historic hostilities between the French and English traditional sayings reflect a certain malice.

Fresh   Fresh as a daisy   see Daisy

Fresh   Fresh woods and pastures new

A new venture or place. This quotation from Milton s *Lycidas* (1637) is frequently misquoted as fresh fields and pastures new .

Friday   Girl Friday (or Man Friday)   see Girl

Friends   Friends in high places

Important friends who can use their influence on your behalf.

From   From bad to worse

Deteriorating. The comparison appears in Edmund Spenser s *Shepherd s Calendar* (1579) where he speaks of the end of the world: From good to badde, and from badde to worse.

From   From pillar to post

From one place to another. The expression may have originated in lawn tennis, the pillar and post being the fittings used in the old version of the game. However, it may refer to the whipping post and pillory used to punish criminals in the past.

Frying   From the frying pan into the fire
Going from one bad situation only to end up in another which is even worse.

Fuel   To add fuel to the flames   see Add

Full   Full and frank discussion
An official meeting between heads of state or senior politicians. This twentieth-century euphemism usually covers up considerable disagreement.

Full   In full cry
In pursuit. This is a fox-hunting term for the time when the hounds have scented the fox and start to bay in a chorus as they give chase.

Full   Full steam ahead!
Carry on at top speed!

Full   To come full circle
Events have run their course, finishing much as they started. This image probably originated in Shakespeare s *King Lear*, when the dying Edmund meets his brother Edgar: The wheel is come full circle.

Funny   Funny money
Currency which is suspect, or a very large sum of money. The term arose in America in the 1930s to describe money from crime. It was later extended to mean any foreign money and in the early 1970s in Britain the new decimal coinage was so described.

Funny   It's a funny old world
Life is strange. This rueful comment has been current in the twentieth century and was used notably by Margaret Thatcher on being voted out of office by her own ministers in 1990.

G

Gab   The gift of the gab
The ability to speak effortlessly and convincingly, usually on trivial matters. The word gab is from the dialect term gob meaning mouth , itself probably from Irish Gaelic.

Gaff   To blow the gaff
To let out the truth about a matter which has been (usually wrongly) concealed. The origin is uncertain and may be connected with the penny gaff , meaning a show of a very low quality in the nineteenth-century theatre where the plot was so crude that there was no suspense. It may, however, be connected with the French *gaffe*, meaning a blunder which was blown or exposed.

Gallery   To play to the gallery
To do or say something with an eye to maximum popularity or effect rather than genuine conviction. Traditionally the gallery in a theatre has offered the cheapest seats and, by implication, contains the least intelligent spectators, so that words directed at them will be appealing to the lowest instincts.

Game   Game for a laugh
Ready to join in something for amusement. The word game is from an Old English word meaning amusement and has also come to mean ready or willing or sporting .

Game   The game is not worth the candle
The project is not worth the risk, effort or expense involved. This is a direct translation from the French essayist Montaigne (1533—92) and compares a costly exercise to a card game at which the players went on into the night using expensive candles for lighting, only to lose the money they had gambled.

Game   The game is up
There is no chance of success now. This was a traditional cry at the end of several sports, including greyhound racing, when one had won and the others had to concede. In modern times detective writers have put these triumphant words into the mouth of the policeman or detective

who has identified the criminal.

Gamut   Run the gamut

To go through a whole range or scale, for example of emotions. The reference is to the musical scale invented by Guido d Arezzo in the tenth century. The Greek letter gamma was used to name the lowest note and ut (now doh) the first note, so the scale became known as gamma ut and then as gamut .

Gang   The gang of four

A group of four working together with a common purpose. Often the implication is that the purpose is suspect. The original Gang of Four were a group in China, led by Jiang Qing, wife of Chairman Mao Tsetung, in the 1970s and found guilty of treason. The label caught people s fancy and in Britain it was applied to the four founders of the Social Democratic Party in 1981 and since then has been extended to other gangs of three, five and so on.

Gang   To gang up on someone

To conspire with others to intimidate another person. The Old English word gangan simply meant to go together, but a gang of people often came to imply that they had a common bad purpose.

Gap   A credibility gap   see Credibility

Garden   To lead someone up the garden path

To deceive someone. Early in the twentieth century this seemed to have mainly sexual implications, the idea being that a man would lure a girl into the garden for seduction.

Gasp   At the last gasp

The end. This biblical phrase is from 1 Maccabees (7 : 9): when he was at the last gasp .

Gate   Irangate, Squidgygate, Thatchergate, etc.

The suffix gate added to the name of a politician or place connected with an event, indicating that there is a scandal. The practice of adding the suffix began after the Watergate scandal in the USA in 1974, when President Nixon was implicated in an intrigue to get himself re-elected. It involved burglary of documents from the Watergate apartment block, attempts at a cover-up and Nixon s eventual resignation.

Gatepost   Between you, me and the gatepost   see Between

Gauntlet   To run the gauntlet
To be exposed to hardship, risk or danger. The word gauntlet is a corruption of the Swedish *gantlope*, the term for a form of military punishment which involved the wrongdoer in a run between rows of soldiers who beat him with knotted cords or sticks. It was adopted by the British in the early American colonies.

Gentle   The gentle sex
Women. This was probably serious at one time but is now used rather ironically.

Get   To get a buzz out of something   see **Buzz**

Get   To get a grip on yourself   see **Grip**

Get   To get a kick out of something   see **Kick**

Get   To get down to brass tacks   see **Brass**

Get   To get in on the act   see **Act**

Get   To get in on the ground floor   see **Ground**

Get   To get in someone's hair   see **Hair**

Get   To get into deep water   see **Water**

Get   To get into hot water   see **Water**

Get   To get into the swing   see **Swing**

Get   To get someone's back up   see **Back**

Get   To get someone's goat   see **Goat**

Get   To get something off your chest   see **Chest**

Get   To get under someone's skin   see **Skin**

Get   To get up and go
To act with energy and decision. Originally used as a noun, get-up-and-go , the phrase was American and was often used to typify the pioneering spirit of the early immigrants to that country.

Get   To get wind of something   see **Wind**

Get   To get your dander up   see **Dander**

Ghost   The ghost of a chance
A very faint possibility. This image is nearly always negative, as in not

the ghost of a chance and dates from the nineteenth century. In *Tom Brown s Schooldays* (1857), Thomas Hughes stresses the hopelessness of Williams s chance of beating Tom at wrestling: Williams hadn t the ghost of a chance.

Ghost   To give up the ghost

To stop trying. In the Bible this expression simply means die , as in Job (14 : 10): Man dieth and wasteth away: yea, man giveth up the ghost. Here ghost means the soul which leaves the body at the moment of death.

Ghost   To lay a ghost

To dispel finally a problem or anxiety which has, like an unquiet spirit, tormented someone s mind for a long time.

Giant   A giant leap for mankind

A great discovery or rapid progress in an important sphere. The words are part of the sentence uttered by the American astronaut Neil Armstrong when he stepped on to the surface of the moon in 1969: That s one small step for [a] man, one giant leap for mankind.

Gift   The gift of the gab   see Gab

Gild   To gild the lily

To try to decorate something which is already beautiful. This image is an abbreviation of Shakespeare s words in *King John* (Act v1, Sc. 2): To gild refined gold, to paint the lily . . . is wasteful and ridiculous excess.

Gild   To gild the pill

To soften the effect of something unpleasant. The concept of putting sugar or some enticing substance on pills has always been common and this expression dates from the seventeenth century.

Gilt   To take the gilt off the gingerbread

To show something as much less valuable than it seems, to destroy an illusion. In the past, stalls at country fairs often displayed gingerbread decorated with imitation gold leaf, which when removed revealed a very ordinary biscuit.

Gird   To gird up your loins

To get ready for action. The expression is frequently found in the Bible, since the Israelites would wear flowing garments unless engaged in travel or hard work, when they would wear a girdle and loin cloth. Thus, in 1 Kings (18 : 76): He girded up his loins and ran.

Girl   Girl Friday (or Man Friday)

A helper who will turn her or his hand to anything. This was inspired by Man Friday, the faithful savage in Daniel Defoe s *Robinson Crusoe* (1719), so named because he was found on a Friday. Since the mid-twentieth century it has been common for executives to place advertisements for a Girl Friday (much less commonly for a Man Friday) to work in a busy office.

Girl   Girl meets boy

A typical romantic story. This phrase is used rather cynically to describe films or novels which deal with falling in love.

Give   Give them an inch and they'll take a mile

If you make any concessions people will take advantage of you. The original expression known in the sixteenth century was: Give them an inch and they ll take an ell , the latter being an old unit of measurement equal to forty-five inches. When the ell became obsolete people tended to understand the word as mile .

Give   To give and take

To make concessions. This may have come from horse-racing in the past where under certain circumstances the rules were relaxed so that large horses were allowed to carry heavier riders than regulations normally allowed and smaller horses could take jockeys who were lighter than usual.

Give   To give someone a wide berth   see Berth

Give   To give someone short shrift   see Shrift

Give   To give the devil his due   see Devil

Give   To give the shirt off your back   see Shirt

Give   To give up the ghost   see Ghost

Glad   A glad hand or to glad-hand

A welcoming handshake, to shake hands with people one after the other in a welcoming way. The term is now used of politicians going amongst people on their election campaigns.

Glad   To give someone the glad eye

To look at someone of the opposite sex seductively or invitingly. The meaning of glad here is bright, welcoming .

Glad   To put on your glad rags
To wear your best clothes. The word glad is used here in its older meaning of bright .

Glasshouses   People who live in glasshouses shouldn't throw stones
People who are themselves open to criticism ought not to attack others.

Glove   To be hand in glove with someone   see Hand

Glutton   A glutton for punishment
A person who seems to invite hard work and burdens.

Go   A no go area   see No

Go   From the word go
From the very beginning. The reference is to racing where the starter shouts go!

Go   To go by the board   see Board

Go   To go by the book   see Book

Go   To go haywire   see Haywire

Go   To go native   see Native

Go   To go off half-cocked   see Half-cocked

Go   To go off your chump/rocker   see Chump

Go   To go overboard   see Overboard

Go   To go round in circles   see Circles

Go   To go scot-free   see Scot-free

Go   To go straight   see Straight

Go   To go the whole hog   see Hog

Go   To go through the roof   see Roof

Go   To go to pot   see Pot

Go   To go to someone's head   see Head

Go   To go to the devil   see Devil

Go   To go to the dogs   see Dogs

Go   To go to town on something   see Town

Go   To go with the flow   see Flow

Goal   To score an own goal

To bring harm to yourself by your own actions. The image is from football where a goal is accidentally scored by a player against his own team.

Goalposts   To shift the goalposts

To change the primary objective or guidelines, at the expense of the opposition or just to be awkward.

Goat   To get someone's goat

To exasperate someone. According to the writer H. L. Mencken in *American Language* (1945), this comes from the horse-racing trainers who used to place a goat inside the stable of a nervous racehorse to calm it down before a race. Anyone who wanted to rattle the horse and thus spoil its chances of winning could take the goat away.

God   God's gift

A person who is specially attractive or helpful. The phrase is an ironical comment on a person who believes themselves to bring special advantage to anyone in their company. A man may consider himself God s gift to women .

God   God's own country

A place which is considered very dear to someone. The term began as a serious description of North America in the early nineteenth century, as in R. H. Kellogg s *Rebel Prisons* (1865): If I could only get out of that horrible den (the South), into God s own country once more. It has become a mainly ironical way of referring to people s native land.

Goes   It goes without saying

It can be taken as a matter of course. This is a translation of a French proverb: *Cela va sans dire* , imported into English in the late nineteenth century.

Golden   A golden handshake

A large lump sum given to an employee on retirement. This is a jocular reference to the formal handshake and presentation ceremony which is traditional.

Golden   The golden age

A period when a culture produces its best arts or skills. Greek and Roman poets used the term for a legendary age of harmony and happiness. It was later used in Western Europe to describe the high peak of Latin literature. It has now been extended to any time of notable achievement and excellence, such as the golden age of cinema .

Good   A good Samaritan

A person who helps others, especially those who are neglected by most people. The biblical parable of the Samaritan (Luke 10 : 30—37) gave rise to this term. It tells of a man who had been attacked, robbed and left for dead. Passers-by ignored his plight, but a man from Samaria took pity and helped him. Jesus told his listeners to do likewise. The modern organisation, the Samaritans, which counsels those in despair, is named after the biblical Samaritan.

Good   Good as gold

Excellent. In most cultures gold is synonymous with enduring value. An interesting extension of the idea is in the New Zealand use of the phrase to mean Yes, that s fine or I agree .

Good   Good, bad or indifferent

Just as it is, for better or worse. A common saying since at least the seventeenth century. It has probably endured because of its jingle quality.

Good   In someone's good graces

To be favoured by somebody.

Good   The good old days   see Days

Good   To have a good head on your shoulders

To be sensible, practical.

Goods   Goods and chattels

Possessions. This is an old legal term.

Goody   Goody-two-shoes

A smug virtuous person. This is the name of the main character of Oliver Goldsmith s *History of Goody Two Shoes* (1765). Having owned only one shoe for some time she went about bragging of her two shoes when at last she acquired a pair.

Goose   To cook someone's goose   see Cook

Goose   To kill the goose that laid the golden egg

To destroy the very source of your prosperity or good fortune through greed. The allusion is to a Greek fable about a farmer whose goose laid golden eggs. He killed the goose, thinking to get all the eggs at once, but realised too late that he had destroyed the fount of his wealth.

Gooseberry   To play gooseberry

To be a third unwanted person accompanying two lovers. The origin is obscure, but guesses include the possibility that it is connected with the fact that Gooseberry was an old name for the Devil. A chaperone might well appear diabolical to a couple in love.

Gordian   The Gordian knot

To solve a tricky problem with one decisive action. According to Greek legend, King Gordius of Phrygia tied his wagon to a tree with a complicated knot. Whoever managed to undo it would rule Asia. Alexander the Great simply slashed the knot with his sword without trying to untie it.

Gory   The gory details

The squalid, shocking parts of a story which might appear tasteless to some people. The word gore, once a common word for blood, especially that shed in fighting, is now often jocular.

Gospel   The gospel truth

An unquestionable fact. This reflects the traditional view that the books of the Bible were held to be sacred repositories of the truth.

Grabs   Up for grabs

Available. In the mid-twentieth century the meaning seems to have been restricted to girls who were accessible, but has now been extended to anything desirable.

Grace   To fall from grace

To lose favour. In the Bible in Galatians (5 : 4) St Paul describes those who lose faith in God as fallen from grace and the term has a strict theological meaning to denote those who are not eligible to enter heaven. It is commonly used for anyone who has offended a benefactor or superior.

Graces   To put on airs and graces   see Airs

Grade   To make the grade

To reach a certain standard. Originally the reference was to levelling a road to a suitable gradient, but it has come to be used in many spheres where a certain level needs to be achieved.

Grain   To go against the grain

To act against your natural inclination. The natural direction or grain of the fibres in wood indicate the easiest way to saw it. If you attempt to saw across instead of along the grain you have difficulties.

Grand   The grand finale

The glorious end of an activity or scheme. The term comes from the closing part of a musical composition, which is usually loud and impressive.

Grand   The grand tour

An extensive visit round a place. The allusion is to the eighteenth-century practice of sending wealthy young men on travels round Europe to broaden their minds on a cultural tour.

Grapevine   To hear something on the grapevine

To get information by way of rumour and gossip.

Grass   Don't let the grass grow under your feet

Make the most of your time. The image of standing so still that grass might grow is an old joke and was incorporated into this saying in the sixteenth century. In *Ralph Roister Doister* (1553), one character boasts of his alertness: There hath growne no grasse on my heel.

Grass   Grass roots

The essentials or the people who represent the essential needs or elements of a community. Originally this referred especially to the ordinary people of rural areas, but now it more commonly refers to those of all areas.

Grasshopper   Knee high to a grasshopper

Very small, very young. Always jocular, this expression became common in the USA in the nineteenth century.

Gravy   The gravy train

A method of getting money or advantages with little effort. This began as American railway slang in the 1920s where an easy run on certain trains meant good pay and light duties. The word gravy came to mean money .

Grease   To grease someone's palm

To bribe someone. This is an ancient concept, known to the Romans as applying ointment in return for favours. The sixteenth-century English version was greasing the hand .

Greasy   A greasy spoon café

An inexpensive restaurant which serves typical British breakfast and lunch dishes, such as bacon and egg, baked beans and cheese on toast.

Great   Going great guns
Proceeding rapidly and noisily. The original British Navy slang was blowing great guns , referring to tempests or strong winds.

Great   The great and the good
Famous people in public life. The term was first applied to the names of those who are considered by the British Government to be eligible for membership of Royal Commissions. It is said that the Treasury actually referred to it as the G and G list. Now it is often used ironically to refer to public figures.

Great   The great outdoors   see Outdoors

Great   The great unwashed
The poor. The term was probably invented by Edmund Burke, British Whig statesman (1727—97), but was also used by William Thackeray (1811—63).

Greek   It's all Greek to me
Impossible to understand. In Shakespeare s *Julius Caesar* (Act 1, Sc. 2), Casca comments on a speech which Seneca had spoken in Greek to make it unintelligible to most people: For mine own part, it was all Greek to me. This has come to refer to any unintelligible spoken words.

Greeks   Beware of Greeks bearing gifts
Look out when enemies suddenly turn friendly. This refers to Virgil s story of the Trojan horse in the *Aeneid*. Ten years into the Trojan War the Greeks abandoned their siege of Troy and left behind an offering of a wooden horse, which was dragged into the city. It turned out to contain Greek warriors who stole out at night and set fire to the city.

Green   Green with envy
Envious or jealous. The colour green has long been associated with jealousy and envy, possibly because according to medieval theory green bile was considered to cause melancholy.

Green   The green shoots of recovery
Signs of an improvement in the economy. These words became the catch phrase of the government of Margaret Thatcher (1979—90) during the late 1980s when her ministers tried to persuade the public that the economy was getting better.

Green   The green-eyed monster
Jealousy. In Shakespeare s *Othello* Iago says of jealousy: It is the green-eyed monster.

Green   To give the green light
Permission to go ahead. The allusion is to traffic lights where the green light is the signal to drive on.

Green fingers   To have green fingers
To be good at gardening.

Grey   A grey area
An issue which is difficult to make rules about because it cannot easily be classified. The colour grey has always lent itself to descriptions of doubtful, shadowy or boring matters.

Grey   A grey eminence
The power behind the throne. Aldous Huxley popularised the phrase when he wrote *Grey Eminence* (1941). The title was a translation of the nickname of the Capuchin monk who was secret adviser to Cardinal Richlieu in seventeenth-century France.

Grey   Men in grey suits
Members of the influential 1922 Committee of senior Conservative MPs who have, amongst other functions, the duty of informing a prime minister that he or she is no longer required to serve the country. This happened in 1990 when Margaret Thatcher was asked to resign. The image is of discreet, shadowy figures, acting not as individuals but as representatives of a party.

Grim   The grim reaper
Death. This is from the traditional portrayal of Death cutting down lives like corn.

Grim   To hang on like grim death
To persist. The traditional picture of Death as a sinister figure with a scythe is coupled with the idea of the tenacity of Death in claiming all humans in the end. See also **Grim reaper**.

Grin   To grin and bear it
To put up with difficulties with good humour. This has been in use for several centuries and was rendered as grin and abide in the seventeenth century.

Grin   To grin from ear to ear
To smile broadly. This was probably once a lively description of a wide grin but has lost its effect through over-use.

Grin   To grin like a Cheshire cat   see **Cheshire**

Grind   To grind the faces of the poor

To oppress poor people and exploit them. The image comes from the Bible from Isaiah (3 : 15): What mean ye that beat my people to pieces and grind the faces of the poor?

Grind   To grind to a halt

To come to a stop slowly and laboriously. The image is of a ship s engine or a train with a failing or clogged mechanism.

Grinding   Grinding poverty

Extreme poverty, usually combined with unjust treatment by the rich. See also **Grind**.

Grip   To get a grip on yourself

To control yourself.

Grip   To lose your grip

To lose your skill or to lose self-control

Grist   That's all grist to the mill

Something which can be turned to account. The portion of corn which a person took to be ground into flour at the mill was called the grist . The idea was that all grains of corn should be gathered to make a portion for grinding.

Grit   To grit your teeth

To get ready to endure hardship. The act of clamping the teeth together in the face of an unpleasant experience seems to be a universal human gesture, as it is mentioned in Latin and Greek literature. About 300 BC Menander used the expression in *The Girl from Samos*.

Grit   True grit

Courage and determination. The word grit is from an Old Norse word meaning pebble and the allusion is to the quality of toughness in the stone.

Groove   In the groove

Playing music well with a good beat or performing well in some other sphere. The term is from the mid-twentieth-century jazz world and refers to the way the stylus on a record player fitted into the grooves of the record.

Ground   Stamping ground

A favourite haunt frequented for a period of someone s life. This eighteenth-century American expression comes from cattle-farming and the habit of cows and horses to gather in one shady spot trampling the ground around them.

Ground   To get in on the ground floor
To join a project at its start and therefore gain an advantage. The expression is thought to have originated in nineteenth-century American business circles.

Ground   To get something off the ground
To get a project started. This expression comes from flying and refers to the successful launching of a new plane.

Groves   The groves of academe
Any institute of higher education and the people connected with it. The Grove of Academus was an olive grove and garden outside Athens where in the fourth century BC Plato held his school of philosophy.

Guard   The old guard   see Old

Gubbins   The gubbins
A collection of trivial objects. Ultimately the word comes from gobbet meaning a small piece or morsel .

Guiding   A guiding light
A principle to help someone through life, or a person who acts as a moral guide. The reference is religious and is in line with the idea in many hymns and prayers of spiritual aid resembling a light.

Gum   Up a gum tree
In a dangerous position from which escape is almost impossible. In the past in New Zealand solitary foresters sometimes dropped their rope while climbing giant kauri trees for wood or gum. Some died while stranded in the tree, which has a smooth trunk that is difficult to climb down.

Guns   Going great guns   see Great

Gutter   The gutter press
The tabloid newspapers, especially the more sensational ones. There has been in Britain a long tradition of associating less scrupulous journalists with sewers and gutters.

H

Habit   To kick the habit   see **Kick**

Habits   Old habits die hard
People do not easily change. This observation was common in the sixteenth century when it appeared as: Olde custom is hard to breke.

Hackles   To feel your hackles rise
To be angry or resentful. The hackles or hairs on the back of a dog s neck stand on end when the animal is angered.

Hail   Hail-fellow-well-met
Friendly and open. The whole phrase has been used mainly as an adjective and was over-used in early twentieth-century schoolgirl stories. It began as a greeting, but as early as the sixteenth century it was in use as a description of genial, welcoming behaviour.

Hair   A hair of the dog that bit you
A small amount of something that made you ill used as a remedy, especially alcohol which is sometimes advised to cure a hangover. The idea behind this sort of remedy is ancient and persists to this day. There is no evidence that alcohol taken the morning after a drinking bout is efficacious, but a hair of the dog is still offered as a treatment.

Hair   A hair shirt
A penance which you impose on yourself. The original was a garment made of rough material worn by sinners from the Middle Ages onwards in atonement.

Hair   Keep your hair on
Keep calm. In extreme stress people are supposed to tear their own hair out.

Hair   To get into someone's hair
To annoy someone. Possibly this echoes an old idea that bats were likely to tangle in people s hair and frighten them.

Hair   To let your hair down
To behave in an informal, free way. For centuries it was the custom for women to wear their hair pinned up or back in formal styles. At night

they would brush it loose.

Hair   To make someone's hair stand on end
To terrify someone. In many animals, hairs on the back of the neck literally become upright in times of stress.

Hairs   To split hairs
To make niggling distinctions, to fuss about details. In *Henry IV, Part 1*, Shakespeare used the image of the hair as one of the least divisible materials: I ll cavil on the ninth part of hair.

Half   A half-baked scheme
An ill-thought-out idea. The concept of something unviable being like an uncooked dish is an old one. Originally half-baked more often referred to a half-witted person.

Half   Half a loaf is better than none
Even if something does not fit all your requirements it is better than nothing. This saying was included in John Heywood s collection of proverbs (1546).

Half   Half a mind   see Mind

Half   Half cocked
Unsuccessful because of poor preparation or too early a start. This refers to the halfway position of the hammer on a firearm when the trigger is fixed and the weapon cannot be fired.

Half   Half the battle   see Battle

Hammer   To go at it hammer and tongs
To do something with all your energy. The expression is from the blacksmith s trade in which the smith used tongs to lift hot metal from the flame and a hammer to beat it into shape with all speed.

Hand   Hand in glove
Working closely together, on very familiar terms. The expression was known in the sixteenth century when it was hand and glove .

Hand   Hand over fist
Happening with amazing speed. This is a sailing term which alludes to the rapid hand action of sailors pulling on the ropes. It often refers to the making of money quickly and easily.

Hand   To live from hand to mouth
To live on the bare minimum of food and resources. The idea is that whatever comes to hand is used with nothing to spare and no choice.

Hand   To wait on someone hand and foot
To look after someone slavishly, serving their every whim.

Handbag   To handbag someone
To scold someone shrewishly. The phrase became common when Margaret Thatcher was prime minister of Britain from 1979 to 1990 and her handbag was jokingly referred to by cartoonists and comedians as the symbol of her power. She was considered to be particularly harsh, for a woman, in dealing with her own ministers and opponents alike.

Hands   Hands down
To win some kind of competition effortlessly. The term is from horse-racing when a jockey is so sure of winning that he can drop his hands, relaxing his hold on the reins.

Hands   Hands on
Direct practical experience of a skill or trade. This is a computing expression meaning that you can learn by sitting at the computer and mastering the skill by actually practising all its functions.

Hands   Many hands make light work
Plenty of helpers make the task easier. A traditional proverb.

Hands   My hands are tied
I am not free to act as I wish.

Hands   To have one's hands full
To be very busy.

Handshake   A golden handshake   see Golden

Handsome   Handsome is as handsome does
Actions, not appearance, are important. The concept is an old one and appears in proverb collections from the sixteenth century onwards.

Hang   Hang (on) in there
Try to keep going even if things are difficult. The expression is probably from boxing, when a boxer threatened with defeat holds on grimly to the ropes or grasps his opponent.

Hang   Let it all hang out
Don t be ashamed or embarrassed, behave as your instincts dictate. This twentieth-century expression is said to have originated in the USA and refers to the male sexual organ.

Hang   To get the hang of something
To understand how something functions or what it means. Here the hang means the natural flow or direction.

Hang   To hang by a thread
To be precarious. The allusion is to the story of Dionysius and Damocles. See also **Damocles**.

Hang   To hang in the balance
To be of uncertain outcome. The image is of the old balance scales with two pans, one of which had weights of fixed quantities to balance against the objects of unknown weight in the other pan.

Hanged   You might as well be hanged for a sheep as a lamb
You might as well commit a big crime as a small one if the punishment is the same. Sheep feature in this saying because until modern times sheep stealing incurred heavy penalties, even death.

Hanging   Hanging fire
Not sure to happen. The action of the seventeenth-century flintlock musket gave rise to this phrase because of its tendency to fail to fire first time. See also **Flash in the Pan**.

Happy   Happy hunting ground
Heaven, or an idyllic place. The belief of the North American Indians was that they would proceed after death to a paradise where there would be ideal hunting conditions and an easy life.

Hard   A hard act to follow
A superb achievement or a person of outstanding ability. This theatrical term describes a show which is so good that the following acts look feeble by comparison.

Hard   A hard nut to crack   see **Nut**

Hard   Hard and fast
Strictly according to the rules. This phrase is nearly always used in the negative, as in: There is no hard and fast rule. The original reference was to a ship that was immobilised either because it was in dry dock or because it had run aground and was fast or stuck.

Hard   Hard as nails
Tough, unsentimental. This must refer to the nail s capacity to resist fierce blows from the hammer.

Hard   Hard on someone's heels
Right behind someone. In close pursuit.

Hare   A hare-brained scheme
A crazy project doomed to failure. Perhaps because of its wild-seeming courtship displays the hare is traditionally thought of as mad.

Hare   To run with the hare and hunt with the hounds
To play a double game, keeping in favour with two opposing sides at the same time. This hunting image has been in use since the fifteenth century.

Hark   To hark back
To return to an earlier point or position or mention of something. This is from a command to the hounds in fox hunting when they have overrun the scent. They are required to hark , that is listen , and to go back.

Harness   To die in harness   see Die

Hash   To make a hash of something
To make a mess of something, to botch it. See also To settle someone's hash.

Hash   To settle someone's hash
To put a stop to the mess that someone is making, to subdue someone who is causing difficulties. The meat dish hash is a mixture of chopped meat and vegetables which has given its name to any mess or confusion.

Hat   A hat trick
A triple success. This is a cricket term meaning the taking of three wickets with successive balls. In the past a bowler who achieved this was presented with a new hat.

Hat   At the drop of a hat   see Drop

Hat   Old hat   see Old

Hat   see also Cap

Hat   To eat your hat   see Eat

Hat   To keep it under your hat

To keep secret. In the days when hats were worn more often, the hat could indeed be a useful place to conceal small items. A popular song in the 1920s went: Keep it under your hat, you must agree to that!

Hat   To talk through your hat

To talk nonsense. It has been suggested that the sheer absurdity of the image accounts for the origin of this expression; otherwise it may be a corruption of talk through your hand , meaning that if you have your hand over your mouth what comes out is not clear.

Hat   To throw your hat in the ring

To announce that you are a candidate or competitor. In boxing or wrestling a man might challenge his opponent or accept a challenge from a fighter by throwing his hat into the ring.

Hat   To wear two hats

To have two different roles (often with conflicting loyalties). The hat has traditionally been an important part of all uniforms. This expression has been popular in the latter part of the twentieth century and was referred to by *The Times* (1963) as the Whitehall idiom of wearing two hats .

Hat   With hat in hand   see Cap

Hatch   Down the hatch

Cheers! Your health! The hatch or trap door on a boat is one of many slang terms for the mouth.

Hatches   To batten down the hatches   see Batten

Hatchet   To bury the hatchet   see Bury

Hatter   Mad as a hatter

Crazy. The Mad Hatter in Lewis Carroll s *Alice in Wonderland* is evidence of the strength of the traditional belief that hat-makers were prone to insanity. There is probably a basis for this as mercury was used in the making of felt hats and one of the symptoms of mercury poisoning is trembling and twitching.

Haul   To haul someone over the coals   see Coals

Have   see also Get

Have   To have a bone to pick   see Bone

Have   To have half a mind (or a good mind)   see Mind

Have   To have it in for someone
To be full of resentment against another person.

Have   To have other fish to fry   see **Fish**

Have   To have something at your fingertips   see **Finger**

Have   To have your hands full   see **Hands**

Have   To have your wits about you   see **Wits**

Have   To have your work cut out (for you)   see **Work**

Have   To have your ear to the ground   see **Ear**

Haves   The haves and the have-nots
The advantaged and the disadvantaged in society. In *Athens* (1836), Edward Bulwer-Lytton wrote about the division between the Rich and the Poor — the have-nots and the haves .

Havoc   To play havoc
To cause confusion and destruction. The word havoc is rarely used outside this expression. It comes from Old French *havot* meaning pillage and looting .

Hay   To make hay while the sun shines
Take advantage of good opportunities as soon as they occur as they may not last. This ancient saying arises from the farming practice which is as sound today as it always was, to cut the grass as soon as dry weather comes.

Haystack   A needle in a haystack   see **Needle**

Haywire   To go haywire
To get out of control, to go wrong. Bales of hay, now usually fastened with twine, were often bound with a thin wire which sprang apart and scattered when cut open.

Head   Head and shoulders above (the rest)
Superior. The expression is now used in the obvious sense of comparing physical height to moral or intellectual greatness, but it originally referred to someone being thrust ahead of others by someone s help, or just good luck.

Head   To be unable to make head or tail of something
To be unable to understand something. The idea of being so confused as to be unable to know which way up something should be is as old as Cicero who spoke of being able to make out neither head nor feet .

Head   To fall head over heels (in love) see **Fall**

Head   To have something go to your head
To let praise or success cloud your judgement. The analogy is with consumption of alcohol which, in excess, affects your intellectual prowess.

Head   To have your head in the clouds
To be unrealistic or absent-minded. The expression is twentieth-century, but clouds have been associated with fantasy for much longer.

Head   To keep your head
Remain calm and in control in a crisis.

Headless   To run around like a headless chicken
To be wildly active and excited without achieving anything. This refers to the fact that the limbs of a decapitated creature continue to move in an uncoordinated way for a short time afterwards.

Health   A clean bill of health see **Clean**

Hear   To be able to hear a pin drop
To be in an atmosphere of total silence and attention. The image has been attributed to Leigh Hunt in *The Story of Rimini* (1816) where he writes of a pin-drop silence .

Heart   A change of heart
A reversal of a former opinion or attitude. This nineteenth-century expression was based on many similar, older forms.

Heart   A heart of gold
A generous person. The expression was used by Shakespeare in *Henry V*, Act 1v, Sc. 1, where Pistol attributes to the king a heart of gold .

Heart   A heart of stone
A cold pitiless person. The image can be traced to Homer and was also used in the Bible in Job (41 : 24): His heart is as firm as stone; yea, as hard as a piece of nether millstone (the nether being the grinding face of the stone).

Heart   A man (or woman) after my own heart see **After**

Heart   It does my heart good
It encourages or gratifies me. In the Middle Ages the heart was thought to be the seat of the emotions and positive news was therefore good for the heart.

Heart   My heart bleeds (for someone)
I pity someone. The image of blood dripping from the heart to indicate sorrow is traditional religious symbolism. Nowadays the expression is almost always ironical and indicates that the person spoken of is in no need of pity.

Heart   To have a heart-to-heart (talk)
An intimate, confidential discussion, usually to clarify a misunderstanding or a painful topic. The expression has become popular in the twentieth century.

Heart   To have your heart in the right place
To have excellent intentions even if you do not always fulfil them.

Heart   To have your heart in your mouth
To be very scared. This idea of fear gagging a person has been in use since the ancient Greek writers up to the present day.

Heart   To warm the cockles of one's heart   see **Cockles**

Heart   To your heart's content
To your entire satisfaction. This was a favourite expression of Shakespeare s and appears, for example, in *King Henry VI* and *The Merchant of Venice*.

Heartlands   The Tory (or Labour, or Liberal Democrat) heartlands
The place where the main supporters of a political party live. This expression, popular in the late 1990s, conveys the idea of a geographical centre of support, but also implies the fervent feeling associated with the word heart .

Heaven   Manna from heaven   see **Manna**

Heaven   Seventh heaven
A state of great happiness. Judaism and Islam recognise seven heavens corresponding to the seven planets. God s abode is considered to be in the highest heaven, that is, the seventh.

Heavily   Heavily pregnant
Very obviously expecting a baby. Since the mid-twentieth century the word heavily has over-frequently been used to qualify the state of any woman more than a few months pregnant.

Heavy   With a heavy heart
Extremely sadly.

Hedge   To hedge your bets

To reduce the risk of loss by having an alternative in operation, or ready to operate. The term originated in horse-racing where a person would seek to guard against loss, often by placing bets with several bookmakers.

Heel   Achilles' heel   see Achilles

Heel   Down at heel   see Down

Hell   All hell let (or broke) loose

Noise, confusion and fury. The words come from Milton s *Paradise Lost* (1667), in which the poet tells of the battle between Satan and the good angels and the Fall of Adam.

Hell   Come hell or high water

No matter what happens. This exclamation was well known by the start of the twentieth century, but its origin is unknown.

Hell   Hell for leather

To do something with desperate urgency. Originally the full phrase referred to riding hell for leather. The word hell expresses frenzied action and leather probably comes from its meaning of to whip, giving a picture of a rider whipping his horse into a mad speed.

Hell   Hell hath no fury like a woman scorned

A woman spurned can turn into a powerful enemy. This is based on a quotation from William Congreve s play *The Mourning Bride* (1697) which contains the lines: Heav n has no rage . . . Nor Hell a fury, like a woman scorned.

Hell   Hell to pay

Severe consequences. Since the early nineteenth century this expression has shifted its meaning; it originally meant simply trouble .

Hell   The road to hell is paved with good intentions

It is not enough to mean well, the important thing is to do good.

Hell   Till (or when) hell freezes over

Forever. This jocular expression was vivid until over-used soon after it emerged at the start of the century. The writer Scott Fitzgerald used it to sign off letters: Yours till hell freezes over.

Hell   To be hell-bent on doing something

Determined, whatever the consequences. The idea was originally a religious one from the Calvinists who divided mankind into the elect who would be saved and the hell-bent or those who were destined for eternal damnation.

Hem   To hem (or hum) and haw

To avoid saying anything definite. These throat-clearing noises are often used to play for time and the expression was confirmed in use in Jonathan Swift s *My Lady s Lamentation* (1728).

Here   Here today and gone tomorrow

A passing fancy or a flighty person. The saying was known in the seventeenth century and originally alluded to the brevity of human life but is now a rather derogatory remark about something or somebody lacking in solid worth.

Here   Here, there and everywhere

Difficult to find, all over the place. The expression dates from the sixteenth century.

Heroes   Unsung heroes

People who have performed great feats but are not known. The sung heroes are those immortalised in great poems like the *Odyssey* or the *Aeneid*. In *The Lay of the Last Minstrel* (1805) Sir Walter Scott wrote of the hero unwept, unhonoured and unsung .

Herring   A red herring

A diversionary tactic, a deliberate wrong clue. Smoked herrings with their bright colour and strong smell were used in the past to train hounds to pick up a scent. The same trick could also be used to lead them astray.

Hide   Neither hide nor hair

Showing no trace of being there. In the Middle Ages the expression was used in a positive sense, often to refer to farm animals for sale. If it was there hide and hair it was very much in evidence. The addition of neither is much more modern, as is the negative sense.

Hide   To hide one's head in the sand

To pretend not to be aware of a problem or unpleasantness. Early observers of ostriches used to consider that the birds buried their heads in the sand in the belief that they would render themselves invisible to predators. However the ostrich actually needs to consume sand and grit to digest food.

Hide   To hide your light under a bushel

To be modest. This is a biblical reference from Matthew (5 : 15): Neither do men light a candle and put it under a bushel, but on a candlestick. The bushel referred to is a container which would hide the light of a candle.

Hiding   To be on a hiding to nothing

To be in a no-win situation. The idea is that you are either about to get a hiding, that is a beating, or face impossible odds. The expression is thought to come from horse-racing.

High   A high old time

A very enjoyable activity or occasion with few restraints. This seems to be connected with the German word for a wedding *hochzeit* which literally means high time . There are similar uses of high for special occasions in English, such as high days and holy days .

High   An all-time high   see All-time

High   High and dry

Stranded. It originally referred to a ship that had run aground.

High   High and mighty

Conceited, arrogant. The words were used seriously in addressing and alluding to kings, but in the nineteenth century they took on an ironical meaning.

High   In high dudgeon   see Dudgeon

High   On your high horse

Behaving arrogantly. The image comes from the practice of mounting a particularly tall horse if you were of high rank to underline your importance. The metaphorical sense was commonly used from the eighteenth century.

High   The high-water mark

The peak of a certain activity or event. When seas and rivers flood, the highest level the flood water reaches is marked on the shore so that it is clear when the water has subsided.

Highway   Highway robbery

Exorbitant in price. The comparison is with the activities of highwaymen who rode the stagecoach routes to rob the passengers.

Hill   Not worth a hill of beans   see Beans

Hill   Over the hill

Past your best. Too old. The metaphor is of life as a hill to be climbed; once over the summit you are thought to be in decline.

Hilt   Up to the hilt

Thoroughly, inextricably. The comparison is with a sword which goes so deep into a wound that only the hilt checks it. The expression is often used in connection with debt or mortgage.

Hit   Hit or miss

Haphazard. The phrase is from sports where a target is aimed at. A shot can be made on the offchance that it may hit the mark.

Hit   To hit below the belt

To make an unfair attack on someone using dishonest methods. The term is from boxing, where it is forbidden to punch below the waist.

Hit   To hit it off with someone

To get on well with someone. The image is an old one and may come from target sports.

Hit   To hit the jackpot

To win an enormous prize or success. The term is from a form of poker game which cannot be started until someone holds a hand good enough to open, that is a pair of jacks or high-value cards. The money put up for each round is in a so-called jackpot and can be a considerable sum.

Hit   To hit the roof

To explode with anger or to reach a very high level of cost or expense.

Hitch   To hitch your wagon to a star

To aim very high. In *Society and Solitude* —Civilisation (1870), Ralph Waldo Emerson invented the image: Hitch your wagon to a star, Let us not fag in paltry works which serve our pot and bag alone.

Hobby-horse   To ride your hobby horse

To dwell on your own particular interest or obsession. The original hobby-horse was a toy consisting of a stick mounted with a horse s head.

Hobson   Hobson's choice

The choice of taking what is offered, or no choice at all. The term arose from the name of Thomas Hobson, a sixteenth-century livery man who hired out horses but gave customers no choice at all.

Hog   To go the whole hog

To do something unreservedly. Many origins have been suggested, including that a hog or pig is greedy and will eat until nothing is left and that a hog was once the name of a coin and therefore could be spent entirely. It may also be connected with the idea of giving a ship a hogging which meant a thorough scrubbing with a stiff brush called a hog .

Hog   To hog the limelight   see Limelight

Hoist   To be hoist with your own petard

To be a victim of your own schemes. The petard was an ancient explosive device for breaching gates and barricades, but all too often it killed the engineer who set it off. The word hoist in this context is the past form of hoise , an Old English word meaning catch or raise . Shakespeare first used the expression figuratively in *Hamlet:* Tis sport to have the engineer hoist with his own petard.

Hold   Hold your horses!

Not so fast! From pre-car days when it was also used as a command to wait.

Hold   Hold your tongue

Be quiet! The expression was in common use in the Middle Ages.

Hold   Not fit to hold a candle to someone

Inferior to the other person. Throughout the centuries when candles were the main source of artificial light holding one for another person was in itself a lowly task. If you were not fit even for that you were indeed contemptible.

Hold   That will not hold water

It is not sound or valid. The analogy of validity and a container which will not leak is four centuries old. In *The Yorkshire Spaw* (1626), John French challenged someone to: produce a rational account . . . one that will hold water .

Hold   To be left holding the baby   see Baby

Hold   To hold no brief for someone or something

To refuse to support a certain person or point of view. This is a legal term where to hold a brief for someone means that you are employed as his or her counsel and will argue his or her case.

Hold   To hold the fort

To look after everything while the person in authority is absent. This is said to have been a message signalled by General Sherman to General Gorse during a battle in the American Civil War in 1864.

Hold   To hold your own

To resist attack or criticism. The expression has been in use since the sixteenth century and, meaning hold your position, is probably military in origin.

Hole   A black hole

Infinite emptiness, a place where someone or something has disappeared. In astronomy this is the term for what is left when a star collapses leaving a field from which neither matter nor radiation can escape. Since the 1960s it has been used generally to indicate a void of any kind.

Hole   Hole and corner

Clandestine and underhand.

Hole   To be in a hole

To be in difficulties.

Hole   To need something like a hole in the head

To be faced with a very unwelcome prospect. This is a translation from Yiddish and was probably brought into wider circulation by Arnold Schuman s play *A Hole in the Head* (1957).

Holes   To pick holes

To be too critical.

Home   An Englishman's home is his castle   see Englishman

Home   Home is where the heart is

Your real home is where your affection is engaged, either by the place or the people. The Roman writer Pliny used the expression, but it appears in English in Elbert Hubbard s *A Thousand and One Epigrams* (1914).

Home   Home, sweet home

Home is the most desirable place. Such sayings exist throughout the ages in many languages, but it was immortalised in English in 1823 with the opera *Clari, or The Maid of Milan* which contained a song *Home, Sweet Home* written by Henry Bishop. It was made popular by leading singers and the phrase was enshrined in the language.

Honest   To be honest

To tell the truth. This common verbal gesture is often thought to precede words which are far from the truth!

Honest   To make an honest women of someone

To marry the woman who is pregnant with your child. Although now it is usually jocular because of changing moral and social standards, the expression captures the traditional principle that birth out of wedlock is unacceptable.

Honesty   Honesty is the best policy

It pays to be honest.

Honeymoon   The honeymoon is over

The good times are over. The word honeymoon , the holiday taken by newlywed couples, comes from the old practice of drinking mead (a honey drink) during the first month. The word has come to mean any initial pleasant period of an activity.

Hook   By hook or by crook

Using all possible means. This referred in the past to the rights of villagers in the Middle Ages to gather firewood in any way possible as long as they did not chop at the trunk or large branches. The smaller branches could be lopped with a hook and dead ones pulled down with a crook.

Hook   Hook, line and sinker

Everything. A gullible person who believes a highly improbable story is like a fish that is so eager to swallow the bait that it takes in most of the fishing line and lead weight as well.

Hook   To let someone off the hook

To release someone from guilt or further obligation. The image is from fishing where a fish caught on the hook can be thrown back into the water.

Hooked   To be hooked

To be in someone s power or unable to resist something. The image, from fishing, is of a fish fast caught in the hook on the end of the fisherman s line.

Hope   A forlorn hope   see Forlorn

Hope   Hope springs eternal

Many people are optimistic in even the worst situations. This is a quotation from Alexander Pope s *Essay on Man* (1733): Hope springs eternal in the human breast.

Hope   To hope against hope

To be optimistic when there are hardly any grounds for being so. This is a biblical quotation from Romans (4 : 18), where St Paul speaks of Abraham who against hope believed in hope .

Hopping   Hopping mad

Furious. This early nineteenth-century American expression originated with Seba Smith s *The Life and Writings of Major Jack Downing* (1833) in which the General was hopping mad .

Hornet   To stir up a hornet's nest

To cause consternation and anger by introducing a controversial topic or news. The image, though often used, retains a lively impact.

Horns   On the horns of a dilemma

Faced with two equally unpleasant alternatives. The term comes from logic where dilemma was the Greek term for a certain type of argument which faced the listener with an either or proposition. The Romans called this a horned question because you risked being caught on either horn. From there the image of being caught on the horns of a dilemma gradually evolved in English.

Horse   A dark horse   see Dark

Horse   A horse of a different colour

An entirely different matter from the one you thought to be under discussion. Apparently the earlier expression was a horse of that colour which would seem to come from identifying horses when selling or racing. In *Twelfth Night* Shakespeare has Maria use it in this way when asked about her plan to trick Malvolio: My purpose is indeed a horse of that colour.

Horse   Horseplay

Boisterous activity, a wild romp. Traditionally riders of hobby-horses accompanied Morris dancers and village processions to provide a touch of farce.

Horse   Horse sense

Common sense. The phrase is supposed to have originated in the American West, according to the *Nation* (1870), to describe men who exceeded others in practical wisdom. Opinions are divided as to whether it comes from the notion that horses are practical animals, or whether it refers to the shrewdness of horse-dealers.

Horse   Horses for courses

Pairing up things, schemes or people with suitable situations to function in or people to work with. This expression originates from racing when some horses perform much better on certain tracks or courses. The popularity of the phrase is probably due to the rhyme.

Horse   Straight from the horse's mouth

From an accurate, reliable source. This usually refers to authoritative information and comes from the practice of examining the teeth of a horse before buying the animal, as this is the most reliable way to check up on its age and health.

Horse   To flog a dead horse   see Flog

Horse   To get on your high horse   see High

Hot   A hot bed

Ideal conditions for the planning of an activity or operation (usually bad from the point of view of the speaker) such as a revolution. The original was a horticultural term for a glass-covered bed of soil specially fertilised for propagating plants.

Hot   Hot air

Pretentious, silly, empty talk. Air has long been associated with emptiness and perhaps because hot air rises it suggests bombastic words which fly out of the mouth without achieving anything.

Hot   Hot on the trail

Close to catching the animal or person you are pursuing. The idea is that the clues, scents and footprints are still warm, indicating the prey is not far away.

Hot stuff

A person or idea that is extremely valuable or attractive. The phrase was nineteenth-century American slang which has remained in use.

Hot   To sell like hot cakes

To be a commercial success. The expression was known in the sixteenth century when hot bread and pancakes were particularly enticing to a population without quick ovens and good food-storage systems. Even today advertisements for hot, fresh bread attract many customers.

Hot under the collar

Embarrassed, uneasy. Anything round the neck, such as a starched collar, is notoriously uncomfortable and when people flush round the throat region the problem is aggravated.

Hounds   To run with hare and hounds   see Hare

Hour   Zero hour   see Zero

House   Like a house on fire

Very quickly, with great efficiency. Strangely the meaning is positive, being used in admiration, whereas the object of comparison, a burning home, is a disaster.

Household   A household word (or name)

Famous. The expression came with the growth of advertising when manufacturers sought to make their product s name familiar to everyone.

Hue   A hue and cry

An uproar, indignation or fuss. The medieval expression meant an obligation on every person witnessing a crime or called to help. He or she had to take part in the hue and cry or loud pursuit of the wrongdoer. Hue is from Old French *huer* meaning to shout .

Hum   To hum and Haw   see Hem

Humble   To eat humble pie   see Eat

Hundred   Not a hundred (or million) miles away

Close by. This twentieth-century ironical expression is often invoked to draw people s attention to something near to where they live, but which they do not know about or choose to ignore because it makes them feel uncomfortable.

Hunt   A witch hunt   see Witch

Hunting   Happy hunting ground   see Happy

Hype   Media hype

Publicity in the newspapers or on TV which makes a person or thing much more talented, attractive or valuable than they are in reality. The slang word hype may either be a short form of hyperbole or of hypodermic , the thinking behind the latter being that something is given an unnatural boost, such as an injected drug may give a person.

I

Ice An ice maiden
A cold, intimidating woman. The term comes from Scandinavian legends of supernatural beings who live in the frozen lands. It frequently now implies that the woman is sexually frigid.

Ice To break the ice   see Break

Ice To cut no ice   see Cut

Ice To skate on thin ice
To take a risk, to put forward weak arguments. Some skaters deliberately choose to take the risk of skating fast over a thin stretch of ice to show their skill.

Icing The icing on the cake
A luxury or extra treat in addition to what could normally be expected in a certain situation.

Idle Idle chitchat
Empty talk or meaningless conversation. The original sixteenth-century phrase was idle chat , but like all such rhythmic pairs, chitchat fixed itself in people s minds.

If If the cap fits, wear it   see Cap

If If the worst comes to the worst   see Worst

Iffy A bit iffy
The situation is dubious, the outcome is uncertain, or I am not sure about it. This is a late-twentieth-century expression.

Ifs Ifs and buts
Excuses, hesitations, delaying tactics. The meaning has changed since the sixteenth century, when it meant wishful thinking . It tends to be used now in the context of a warning to someone, especially a child, to do as they are told without any ifs and buts .

Ilk Of that ilk
Of that type or class. This common usage is a misunderstanding of a Scottish term meaning of the place of the same name , as in Moncrieff

of that ilk referring to a person called Moncrieff from the place called Moncrieff. However the meaning of that type is much more common now.

Ill Ill-gotten gains
Profits or advantages which have been procured dishonestly. This phrase is part of an old proverb: Ill-gotten gains never prosper.

Ill It's an ill wind that blows nobody any good
There is always someone or something that benefits from a disaster. This is an old proverb in use since the sixteenth century.

Imagination To let your imagination run riot
To go too far, to indulge in a fantastic idea or project. The writer Hugh Miller wrote in *First Impressions of England* (1847): The sculptor seems to have let his imagination altogether run riot.

Immemorial From time immemorial
Since very early times, before living memory. The term was originally legal and signified the time before there could be. said to be legal memory, that was fixed as being any period before the reign of Richard I (1189—90).

In In a jiffy see Jiffy

In In a nutshell see Nutshell

In In a pickle see Pickle

In In a rut see Rut

In In a word see Word

In In at the death see Death

In In deep water see Water

In In for a penny, in for a pound see Penny

In In full cry see Full

In In hot water see Water

In In one ear and out the other see Ear

In In the arms of Morpheus see Morpheus

In In the bag see Bag

In   In the dog house   see **Dog**

In   In the groove   see **Groove**

In   In the heat of the moment   see **Moment**

In   In the long run   see **Run**

In   In the pink   see **Pink**

In   In the thick of it   see **Thick**

In   In the twinkling of an eye   see **Twinkling**

In   In your element   see **Element**

In   The in thing
Whatever is in fashion. For centuries to be in has meant to be in fashion.

In   To have it in for someone   see **Have**

Inch   Give someone an inch and they take a mile   see **Give**

Indifferent   Good, bad and indifferent   see **Good**

Inferno   A raging inferno
A big destructive fire. This is an Italian word meaning hell and made famous as such by the poet Dante Alighieri (1265—1321) in his *Divine Comedy*.

Injury   To add insult to injury   see **Add**

Innings   To have had a good innings
To have enjoyed a period of fruitful activity or work, or to have lived a long time. This is a term from the game of cricket, meaning the batting turn of a player.

Innocent   Innocent as a lamb
Pure and sinless. The lamb is traditionally the symbol of innocence. In *Henry IV*, Shakespeare has King Henry say: Gloucester is as innocent from meaning treason to our royal person as is the suckling lamb.

Ins   The ins and outs
The small details and complications of a situation. From the Middle Ages until the nineteenth century this phrase meant those in power or favour and those out of power but it had clearly changed by the time Thomas Hood wrote in *Laying Down the Law* about a celebrated judge who was prone to hesitate on devious ins and outs .

Inside   An inside job

A crime committed by a person within the building, group or organisation concerned. A police term much used in newspapers and detective stories.

Inside   The inside story

The reality of a situation as opposed to the public perception of it. A phrase from journalism where newspapers are keen to show that their reporters are the ones with access to the hidden information.

Insolence   Dumb insolence

Showing defiance and derision by remaining silent, usually under interrogation. A favourite accusation of schoolteachers about insubordinate pupils.

Instant   Instant sunshine

Immediate satisfaction and happiness. This was the name of a British cabaret group formed in 1966. In the twentieth century the word instant has become a component of many a formula, such as instant coffee, instant tan and instant soup.

Intents   To all intents and purposes

For all practical purposes, in effect, virtually. This is a legal term in origin.

Interests   In someone's best interests

Advantageous for someone.

Interest   Vested interest

A strong personal concern in something, usually because you stand to gain from it. The term in property law means having an existing or disposable right to the immediate or future enjoyment or use of a property.

Internet   To surf the internet

To scan the international communications network randomly to extract information or for entertainment. The internet is a computer network which has enormous interconnectiveness because it works through telephone links, allowing users to communicate and pass information from anywhere in the world. This expression has become the catchline of many articles and discussions about the internet and reflects the trendy image which it has brought to the world of computing.

Iron   An iron hand in a velvet glove

Fierce determination concealed by a gentle manner. The image is said to have been invented by Napoleon Bonaparte.

Iron   Iron rations
Emergency food supplies. As the first use of these was probably military they would have been kept in metal containers and, in the twentieth century, in sealed cans.

Iron   The Iron Duke, the Iron Chancellor, the Iron Lady
A firm and powerful public figure. The tough quality of the metal has provided a formula for describing the personalities of certain leaders, such as the Duke of Wellington (1769—1852), Otto Bismarck (1815—98) and twentieth-century British prime minister Margaret Thatcher.

Iron   To iron out problems
To solve problems.

Iron   To rule with a rod of iron
To direct people in a stern or tyrannical way. The words are from Tyndall s translation of the Bible (1526): And he shall rule them with a rodde of iron.

Iron   To strike while the iron is hot
To take the opportunity of doing something when circumstances are most favourable. This saying has been in use since the Middle Ages and comes from blacksmithing where the iron is most malleable when heated.

Irons   To have too many irons in the fire
To be involved in too many different projects. The image is from blacksmithing where the smith risks spoiling his work if he tries to heat and deal with too many pieces of iron at the same time.

It   It never rains but it pours   see Rain

It   It'll all come out in the wash   see Wash

Itching   Itching for a fight
Quarrelsome.

Itchy   Itchy feet
Unable to settle in one place, longing to travel.

Itchy   Itchy palm
Corrupt, ready to take bribes. In *Julius Caesar* Shakespeare invented this phrase to describe Cassius: You yourself are much condemned to have an itching palm.

Itsy bitsy

Superficial or uncoordinated. The term is often used of a woman s style of dress. Amongst American journalists it was sometimes used to describe Nancy Reagan, wife of Ronald Reagan, President of the USA.

Ivory   An ivory tower

A state of mind in which a person is remote from ordinary problems. The allusion is to fairy-tale characters dwelling in towers far from lowly people. The French writer Saint-Beuve used the expression to describe another writer, Alfred de Vigny, whom he regarded as out of touch with reality.

J

Jack   Every man jack of them   see **Every**

Jack   I'm all right Jack

The philosophy of looking after your own interests exclusively. This is probably connected with the Australian meaning of Jack as a smart or cunning person.

Jack   Jack of all trades

A person who is good at everything. This term was known in the sixteenth century. Much later master of none was added to the original, signifying that a person who does everything may be mediocre in all skills.

Jackpot   To hit the jackpot   see **Hit**

Jam   Money for jam

Financial gain for no effort at all.

Jam   To be in a jam

To be in a difficult situation. This is from the meaning of a jam in the sense of being stuck fast.

Jaundiced   A jaundiced eye   see **Eye**

Jaws   To snatch someone from the jaws of death
To rescue from a very dangerous situation.

Je   A certain *je ne sais quoi*
A special fascinating quality that is hard to describe. What was once an affected use of a French phrase meaning I don t know what has become a joking remark.

Jet   The jet set
Rich, fashionable people who travel a lot. The phrase came into use soon after travelling by jet plane became possible in the mid-twentieth century and the rhyming words caught the popular imagination.

Jetsam   Flotsam and jetsam   see Flotsam

Jewel   The jewel in the crown
The most precious part of something. The phrase was in use in the early part of the nineteenth century, but it has become popular in the late twentieth century because it was used as the title of a television adaptation of a novel by Paul Scott. Here the jewel in the crown was India, of which Queen Victoria became Empress in 1877.

Jiffy   In a jiffy
In a very short time. The use of jiffy for a moment has been common since the early nineteenth century but its origin is unknown.

Jinks   High jinks
Boisterous activity. The ancient game of jinks resembled the game of forfeits. A throw of the dice determined which player should perform an act or sing. This led to crude jokes and noise.

Jitters   To have the jitters
To be nervous and excitable. This is probable popular because the sound suggests the meaning.

Job   It is a good job
A satisfactory state of affairs. The very common word job is of uncertain origin, possibly connected with gob meaning mouth or mouthful or a lump of something.

Job   More than one's job is worth
Too risky.

Job   To make the best of a bad job
To be resigned to something which is not an ideal state of affairs. See also It is a good job.

Jockey   To jockey for position
To obtain an advantage by manoeuvring. This is from horse-racing where a rider might use shrewd moves to get ahead of the others.

John   A Dear John letter   see Dear

Joint   To put someone's nose out of joint   see Nose

Joking   Joking apart
To be serious now, after joking. This is often a preliminary remark used before adopting a more serious tone in conversation, or it can be almost meaningless, simply a conversational filler.

Joneses   To keep up with the Joneses
Make sure that you are not outdone in wealth, smartness or possessions by your neighbours. This was the title of a comic strip in the *New York Globe* until 1931. The author, Arthur Momand, told the exploits of a family and their neighbours, giving them one of the most common surnames.

Jot   Every jot and tittle
Every small item or detail. The words are from the Bible from Matthew (5 : 18): Till heaven and earth pass, one jot or tittle shall in no wise pass from the law, till all be fulfilled . The word jot is from a translation of iota , the smallest Greek letter and tittle is the dot over the letter.

Jowl   Cheek by jowl   see Cheek

Joy   To get no joy
To get no satisfaction.

Jugular   To go for the jugular
To attack or argue by aiming at your opponent s weakest point. The jugular veins are those in the neck which carry blood from the face and neck to the heart.

Jump   To jump at the chance
To seize an opportunity.

Jump   To jump down someone's throat
To reproach someone harshly and suddenly. The expression seems to have come into use in the nineteenth century.

Jump   To jump for joy
To show your pleasure.

Jump   To jump on someone
To reproach or reprimand someone.

Jump   To jump the gun
To act prematurely or rashly. This is from a term used in athletics when a runner starts before the starter s gun has gone off.

Jungle   The jungle telegraph
The spread of news by means of gossip and rumour. The image is of native drum beats or smoke signals used by primitive peoples to convey information.

Jungle   The law of the jungle
Lawless and uncivilised.

Junk   Junk food
Processed food which requires little or no cooking and is of poor nutritional value. The word junk is from the Latin *juncus* meaning rushes , and junk was a sailor s term for odds and ends of rope and fibre, therefore something of little value.

Junk   To junk something
To criticise an idea or project as being of no value.

Just   Just one of those things
The sort of thing that happens in life, for no particular reason. A Cole Porter song which came out in 1935 fixed this expression in the English language.

Just   To get one's just deserts   see **Deserts**

K

Keel   On an even keel
Well balanced, steady. The keel is the lowest structural part of a boat, maintaining its stability in the water.

Keep   Keep a stiff upper lip   see **Lip**

Keep   Keep it under your hat   see **Hat**

Keep   Keep your hair on   see **Hair**

Keep   To keep a straight face   see **Face**

Keep   To keep an eye on someone or something   see **Eye**

Keep   To keep body and soul together   see **Body**

Keep   To keep someone at arm's length   see **Arm**

Keep   To keep someone posted   see **Posted**

Keep   To keep the ball rolling   see **Ball**

Keep   To keep up with the Joneses   see **Joneses**

Keep   To keep your ear to the ground   see **Ear**

Keep   To keep your fingers crossed   see **Fingers**

Keep   To keep your head above water   see **Water**

Keep   To keep your nose clean   see **Nose**

Keep   To keep yourself to yourself
To stay aloof from other people.

Kettle   A fine kettle of fish   see **Fine**

Key   To have the key of the door
To be an adult. Traditionally in Britain a person came of age at twenty-one and afterwards could come in and out as he or she pleased. The notion is enshrined in a popular song: I've got the key of the door. Never been twenty-one before.

Kibosh   To put the kibosh on something
To put a stop to it, to veto a project. It has been suggested that the origin is the Irish Gaelic phrase *cie bais* meaning the cap of death .

Kick   A kick in the pants
A reprimand. The image was in use in the seventeenth century.

Kick   A kick in the teeth
A reprimand. A later version of a kick in the pants .

Kick   A kick start
A vigorous stimulus to revive a project which is not thriving. This is from the vigorous method of starting an engine by pressing or kicking a pedal, as in motor bikes.

Kick   Better than a kick in the pants
What is on offer should not be scorned because it is better than a reprimand. This is a twentieth-century variation on a much older image. See also **A kick in the pants.**

Kick   To get a kick out of something
To be stimulated or exhilarated by something.

Kick   To kick the habit
To give up a habit which is potentially very harmful. Here kick has the sense of rebel against something .

Kick   To kick a man when he's down
To scold or criticise someone when they are already sad or unfortunate from some other cause.

Kick   To kick the bucket
To die. The word bucket here probably refers to a bucket beam in the roof of a slaughter house. After being slaughtered an animal s legs swung against the beam.

Kick   To kick up a fuss
To be very demanding or to complain loudly.

Kicking   Alive and kicking   see Alive

Kid   To handle someone with kid gloves
To treat someone with great tact or care. In the past, gloves made from the skin of a young goat were highly prized for their softness and fine appearance.

Kill   If looks could kill

Someone s facial expression registering hate and resentment. This phrase is used in the twentieth century to dramatise a piece of gossip or account of an event.

Kill   Kill or cure

The medicine or solution to a problem is so drastic that it will either destroy the user or have an outstanding success.

Kill   To kill (or shoot) the messenger

To punish the bearer of bad tidings instead of those responsible for the disaster. Shakespeare was well aware of this human tendency and in the last act of *Macbeth* he shows Macbeth s fury against the messengers who bring him news that he is surrounded and defeat is imminent.

Kill   To kill the fatted calf

To prepare a feast of welcome. This biblical quotation is from the parable of the prodigal son told by Jesus in Luke (15 : 11—32). A man had two sons, one of whom stayed at home and worked hard, the other travelled and squandered his money. When the wastrel returned the father ordered the fatted calf to be killed to celebrate his return.

Kill   To kill the goose that lays the golden eggs   see **Goose**

Kill   To kill two birds with one stone

To fulfil two aims with just one effort. The image existed in Latin and was in use in English in the sixteenth century, coming in both cases from a primitive type of hunting by catapult.

Kill   To kill with kindness

To be too generous to somebody for their own good. The full expression was to kill with kindness as fond apes do their young, referring to the possibility of an ape crushing its young to death in an over-enthusiastic hug. The expression was fixed further in the language by Thomas Heywood s play *A Woman Kilde with Kindnesse* (1675).

Killing   The killing fields

A place where massacres or terrible cruelty have taken place. This was the title of a film (1984) about executions in Cambodia by the tyrant Pol Pot who ordered the killing of forced labourers in the paddy fields. Since then the phrase has been used of many scenes of mass execution or torture.

Kilter   Out of kilter

Not in a good frame of mind, out of condition. The word kilter is a form of kelter , a seventeenth-century word meaning in good condition . Its origin is unknown though it may be connected with kelter , the coarse good cloth used for everyday clothes.

Kindred   A kindred spirit
A person with tastes, attitudes and habits like your own. It has been in use since the nineteenth century.

King   King size (or king-sized)
Larger than standard size. Here king is used as an adjective which can be added to almost any commodity, such as a beds, sheets, cigarettes, to indicate a big size. Probably the first such use was in building, where the king post was the large vertical post connecting the apex of a triangular roof-truss to the tie-beam.

King   The king pin
The most important person in a set-up, or the main principle on which a theory or philosophy rests. This is the name of a pivot pin which provides a steering joint in a motor vehicle.

Kingdom   Until kingdom come
Forever, for a long time. The phrase is suggested by the Lord s Prayer where the words Thy kingdom come refer to man s hoped-for salvation at the end of the world when the kingdom of God will triumph.

Kiss   Kiss and tell
To give away an intimate secret, usually about a romantic or sexual liaison. The phrase was invented by Charles Cotton in *Burlesque* (1675): And if he needs must kiss and tell, I ll kick him headlong into hell. Nowadays it describes the activities of former lovers of men in public life who sell details of their affairs to newspapers.

Kiss   The kiss of death
An apparently friendly action or relationship which swiftly brings an end to a project. The allusion is to the kiss with which Judas Iscariot identified and therefore betrayed Jesus to the Romans.

Kiss   The kiss of life
A life-saving action for a person or project. Since the 1960s this name has been used for the mouth-to-mouth method of resuscitation of an unconscious person and has been extended to situations where an emergency measure has been used to revive someone or something.

Kitten   Weak as a kitten
Fragile.

Knee   Knee-high to a grasshopper   see Grasshopper

Knees   The bee's knees

The best, most attractive, talented person. Originating in the early nineteenth century, this may be connected with an eighteenth-century saying: As big as a bee s knee , a jocular allusion to a small thing or person, but its main attraction seems to be the rhyme and the ludicrous image.

Knees   To be brought to one's knees

To be humiliated and made to ask for mercy.

Knife   On a knife edge

Facing imminent disaster, about to collapse.

Knife   To have your knife into someone

To bear a grudge against someone and wish to harm them.

Knight   A knight in shining armour

Someone who will deliver you from your difficulties or a dashing romantic lover. The expression is twentieth-century, but the image is from the Middle Ages and the tales of courtly love, still known to us through fairy tales, of fair ladies who are rescued from danger by handsome knights.

Knives   The night of the long knives

A surprise purge of unwanted members of a government or any body in authority. The name was given to the time in 1934 when Hitler liquidated the leaders of the SS storm-troopers who had helped him to power. Since then it has been used, for example, to describe ruthless reorganisations of the cabinets of Harold Macmillan and Margaret Thatcher.

Knock   To knock for six

To demolish an opponent s argument or plan completely. This is a cricketing term to describe a batsman hitting the ball over the boundary and scoring six runs.

Knock   To knock sense into someone

To use brusque or harsh methods to make someone see reason.

Knock   To knock spots off someone

To defeat or outdo someone. This nineteenth-century expression arose from the habit of using playing cards for target practice, the object being to aim well enough to hit all the spots and pips from a card.

Knock   You could have knocked me down with a feather

I was astonished. This is found in the early nineteenth century in the writings of William Cobbett in *Rural Rides* (1821).

Knocks   The school (or university) of hard knocks

The sort of life experience which teaches you how to deal with hardship. The term arose at the start of the twentieth century and in various forms has been used by self-educated but successful figures, such as Frank Sinatra, who described himself as a graduate of the school of hard knocks.

Knot   The Gordian knot   see Gordian

Knot   To tie the knot

To get married. The expression existed in the seventeenth century as part of a longer one: To tie a knot with one s tongue that one cannot untie with one s teeth. It remained in this form until the early twentieth century but was later abbreviated.

Know   Not to know someone from Adam   see Adam

Know   To know the ropes

To have expert knowledge of an operation or task. This is a sailing term describing the knowledge required of a sailor who had to know the rigging of a ship to handle the ropes.

Know   To know which side your bread is buttered

To know where your own best interests are served. The expression was known in proverb collections of the sixteenth century.

Know   To know what's what

To understand all the implications of a situation. Samuel Butler may have invented the expression in *Hudibras* (1663): He knew what s what and that s as high as metaphysic wit can fly.

Knuckle   To knuckle down

To settle down to do some hard work. To knuckle refers to the act of bending your joints in an act of submission.

Knuckle   To knuckle under

To accept your inferior position. See also **To knuckle down**

Knuckles   A rap on the knuckles

A reprimand. Through the ages teachers have brought children to order with a sharp tap on the knuckles with a pointer or ruler.

L

Labour   A labour of love
Something done out of affection and without thought of personal gain. These words are from the Bible, from St Paul s epistle to the Thessalonians where he thanks them for their unstinting work — remembering without ceasing your work of faith and labour of love .

Lady   A lady of leisure
A woman who has sufficient income to be able not to work. The term is used ironically.

Lady   Lady Bountiful
A woman who helps others in a patronising manner. The original was a character in George Farquhar s play *The Beaux Stratagem* (1707) who was sincerely generous and helpful to others, especially to the sick. It later became an ironical term.

Lady   The Iron Lady   see Iron

Lady   The lady's not for turning
She will not change her mind. In 1980, Margaret Thatcher invented this expression to deny that she would indulge in policy changes or U turns as prime minister. She was punning on the title of Christopher Fry s play *The Lady s not for Burning* (1948). In later years this expression has been used in other situations.

Lamb   Like a lamb to the slaughter
Going meekly into a harsh ordeal without protest.

Lame   A lame duck   see Duck

Land   Land of milk and honey
A place abundant in food and all human needs. These words from the Bible form part of the Lord s promise to Moses about his chosen people: And I am come to deliver them out of the land of the Egyptians, and to bring them up out of that land unto a good land and large, unto a land flowing with milk and honey.

Lap   In the lap of luxury

In rich, easy circumstances. Luxury is personified as an indulgent parent holding the lucky rich person like a child on his or her knee. Maria Edgeworth used this expression in her *Moral Tales* (1802) of someone brought up in the lap of luxury .

Last   Last but not least

The final person or item mentioned is certainly not the least important just because of their place on the list. Research in the twentieth century seems to hint that there may be a real need to stress this point, as there is evidence that, for example, children whose names are towards the end of class registers receive less attention and do less well.

Last   Last gasp   see Gasp

Last   Last-ditch effort   see Ditch

Last   On his (or its) last legs

Near to death or to the end of his or its useful life. The expression was used in the sixteenth century and probably refers to the buckling of an animal s back legs when it is weak.

Last   The last resort

The final place to go to for help. In 1672 Sir William Temple used it thus: All government is a restraint upon liberty: and under all the dominions equally absolute, where it is in the last resort.

Last   The last straw

One hardship too many, the final extra burden which makes everything intolerable. The seventeenth-century version seems to have been the last feather that breaks the horse s back . In *Dombey and Son* (1848), Charles Dickens speaks of: The straw that broke the camel s back , but the simple phrase the last straw is now part of the language.

Last   To have the last laugh

To be triumphant in the end, despite earlier humiliations. This notion exists in most European languages.

Late   The late lamented

The dead person. Once a serious way of referring to a deceased person, this is now ironical.

Late   Too little too late   see Little

Laugh   Don't know whether to laugh or cry

The present situation is painful, but it has ludicrous, astonishing elements. This remark is always appropriate for certain situations and a similar observation was made by the Russian poet Alexander Pushkin (1799—1837): All this would be laughable, were it not so sad.

Laugh   Game for a laugh   see **Game**

Laugh   To laugh all the way to the bank   see **Cry**

Laugh   To laugh on the other side of your face

To be forced to change from amusement to sadness or anger. An Italian collector of proverbs noted in the seventeenth century that this was an English expression used by people who got revenge on someone who was jeering at them. It is a favourite of schoolteachers when dealing with giggling pupils.

Laugh   To laugh someone out of court

To pour scorn on an argument and show that it is untenable. The idea is that the opponent s views would not stand examination in a court of law.

Laugh   To laugh up your sleeve

To be secretly amused, to gloat over knowledge that you alone possess. This image was more feasible in the sixteenth and seventeenth centuries when wide, complicated sleeves were fashionable.

Laugh   To laugh your head off

To be wildly amused.

Laurels   To rest on your laurels

To be too ready to relax your efforts on the strength of having made great achievements in the past. The laurels referred to are the wreaths of the bay tree worn in ancient Rome by star athletes, poets and high achievers in many fields.

Law   Law and order

The accepted way a society is run so that its rules are made and obeyed. The words are similar in meaning but are used as a rallying cry at political meetings, especially when society s moral codes seem threatened.

Law   The law of the land

The accepted way society is run. See also **Law and order** above. The alliteration here helps to make the phrase popular.

Law   To lay down the law
To make dogmatic statements, usually when you are not in a position to do so.

Law   To take the law into your own hands
To act against a transgressor on your own initiative without reference to those in authority. The most serious example of this is probably lynching whereby a mob of people seize a prisoner and execute him before trial.

Lay   To lay a ghost
To settle or come to terms with a long-standing problem or painful memory. This is another term for exorcising a spirit which has allegedly possessed a person, and ministers of some churches still perform a religious ceremony for this purpose.

Lay   To lay it on the line
To speak sincerely, often about risks involved in an enterprise. The early twentieth-century meaning was associated with being frank and honest about money. A rather different meaning has arisen latterly, as it now sometimes means to be ready to sacrifice yourself for your principles.

Lay   To lay it on thick
To exaggerate. The earlier expression was to lay it on with a trowel and appears in Shakespeare s *As You Like It* (Act 1, Sc. 2).

Lay   To lay your cards on the table   see Cards

Lead   To lead by the nose
To make someone follow your wishes blindly. The reference is to farm animals being led by means of a ring in their nose. The expression appears in the Bible and in sixteenth-century works.

Leading   A leading edge
A top position usually in the world of technology and science. This was originally the name of the edge of an aeroplane s propeller which faced the direction of motion, then it was extended to any other device which improved a plane s capability. Now it is used about any device or system which puts you in the forefront,

Leading   A leading question   see Question

Leaf   To turn over a new leaf
To reform your behaviour. The image is of the reader or writer of a book starting afresh on a new page or leaf.

Lean   A lean and hungry look

A dangerous aspect. In Shakespeare s *Julius Caesar* Caesar says of Cassius that he has a lean and hungry look , rightly suspecting him of conspiracy.

Leap   A leap in the dark

A venture undertaken without being able to foresee the consequences. In the writings of Thomas Brown (1663—1704) and others the expression referred to death, but since the nineteenth century it has been used figuratively for any risky step. When Disraeli sought to extend the franchise in 1876 he was said to be taking a leap in the dark.

Leave   French leave   see French

Leave   Leave someone in the dark

Not to let them know what your intentions are.

Leave   To leave in the lurch

To abandon someone in a difficult position. The expression comes from the French dice game called *lourche* which was similar to backgammon. To incur a lourche meant to be penalised or left behind in the game, and after the seventeenth century was used outside the game to refer to any kind of abandonment.

Leave   To leave no stone unturned

Make all possible effort to find or achieve something. The expression comes from translations of the Greek playwright Euripedes who told the story of Polycrates of Thebes who had heard that General Mardonius had abandoned a fabulous treasure in his tent after being defeated in battle. Polycrates turned to the Oracle of Delphi for help and the reply was: Leave no stone unturned.

Leave   To leave out in the cold

To exclude someone from his own group or society. The expression was already in constant use by the mid-1960s when John Le Carr wrote *The Spy Who Came in from the Cold* in which the main character returns to the West from communist East Germany.

Leave   To leave to his or her own devices

To let someone do as she or he wants. Here the word devices carries an obsolete meaning of plans or projects, as it does in the Anglican *Book of Common Prayer*: We have followed too much the devices and desires of our own hearts ...

Left   The left hand doesn't know what the right hand is doing

Lack of coordination and communication in a group or company. The notion is from the Bible from Matthew (6 : 3) which, however, had a different meaning from the one which has evolved: Let not thy right hand know what thy left hand doeth: that thine alms may be in secret. The injunction was to be deliberately discreet about your charity.

Left   Two left feet

Clumsy. This is a description given to an incompetent dancing partner.

Leg   Without a leg to stand on

Having no support or proof for your standpoint.

Legend   A legend in his or her lifetime

Someone who is extremely famous and the subject of people s fantasies.

Legs   On your last legs   see Last

Lend   Lend me your ears

Listen to me. The words are from Shakespeare s *Julius Caesar* (Act III, Sc. 2) where Mark Antony addresses the people of Rome after Caesar s assassination: Friends Romans countrymen, lend me your ears. It is now used jokingly.

Lesser   The lesser of two evils

The least unpleasant of two very undesirable choices. The expression existed in ancient Greece and in medieval England, as in Chaucer s *Troilus and Criseyde:* Of harmes two, the lesse is for to chese.

Let   Let bygones be bygones   see Bygones

Let   Let it all hang out   see Hang

Let   Let's get this show on the road

Let us plan things and start the project quickly so that our enterprise will function well.

Let   To let off steam

To release pent-up feelings. The image is from opening the safety valve in a steam engine to avoid an explosion.

Let   To let rip

To go ahead with what you are about to do without any inhibitions. This arose in the early days of steam engines. The order to allow the engine to go as fast as possible was: Let her rip!

Let   To let sleeping dogs lie   see Dogs

Let   To let slip the dogs of war see **Dogs**

Let   To let someone have it
To vent your anger on someone.

Let   To let the cat out of the bag see **Cat**

Let   To let your hair down see **Hair**

Letter   Dear John letter see **Dear**

Level   A level playing field
A fair basis for making a decision or dealing with people. This twentieth-century expression comes from team sports where it is essential for the physical conditions to be the same for each team in their own part of the field.

Level   To do your level best
To perform as well as you can. The expression is associated with the nineteenth-century Californian gold rush when miners who panned for gold had to shake sand and gravel until it was level in order to pick out the gold ore.

Leveller   A great leveller
Something or someone that puts everyone in an equal position. The original levellers were the seventeenth-century republicans who wanted to extend the right to vote. It is applied metaphorically to such things as death, bad weather or illness.

Lick   To lick into shape
To make someone conform. The image derives from the myth that bear cubs are born shapeless and have to be licked by their mother until they achieve the shape of a bear. The myth is found in the work of the tenth-century Arab physician Avicenna.

Lick   To lick your chops (or lips)
To anticipate something with pleasure. The image is of an animal wetting its chops, or lower jaw, at the prospect of a meal.

Lie   A barefaced lie
Unashamed telling of an untruth. Barefaced suggests that a man is clean-shaven. Probably the idea is that a crime committed with no attempt at disguise, such as a beard, shows that the perpetrator is completely shameless.

Lie   A white lie

A harmless fib. Lies are popularly graded according to the damage they do and the lie told in excuse or to save someone pain is thought of as light or mild, qualities associated with the colour white.

Lie   To lie low

To conceal yourself or your intentions. The reference is to a hunter hiding down in the undergrowth waiting for his prey. In the *Uncle Remus* stories of Joel Chandler Harris, Brer Rabbit frequently lay low .

Lie   To lie through one's teeth

To tell obvious, outrageous untruths. Perhaps the teeth signify a smiling, shameless lie. The expression was known in the fourteenth century in the *Romance of Sir Guy of Warwick*: Thou lexst amidward thi teth.

Lies   Lies, damned lies and statistics

There are ordinary lies, very harmful lies and (most shameless of all) statistics which seem to show the truth, but can be exploited to show the opposite. The words in full are: There are three kinds of lies: lies, damned lies and statistics. They are attributed to Benjamin Disraeli (1804—81).

Life   A charmed life   see Charmed

Life   Large as, or larger than, life

Looking life-like, or on a grand scale. Large as life is the English translation of the Latin *ad vivum*, or to the life, indicating that something looked realistic. Much later larger than life emerged as a description of someone or something extraordinary.

Life   Life begins at forty

Even in middle age the future is promising. This was the title of a book in 1932 by an American professor of journalism, William B. Pitkin, who sought to encourage an adventurous optimistic approach in older people. It quickly became a catch phrase and inspired a song with the same title.

Life   Life in the fast lane   see Fast

Life   Life's a bitch

Life is hard, unfair and unpredictable. The word for a female dog has a long history of being used to describe a malicious sort of woman, and more recently a bad situation.

Life   Life's a bowl of cherries

Everything is satisfactory and pleasant. This saying is nearly always ironical. It was the title of a song by Ray Henderson and performed by Ethel Merman in 1931.

Life   Not on your life

Certainly not. This nineteenth-century phrase stems from the idea that you could not bet your life on the truth of what the speaker is telling you.

Life   The life and soul of the party

A person who makes social events pleasant and lively. The use of life and soul to indicate the person or thing that makes an event function well dates back to the seventeenth century. In his translation of *Gils Blas* in 1809 Benjamin Malkin speaks of the life and soul of the ballet .

Life   The life of Riley

An easy, wealthy life with no effort. Since the nineteenth century there have been songs and later television characters to support the idea that a person called Riley once lived a rich and carefree existence, but no historical figure has been found. Probably Riley was supposed to be the archetypal Irishman and prejudiced English people characterised him as a cheerful sponger.

Lift   To lift a finger to help

Make an effort to be useful. The expression is nearly always negative. Someone who cannot make that minimal exertion to raise one finger is indeed unhelpful.

Light   Light at the end of the tunnel

The possibility of a solution or an end to hardship. The image comes from the railway or from mines. It was in use in the early twentieth century when Middleton Murry wrote to his sick wife, the novelist Katherine Mansfield, of daylight at the end of the tunnel .

Light   Out like a light

Fallen into a deep sleep.

Light   To give the green light

To say that a project can go ahead. The reference is to traffic or railway lights where the green is the signal to move forward.

Like   Like a bat out of hell

Fast-moving. The expression was first used in the Air Force during World War I of the fighter planes. In the later part of the twentieth century it has been used to convey someone rushing in a menacing manner.

Like   Like a headless chicken see Headless

Like   Like a hole in the head   see Hole

Like   Like a house on fire   see House

Like   Like a ton of bricks   see Bricks

Like   Like as two peas in a pod   see Peas

Like   Like it or lump it   see Lump

Like   Like the clappers   see Clappers

Limb   Out on a limb

On your own, without the support of your own group or society. This image refers to the branch or limb of a tree where an animal might find itself separated from its group and exposed to predators.

Limelight   To hog the limelight

To insist on being the centre of attention. In the past theatrical spotlights used cylinders of heated lime to create an intense white light, thus the name limelight. An actor who tried to exclude other actors from limelight was said to hog it or monopolise it.

Line   The bottom line

The final result, or the crux of the matter. In accounting terms the bottom line of a financial statement shows the total income after expenses.

Line   To line your pockets

To accept bribes or obtain money in some other dishonest way. The image of ill-gotten money as a lining to your clothes conveys the furtiveness. In *Othello* (Act 1, Sc. 1) Iago mentions dishonest servants who have lined their coats.

Line   To toe the line

To conform strictly to the rules. In racing the runners have to place their toes against a starting line.

Linen   To wash your dirty linen in public

To expose private personal or family affairs to other people s scrutiny. Napoleon Bonaparte popularised this image by commenting in one of his speeches that: It is in the family, not in public, that one washes one s dirty linen.

Link   The missing link

A gap in a series of things or ideas. The image is from the series of links that form a chain, but it came to great prominence during the nineteenth century controversy over the theories of Charles Darwin about the origin of man. Darwin was popularly supposed to have suggested that a half-ape half-man creature once existed and that the discovery of the remains of such a being would prove that man came from the apes.

Lion   Beard the lion   see Beard

Lion   The lion's share

The biggest portion. One of Aesop s fables tells the story of how a lion hunted together with a heifer, a goat and a sheep, having agreed to share the catch. At the end of the day the lion chose the best part for himself, then took a second portion on the grounds that it belonged to the strongest animal, then a third was for him as the biggest. Seizing the remaining part he simply said: Touch it if you dare.

Lip   Stiff upper lip

Stoicism. This refers to the firm clamping together of the lips in a gesture of fortitude.

Lips   My lips are sealed

I cannot reveal anything. This is based on an earlier expression which referred to the sealing up of the lips of another person with a view to preventing them from blabbing secrets. A famous cartoon of the 1930s showed the prime minister, Stanley Baldwin, with his mouth closed with sticking plaster, an allusion to his saying on the Abyssinian crisis: My lips are as yet unsealed.

Lips   Read my lips   see Read

Little   A little bird told me

I have obtained information from a secret source. The idea of birds as messengers is ancient and widespread. This saying is included in John Heywood s 1546 collection. Nowadays it has a rather coy flavour and is used by adults to children.

Little   Little Orphan Annie   see Orphan

Little   Little pitchers have big ears

Be careful what you say in front of little children because they understand more than you think. This warning comparing children s ears to the handles of a jug appears in John Heywood s sixteenth-century proverb collection as: small pitchers have wide eares .

Little   Too little, too late

An inadequate solution which has not even been applied in time. It is commonly used about military matters, especially about hostilities between Britain and Germany in the twentieth century which were said to be exacerbated by too few concessions made too late by Britain after Germany s defeat in 1918.

Live   A live wire

A dynamic enterprising person. The allusion is to a cable with an electric charge passing through it.

Live   Live (or lead, or bear) a charmed life

To be lucky, to come through dangers unharmed. In Shakespeare s *Macbeth*, Macbeth is confident of success against Macduff because he bears a charmed life, which must not yield to one of woman born , but the magic does not work because Macduff turns out to have been born by Caesarean section and therefore not born of a woman in the usual way.

Live   Live and learn

Experience of life is a valuable learning process. The notion is common in many cultures. The saying appeared in the seventeenth-century collection of proverbs compiled by James Howell as: One may live and learn and be hanged and forget all.

Live   Live and let live

Be tolerant. In *The Ancient Law-merchant* (1622), Gerard de Malynes quotes this as a Dutch adage and it later appeared in English proverb collections.

Live   To live dangerously

To be willing to experiment and take chances in life. This was originally in the form of advice given by the German poet Goethe and the philosopher Nietzsche.

Live   To live in sin

To live together as man and wife without being married. The reference is to the strict code of the Roman Catholic Church which is against such co-habiting, as are many religions. However, since the so-called permissive era of the 1960s the practice has become common enough to make the phrase jocular.

Live   To live life to the full

To seek enriching experiences and enjoy your life. In the twentieth century this has been over-used as a tribute to the deceased at funerals.

Live   To live on borrowed time

To live longer than expected. This late nineteenth-century expression is often applied to very ill people who manage to survive, or people whose lives are full of danger.

Living   To beat the living daylights out of someone   see Beat

Lo   Lo and behold

Look! What a surprise! The words are archaic and mean look, from Old English la, and see. The phrase is a formula in fairy tales but is also used nowadays in a jocular way.

Lock   Lock, stock and barrel

Completely, leaving nothing out. The words derive from the main parts of a gun.

Loins   To gird one's loins   see Gird

Long   A long shot

An attempt that has not much chance of success. The image is from shooting either arrows or bullets, for the farther the range the less chance there is of hitting the target.

Long   At long last

Ultimately. An earlier phrase at the long last was used in the seventeenth century but the present form became common in the twentieth century.

Long   Long in the tooth

Quite old. The teeth of horses change their angle and protrude forward as they become older and their gums recede. The phrase has only been applied to humans in the twentieth century.

Long   Long time no see

We have not seen each other for a long time. This now jocular greeting originates in pidgin English, a mixture of English and features of native languages which was used in parts of the former British Empire especially for trading.

Long   The long and short of it

To summarise or in brief. The idea is as old as the Middle Ages when to say langly or schorte appeared in *Langtoft s Chronicle* (1330).

Look   Look down your nose

To scorn someone.

Look   To look daggers at someone   see Daggers

Loony   The loony left

The irresponsible, spendthrift element in the Labour party. This derogatory description with its catchy alliteration has often been used in the late twentieth century by Conservatives wishing to lower the reputation of Labour councils. It has been countered with remarks about the loony right .

Loose   A loose cannon   see Cannon

Loose   A loose tongue

A tendency to talk too much and indiscreetly.

Loose   Loose ends

Details which remain to be settled or explained. The reference is to the ends of rope or string left dangling from a knot. The phrase has been further fixed in the language by Ned Sherrin s radio programme *Loose Ends*, a show containing a mixture of comedy, topical comment and music.

Lose   To lose face   see Face

Lose   To lose your cool

To lose your temper.

Lose   To lose your tongue

To be unable or unwilling to speak. This is usually in the form of a question from an angry person waiting for a response, often from a child.

Losing   A losing battle

Trying to do something which is bound to be unsuccessful. The expression is from a military situation in which the fight is clearly going to be lost.

Lost   A lost cause

A hopeless quest pursued by someone who is unwilling to admit that all their efforts are in vain. In *Essays in Criticism* (1865), Matthew Arnold described Oxford as the home of lost causes .

Loud Loud and clear
Very firmly.

Love Not for love nor money
Impossible.

Low A low profile
Being present without being pushy or conspicuous. This is a favourite expression of the police in the late twentieth century when they wish to convey that they are aware of problems but do not want to provoke trouble by being overbearing.

Low An all-time low see **All-time**

Low The lowest of the low
A despicable person. The alliteration probably gives this phrase lasting appeal.

Low To give someone the low-down
To reveal secret information.

Lumber To be lumbered with something
To be burdened. Probably this use of lumber comes from the noun meaning a collection of unwanted household junk .

Lump You will have to like it or lump it
You will have to tolerate it whether you like it or not. The saying is from the nineteenth century and the meaning of lump as to put up with may come from the idea of having to swallow an unpalatable lump.

Lunatic The lunatic fringe
Extremists in a minority group, usually political. It may have been used first by Theodore Roosevelt, president of the USA in 1913, who spoke of the lunatic fringe amongst the votaries of any movement .

Lurch To leave in the lurch see **Leave**

Lying To take something lying down
To tolerate a wrong done to you without protest. The image is of a beaten animal too cowed to defend itself. George Bernard Shaw used the expression in *Androcles and the Lion* (1914): I should be ashamed if I let myself be struck like that and took it lying down.

M

Mad   Barking mad   see **Barking**

Mad   Mad as a hatter   see **Hatter**

Madding   Far from the madding crowd   see **Far**

Made   You've got it made
You have every advantage.

Made   You've made my day
You have made me happy. This is now mainly used ironically.

Main   An eye to the main chance   see **Eye**

Mainstream   Mainstream Science (or English or Politics)
The strongest trend, the most pervasive ideas on the subject. The main-stream is the main current in a river. The word is now used as an adjective to describe any middle-of-the way fashion in various fields.

Maintain   To maintain the *status quo*
To keep things as they are. The Latin means literally the state in which .

Majority   The silent majority
The great number of people in any society who take no active part in movements of public protest or approval. Like many politicians the US president Richard Nixon claimed (in a speech of 1969, to justify the Vietnam war) that the silent majority of ordinary people were with him.

Make   Make love, not war
Work for peace. This slogan was said to have been invented in the 1960s by the American, G. Legman, a sexologist at the Kinsey Institute. It was used as a rallying call for various movements, mainly the anti-Vietnam war protests in the USA.

Make   To make a clean breast of it   see **Clean**

Make   To make a mountain out of a molehill
To make a fuss about a trivial matter.

Make To make an honest woman of someone see Honest

Make To make ends meet see Ends

Make To make hay while the sun shines see Hay

Make To make neither head nor tail of something see Head

Make To make no bones about it see Bones

Make To make or break
To achieve great success or terrible failure. The more common form of this expression was to make or marr but Charles Dickens introduced the present form in *Barnaby Rudge* (1840).

Make To make someone's hair stand on end see Hair

Make To make the best of a bad job see Job

Make To make the grade see Grade

Make To make tracks see Tracks

Make To make your blood boil see Blood

Malice With malice aforethought
Doing intentional harm to another person. Often used ironically now, this has been a legal term for centuries.

Man A man after my own heart see After

Man A man of the world
A sophisticated experienced man. The term originally meant a married man as opposed to a celibate priest, but by the nineteenth century it had acquired its present meaning.

Man Are you a man or a mouse?
Are you a brave individual or a coward? This appears anonymously in the sixteenth-century *Scholehouse of Women*: Fear not she saith unto her spouse, a man or a mouse whether ye be.

Man Man Friday see Girl

Man Man to man
Frankly. This expression dates from times when certain topics were held to be too crude or complicated for women to hear. Men, on the other hand, could speak together unrestrainedly.

Man   Our man in

Our government s representative in a certain place. Once used seriously in diplomatic circles and also in the title of Graham Greene s novel *Our Man in Havana*, it is now used mainly ironically.

Man   The man in the street

The average man. This phrase is much used by the media. See also **The man on the Clapham omnibus.**

Man   The man on the Clapham omnibus   see **Clapham**

Man   The new man

The modern man. The implication is that concepts of masculine behaviour have changed, usually to mean that today s man is willing to perform tasks once considered exclusively women s work.

Man   Yesterday's man

A failure, a person whose ideas are out-of-date and unpopular. This phrase has been used in political campaigns in the twentieth century, notably that of the Labour party in 1970 describing the Tories as yesterday s men .

Manger   A dog in the manger   see **Dog**

Manna   Manna from heaven

Any unexpected help or surprise gift. The reference is to the biblical manna or bread from heaven which miraculously fell from the sky to feed the hungry Israelites on their journey through the desert with Moses.

Manner   To the manner (manor) born

Displaying an accomplished skill and an air of confidence. This is a quotation from Shakespeare s *Hamlet* when the Prince comments on the acting expertise of the travelling players who have come to perform at court. The title of a British TV series *To the Manor Born* is a pun on the original expression and reflects a common misapprehension as to the meaning.

Marching   To give someone their marching orders

To tell someone to go away. This is a military expression used when soldiers receive a command to move to a new place.

Marines   Tell it to the marines!

I do not believe you! King Charles I is supposed to have originated this expression of incredulity when he was told of flying fish. So as not to offend the marines he later explained that he had referred to them as well-travelled men who would be likely to be able to confirm or deny the existence of such creatures.

Mark   Mark my words!
Pay attention to what I have said. The word mark is simply an archaic word for notice which has persisted in this set expression.

Mark   To mark time
To go through the motions of doing something while actually waiting for further developments. This is from military drills in which one exercise is to get the soldiers to march on the spot, ready to move forward whenever they are commanded.

Mark   Up to the mark
Of acceptable quality or fitness. This refers to the standard of fitness fixed by the assay office for gold and silver articles. Those of approved quality would bear the hallmark.

Marriage   A marriage (match) made in heaven
A happy and successful partnership. Like the term a marriage of convenience this can also be applied to partnerships other than matrimony.

Marriage   A marriage of convenience
A wedding arranged for social or business needs rather than love. The meaning is often extended to other partnerships and associations as well as matrimony.

Matters   To take matters into your own hands   see Take

McCoy   The real McCoy
The genuine person or article. There are two different explanations of this phrase. One is that it referred to the real Mackay, a brand of whisky, the other that it referred to a boxer called McCoy who was challenged to fight by a drunk who had to be convinced that it was unwise to try to fight the real McCoy.

Meal   To make a meal of it
To make a simple procedure too long and complicated.

Medicine   A taste of your own medicine
Being treated as harshly as you have treated others.

Meet   To meet someone halfway
To compromise.

Meet   To meet your maker

To die. The implication is that you will be judged on the life you have led when you die and face God, your Creator.

Meltdown   To reach meltdown

To reach crisis point, to be in a rage, or under unbearable stress. The term is from nuclear engineering accidents where fuel has become so overheated that it has collapsed into or through the fabric of the reactor.

Memory   Down memory lane

In a reminiscing mood. The phrase has become common in publicity for chocolates, old photographs and any articles where nostalgia can be evoked.

Men   Men in grey suits   see **Grey**

Messenger   To kill the messenger   see **Kill**

Method   There's method in (someone's) madness

The behaviour of a mad person sometimes shows an underlying sane logic. The modern expression probably comes from the words of Polonius in Shakespeare s *Hamlet* as he secretly observed the prince: Though this be madness, yet there s method in t.

Midas   The Midas touch

The talent for making any enterprise profitable. According to Greek legend King Midas of Phrygia was granted the gift of making everything he touched turn to gold. When even his food changed he begged the gods to take back the gift.

Middle   Middle England

A class of English people taken (especially by political observers) to be typical in their attitudes and aspirations. The phrase has a similar resonance to names like the Middle Ages, or the Middle Kingdom and has more weight than the average man .

Midnight   To burn the midnight oil   see **Burn**

Milk   The milk of human kindness

Compassion, gentleness. In Shakespeare s *Macbeth*, Lady Macbeth, urging her husband to kill in order to become king, doubts if he is equal to it: Yet do I fear thy nature, it is too full o th milk of human kindness.

Milk   To milk something for all it is worth

To extract as much advantage as you can from a situation. The reference is to milking a cow.

Mill   To put someone through the mill

To make someone suffer. The analogy is with corn which is put through the grinding process in a flour mill.

Millstone   A millstone round the neck

To be burdened with a big problem, especially a financial one. In biblical times the punishment for certain crimes was to hang a millstone round the neck of the offender.

Mince   Let's not mince words

Let us say exactly what we mean. The reference is to the chopping of meat into tiny pieces to make it palatable and easily digestible.

Mincemeat   To make mincemeat of someone

To defeat them in an argument or any competitive situation, to dominate someone. The reference is to meat which is cut small or ground into manageable form.

Mind   In your mind's eye

In your imagination. The metaphor was in use in the fifteenth century. Thomas Hoccleve used it in *De Regime Principum* (1412): Haue often him byfore your mynde s ye.

Mind   Mind over matter

The triumph of willpower over physical limitations.

Mind   Mind your own business

Do not meddle in other people s affairs. This expression appears in English in the sixteenth century as, Mind your business.

Mind   Mind your P's and Q's   see P's

Mind   The mind boggles

The subject under discussion is astonishing or alarming. The verb to boggle originally meant to react to a certain mishievous or evil spirit with a capacity to frighten or shock people.

Mind   To have a good mind to

To be determined to do something.

Mind   To have half a mind

Almost determined on something but not quite.

Mine   A mine of information
A useful source of knowledge to refer to. Just as a mineral mine provides valuable raw materials, so a good reference work or a learned person can be a resource for useful information.

Mint   To make a mint of money
An enormous sum of money. As the mint is where coins and notes are manufactured or stored the idea is that the amount can be constantly replenished. The expression was current in the seventeenth century.

Miss   A miss is as good as a mile
If something fails it makes no difference whether it was a near-success or a total flop, the result is the same. The traditional version was: An inch in a miss is as good as an ell, the ell being an old unit of measurement equal to about forty-five inches.

Miss   Someone doesn't miss a trick
Nothing escapes attention. The reference is to card playing.

Miss   To miss the boat see **Boat**

Missing   The missing link see **Link**

Moment   At this moment in time
Now. This phrase, current in the late twentieth century, has been criticised for being a roundabout way of saying something simple, but it has a resonance which obviously appeals to people.

Moment   In the heat of the moment
Impulsively.

Moment   Never a dull moment
There is always something interesting happening. This is a time-worn comment used as a conversation filler in the twentieth century.

Moment   The moment of truth
The turning point, the time when you have to act on your stated intentions. This is a translation of the Spanish *el momento de la verdad*, which describes the point in a bullfight when the mortal wound is inflicted on the animal.

Moment   Unguarded moment
During a time when you are momentarily not alert.

Monday   That Monday-morning feeling
Depression or general reluctance to face the tasks in hand for the week. This concept originated in advertising in the twentieth century,

probably for a product or remedy which claimed to dispel the gloom felt at the start of the working week.

Money   Funny money see **Funny**

Money   Money burns a hole in someone's pocket
This person is a spendthrift. This image was used by Sir Thomas More in *Works*: a little wanton money . . . which burned out the bottom of his purse .

Money   Money doesn't grow on trees
Prosperity is only won by very hard work. This is a typical remark of parents when their offspring seem not to appreciate the value of money.

Money   Money is the root of all evil
The pursuit of wealth causes problems and crime. This is a biblical quotation from St Paul who said: For the love of money is the root of all evil (Timothy 6 : 10).

Money   Money talks
The rich hold the power. This has been a familiar concept throughout the ages. In his *Adagia* (1523) Erasmus wrote: Against the talking power of money, eloquence is of no avail.

Money   To throw good money after bad
To continue to invest in what is clearly a bad cause.

Monkey   Monkey business
Underhand, silly behaviour. In many cultures monkeys have a reputation for mischief.

Monstrous   Monstrous carbuncle
An ugly architectural or landscape feature. The comparison of unsightly buildings to spots and pimples is not new, but this phrase became fashionable after Prince Charles used it in 1984 to describe the design for a new wing of the National Gallery in London: a monstrous carbuncle on the face of a much-loved and elegant friend .

Month   Not in a month of Sundays
Never. This image of an absurd measure of time was first in print in the early nineteenth century.

Moon   The moon is made of green cheese
The most absurd thing imaginable.

Moot   Moot point

A debatable question. Originally this referred to a case for discussion at a moot, or meeting of law students, but came to mean any matter capable of different interpretations.

Moral   A moral victory

Proved to be right according to generally acknowledged principles of what is good and bad, even though the winner may not gain in material or worldly terms.

Moral   The moral high ground

The advantage of being or seeming more virtuous than your opponent.

More   More than (someone) bargained for

More complicated or difficult than expected. The reference is to shopping where your purchase turns out different from what you thought you were buying.

More   More than one way to skin a cat

There is more than one way of doing something. This expression was known in the mid-nineteenth century and it has been suggested that skinning a cat describes a type of somersault performed on a bar or swing and can be done in various ways.

More   The more the merrier

The activity or situation will be improved if there are more people involved. The traditional version of this saying, recorded by John Heywood in 1546, has another half which has now dropped out of use: Ye but the fewer the better far.

More   There is more to it than meets the eye

The matter is more complex and not as it seems to be on the surface. This has been in use since the nineteenth century.

Morning   Morning, noon and night

All the time This phrase always has negative implications, suggesting that the activity which goes on all round the clock is unwelcome.

Morning   The morning after

A hangover, the result of a binge, usually drinking. The full phrase began in the nineteenth century as the morning after the night before . It has been extended to any unpleasant after-effect of over-indulgence.

Morpheus   In the arms of Morpheus

Asleep. Morpheus was the Greek god of sleep and the phrase originated as a rather pompous Victorian way of referring to sleep.

Mother   The mother of all . . .

The greatest. This is used as a superlative adjective and can be used for emphasis in such expressions as the mother of all wars / rows, etc. .

Mouth   To have your heart in your mouth

To be very apprehensive. The expression existed in Latin literature. In his *Satyricon* (AD 66) Petronius wrote: My heart was in my mouth.

Mouth   To open your big mouth

To blab, to reveal secrets.

Move   Movers and shakers

Influential people. In past centuries God has been described as the Mover or the Shaker. Writing about poets, the nineteenth-century poet A. W. E. O Shaughnessy said, Yet we are the movers and shakers of the world forever, it seems.

Move   To move heaven and earth

To make enormous efforts to get something done.

Moveable   A moveable feast

An exceptional experience, related originally to a certain place, time or situation but having the capacity to influence a person long afterwards and in other places. In the Christian calendar a moveable feast, such as Easter, is one which celebrates a certain event but falls on different dates each year. The writer Ernest Hemingway wrote *A Moveable Feast* (1964) about living in Paris.

Much   Much ado about nothing

Unnecessary fussing over trifles. The expression is at least a century older than Shakespeare s play with this title.

Much   Much of a muchness

Very similar, of the same value. This expression dates from the early nineteenth century and seems to appeal to people s love of alliteration.

Mud   (Someone's) name is mud

His or her reputation is very bad. The assassin of US president Abraham Lincoln was hurt while escaping and a Dr Mudd, unaware of his identity, treated his injuries. The doctor was reviled for helping the criminal and his name became a byword.

Mud   Clear as mud

Not clear at all.

Muddle   To muddle through

To manage somehow despite difficulties.

Muddy   To muddy the waters

To confuse the issue. This early nineteenth-century expression refers to the churning up of the bed of a clear fishing stream by boats or humans.

Mug   To be a mug

To be easily deceived, stupid. The word mug has long been slang for face and was also used often in the theatre as a verb for making up the face. Although the origin of its use for a gullible person is not known, it is possible to guess that the notion of putting on a silly clown face in the theatre gave rise to the idea of mug meaning a stupid person.

Mum   Mum's the word

Nobody must speak about this matter. The only sound that emerges when you keep your lips together is mmm which presumably gave rise to the word mum in this expression.

Museum   A museum piece

An old-fashioned person or thing. The phrase was at first used to describe an object worthy of being exhibited in a museum, then at the beginning of the twentieth century it became ironical.

Music   To face the music   see **Face**

Musical   Musical chairs

Making changes in rapid succession. This comes from the children s game in which the players march to music round a row of chairs which are one fewer in number than the players. When the music stops the players scramble for a seat, the loser being the person left without.

Muster   To pass muster   see **Pass**

Mutton   Mutton dressed as lamb

An older person, especially a woman, trying to appear young. The reference is to tough mutton being sold or served up to seem like tender appetising lamb.

Mutual   A mutual admiration society

Feelings of admiration shared by two people. The phrase was first used by Henry David Thoreau in 1851 and is now used ironically or critically of people who flatter each other or who esteem each other but are not approved of by society in general.

N

Nail   Hard as nails
Physically or mentally tough, having an uncompromising attitude. Charles Dickens used the phrase in *Oliver Twist* (1837), when referring to a gang of thieves.

Nail   On the nail
Immediately or on the spot. This comes from to pay on the nail from the name of a pillar topped by a shallow bowl used in commerce as a receptacle for cash in the Middle Ages. It was probably called a nail because of its shape. Examples of such nails can be seen outside the Bristol Corn Exchange.

Nail   The nail in the coffin
The final act or event that finishes something or someone off.

Nail   To fight tooth and nail
To fight with all your power and energy.

Nail   To nail a lie
To expose a falsehood. The idea of pinning down a liar comes from the Bible (Isaiah 22 : 23): I will fasten him as a nail in a sure place.

Naked   The naked truth
The plain truth, unembellished. According to fable Truth and Falsehood were bathing. Falsehood got out of the water and put on Truth s clothes. Truth did not want to put on Falsehood s clothes and so went naked.

Namby-pamby
Feeble and sentimental. It was originally used of authors. Ambrose Philips (1674—1749) was given this nickname by dramatist Henry Carey for some verses that he wrote in a sentimental style.

Name   (Someone's) name is mud   see Mud

Name   Name-dropping
Embellishing your conversation by frequently mentioning famous acquaintances or people of high status in order to impress your audience.

Name   The name of the game

The essential or significant point about someone or something. It comes from the title of a US film (1966): *The Name of the Game is Fame* and was also the title of a US TV series (1968—71).

Name   To name the day

To set a day for the wedding ceremony. Traditionally this is the privilege of the bride-to-be.

Name   To take someone's name in vain

To be irreverent about somebody. Originally this phrase was used of God s name. In many cultures the deity s name is regarded as his manifestation and is revered as such, so it must not be used inappropriately.

Napping   To be caught napping

To suffer misfortune or be injured when off guard. Hunters often catch game birds while they are sleeping.

Nasty   Nasty, brutish and short

This is a negative view of life, first espoused by the philosopher Thomas Hobbes in *Leviathan* (1651), in which he sees man as a selfish rather than a social being.

Native   To go native

To abandon civilised life and adopt the customs of a more primitive society. Especially in the days of the British Empire the term natives referred not only to the original inhabitants of a country but implied wild or uncivilised people.

Nature   A child of nature   see Child

Nature   The call of nature   see Call

Naughty   Naughty but nice

The pleasure of something that is morally or physically harmful. Many songs have used this phrase as a theme, particularly in the late nineteenth and early twentieth century. It is also the title of a 1939 American film. It may have also sometimes alluded to sexual intercourse.

Near   Too near the bone

Painfully true to life or close to the truth. In anatomical terms the closer to the bone the more painful the injury.

Nearest Nearest and dearest
Close family and friends. The rhyme probably achieved this phrase its status as a common expression.

Neat Neat as a new pin
Particularly tidy or well arranged. John Wolcot in 1796 wrote: How neat was Ellen in her dress! As neat as a new pin!

Necessity Necessity is the mother of invention
The best ideas and inventions are often produced by people when under pressure to do so. An equivalent phrase was recorded by William Horman in his *Vulgaria* in 1519: Nede taught hym wytte. The modern version is cited in *Gulliver s Travels* by Jonathan Swift (1726).

Necessity To make a virtue of necessity
To resign yourself to doing something cheerfully, knowing that you have no option. Chaucer used this phrase in the *Knight s Tale*: Thanne is it wisdom, as it thinketh me / To maken virtu of necessitee.

Neck Neck and neck
Exactly equal, usually referring to positions in a race or contest. The term comes from horse-racing and is suggestive of the horse s neck stretched forward.

Neck Neck of the woods
An area or district. Originally it referred to a settlement in a forest.

Neck To get it in the neck
To be severely reprimanded. The saying is American in origin and is probably an abbreviated form of expressions such as to get it where the chicken got the axe — in the neck .

Neck To stick your neck out
To expose yourself to trouble or danger. As a chicken that extends its neck in front of the axe is asking to be slaughtered.

Nectar Nectar of the gods
Anything delightful to drink, often alcoholic. Nectar in legend was said to be the drink of the gods that bestows immortality.

Need To need (something) like a hole in the head   see Hole

Needle A needle in a haystack
Something extremely hard to find. Physically, something that is so small in relation to what surrounds it that it is impossible to pinpoint. This ancient saying was originally to look for a needle in a meadow .

Needless   Needless to say
Something that is obvious but you are going to say it anyway. Equivalent expressions have been documented from the sixteenth century.

Neither   Neither fish, flesh nor fowl   see Fish

Neither   Neither here nor there
Irrelevant. Of no significance. Edward Fitzgerald lent another interpretation to this phrase in his translation of the *Rubaiyat of Omar Khayyam* in which your reward is neither here nor there signifies neither before birth nor after death but throughout life.

Neither   Neither hide nor hair   see Hide

Neither   Neither rhyme nor reason
Having no good sense or motive — as with something that has no poetic or entertainment value, and no wisdom or educational value. It often refers to a person s actions that cannot be explained.

Nelly   Not on your nelly
Certainly not! Nelly probably comes from rhyming slang Nelly Duff , meaning puff , that is breath or life.

Nerves   A battle of nerves
A psychological contest of endurance or an attempt by two opponents to break each other s will.

Nest   A nest egg
Something carefully reserved or set aside, usually money, for future use. An egg was sometimes placed in a hen s nest to induce her to lay more, so the idea is that a little money kept aside will serve as an incentive to continue saving.

Nest   The empty-nest syndrome
The feeling of depression that a mother is said to feel when her children leave home, or fly the nest .

Network   The old-boy network
Strong allegiance between ex-members of a noted establishment (usually a school or college) who use their influence to help each other.

Never   And never the twain shall meet
The strong difference between eastern and western culture. This comes from *The Ballad of East and West* by Rudyard Kipling: East is east and west is west and never the twain shall meet.

Never   **Never a dull moment**   see **Moment**

Never   **Never darken my doorstep again**   see **Darken**

Never   **Never say die**   see **Die**

Never   **Never-never land**
An imaginary place or concept. It comes from J. M. Barrie s *Peter Pan* (1904) and was the place where the lost boys dwelled. It was also used to describe most of the unsettled parts of Australia but is now only used to refer to remote parts of Queensland.

New   **A new lease of life**
Prolonged life or period of use for someone or something cured, revitalised or repaired.

New   **New brooms sweep clean**   see **Brooms**

New   **The new look**
An innovation. The original new look was a post-war dress fashion of the late 1940s with long full skirts and colourful materials which had not been possible under wartime economy regulations.

News   **First the good news**
Let s begin with pleasant information before going on to less satisfactory items. This is an opening remark popular in the late twentieth century. The speaker may continue with the rest: And now the bad news . . .

News   **No news is good news**
If you are not kept up to date with a situation, you assume that this is because things are going well or that if something bad happened you would be informed.

News   **To be bad news**
Someone or something liable to bring trouble.

Nice   **A nice little earner**
Something which brings a modest but regular income. It could be said of a small business, a business deal (sometimes shady) or a machine, for example. It is also the name of a public house in East London.

Nick   **In the nick of time**
At the final crucial moment. The term nick or nicke has been used at least since the sixteenth century to mean at the crucial moment .

Night   A one-night stand

A casual sexual encounter. It derives from theatre when an act is only shown for one night rather than running for several.

Nine   A nine-day wonder

A passing fad or phase. The expression was familiar to Chaucer and appears in Shakespeare s *Henry VI* where Gloucester mentions that the king s proposed marriage might turn out to be a ten-day wonder . Clarence corrects him: That s a day longer than a wonder lasts. The period of nine days may come from the length of a Catholic *novena*, a nine-day devotion for a specific intention.

Nine   Nine times out of ten

In nearly all cases. It is now so commonly used that it very rarely refers to a real figure or percentage.

Nine   Nine-to-five job

An ordinary job. Standard full-time hours in the UK are between 9 a.m. and 5 p.m., Monday to Friday.

Nines   Dressed up to the nines   see Dressed

Nip   Nip and tuck

Dead even. The origin of this phrase has been lost, but it is probably from nineteenth-century America and has sometimes been documented in the form nip and tack . It is used in the same way as neck and neck . The phrase is also sometimes used to refer jocularly to cosmetic surgery.

Nip   To nip something in the bud

To stop something in its early stages. If there is a frost in late spring it may kill the newly developed buds of flowers. It is at least four centuries old.

Nitty-gritty   To get down to the nitty-gritty

To deal with the root of a problem (usually money). The origin of this phrase is somewhat obscure, but it may be connected with the difficulty of removing small and grit-like lice or nits from the scalp. Another suggestion is that it refers to the hard edible centre of a cereal, that is, the grits.

No   A no-go area

A place or a subject which cannot be safely approached by outsiders, especially those in authority. The term is used especially of quarters of a city which the police hold back from entering so as not to provoke problems.

No   A no-win situation

A position in which no solution seems possible through any course of action.

No   No dice

Useless and ineffective. The phrase comes from gambling with dice in twentieth-century America, referring to when a player fails to score, and it was popularised in many films and books, such as A. Marshall s novel *Some Like it Hot* (1941).

No   No flies on me   see **Flies**

No   No fool like an old fool

Act your age. Youthful or juvenile behaviour is out of place in an older person. It was recorded as a proverb in 1546 by John Heywood.

No   No great shakes

Nothing special. The OED suggests that the phrase may have to do with shakes of the dice. In Thomas Moore s *Tom Crib s Memorial to Congress* (1819) he talks of someone who is no great shakes at learned chat .

No   No laughing matter

A serious matter. This expression dates back to the sixteenth century, and in the eighteenth century the writer Sheridan is quoted as having said: A joke in your mouth is no laughing matter.

No   No love lost between them

They hate each other. It has been used since the sixteenth century to mean both that they love each other and they hate each other, though the former became obsolete during the eighteenth century.

No   No news is good news   see **News**

No   No pain, no gain

You cannot obtain the reward without suffering the process of getting it. The expression is twentieth-century American and derives from proverbial expressions such as, Nothing ventured, nothing gained. Its appeal comes from the simple rhyme.

No   No picnic

Not easy or straightforward, or not enjoyable. It became common in the late nineteenth century.

No   No rest for the wicked   see **Rest**

No   No skin off my nose   see **Nose**

No   No spring chicken
No longer young.

No   No such thing as a free lunch
No such thing as something for nothing. Gifts in the business and political worlds are often either bribes or means of entrapment.

No   No two ways about it
There is no doubt in the matter. There is only one obvious answer.

Nod   On the nod
On credit. In an auction the buyer indicates that he wants to buy by nodding and pays later.

Nodding   A nodding acquaintance   see **Acquaintance**

Non   Non compos mentis
Insane or mentally confused. This is a legal term from Latin meaning not sound of mind .

Nose   Follow your nose
Go straight ahead. Use your initiative. Trust your own intuition. Literally, go in the direction that the smell is coming from.

Nose   No skin off my nose
It does not bother me. The expression comes from the days of bare-fist boxing and implies that if you are not involved in a bout it is so much the better for you because you will avoid injury.

Nose   To have your nose put out of joint
To be angry because someone has taken your place. It suggests the humiliation of a punch on the nose to a defeated boxer. It was in use in the sixteenth century.

Nose   To have your nose to the grindstone
Hard at work. An old and picturesque image of someone so bent over his work that his nose scrapes against it. In *A Merry Dialogue* (1557) Erasmus wrote: I would holden his nose to the grindstone.

Nose   To keep your nose clean
To stay out of trouble. A traditional parental warning to children to use a handkerchief, now more often used figuratively.

Nose   To pay through the nose
To be overcharged. In the ninth century the Danes imposed a poll tax in Ireland and the penalty for non-payment was the slitting of the nose.

Not   Not all it's cracked up to be   see **Cracked**

Not   Not cricket   see **Cricket**

Not   Not for all the tea in China   see **China**

Not   Not for love nor money   see **Love**

Not   Not my cup of tea   see **Cup**

Not   Not on your life   see **Life**

Not   Not on your nelly   see **Nelly**

Not   Not to put too fine a point on it   see **Point**

Not   Not worth the paper it's written on   see **Paper**

Note   To strike the right note
To express an idea or opinion in suitable language. The image comes from playing a musical instrument harmoniously.

Notes   To compare notes
To exchange opinions. An obvious transfer from the idea of comparing written observations.

Nothing   Nothing to write home about
Boring or disappointing. This is an ancient concept expressed by Pliny the Younger two thousand years ago in one of his letters.

Nothing   Nothing ventured, nothing gained   see **No pain, no gain**

Now   Now or never
To be done immediately or not at all.

Nowhere   Out of nowhere
From obscurity into view, perhaps in the case of a public figure. This was said, for example, of John Major who was little known until he became prime minister.

Nut   A hard nut to crack
A tough problem to solve, or a difficult person to negotiate with.

Nutshell   In a nutshell

Summed up briefly, put concisely. The eighteenth-century poet Alexander Pope was jokingly referred to as Homer in a nutshell due to his small deformed body.

Nutty   Nutty as a fruitcake

Crazy or eccentric. Nutty has long been used to mean insane. The phrase has now given rise to the use of a fruitcake as a term for an eccentric person.

Oar   To put your oar in

To interfere in someone s affairs. The image is from rowing where two boats going along their own course would not ordinarily be close enough for the oars to hit each other. A rower going too close to the other boat would be disruptive.

Oats   To sow your wild oats

To indulge in excesses while young. This is an old expression that refers to cultivating grain. Bad grain produces wild oats and good grain produces a cultivated crop. This phrase is often used with reference to youthful sexual indulgence taking the image of planting seeds as a reference to sex.

Odd   Odd man out

The one that does not fit the pattern or stands out. An old gambling game with coins involved rounds in which three people would toss coins and the one whose coin came up tails when the others had heads or vice versa was out of the round.

Odd   Odds and ends

Miscellaneous things, often things you might find lying around. The expression was originally odd ends . An end is the term used for an offcut of cloth.

Odds   That makes no odds

It does not matter, or does not change anything. The phrase comes from betting terminology where the odds are the ratio by which the amount staked by one party to a bet exceeds that of the other. This refers to a situation where the difference is insignificant.

Odds   To shout the odds

To make a loud fuss. The bookmaker has to announce the odds for a race over the noise of the excited crowd trying to place bets.

Odour   In bad odour

Out of favour.

Odour   The odour of sanctity

Saintliness or sham piety. A sweet smell was said to come from the dead body of a holy person. This notion was popular in the Middle Ages and still exists in many cultures.

Off   Off the beaten track   see Beaten

Off   Off the cuff   see Cuff

Off   Off the deep end   see Deep

Off   Off the record   see Record

Off   Off the top of your head

Improvised. Without prior consideration or planning. This twentieth-century American expression appears in Harold Ickes *Secret Diary* (1939): He was impetuous and inclined to think off the top of his head at times.

Off   Off the wall

Unconventional. Impromptu. This expression usually refers to an idea or piece of work. It perhaps alludes to the unpredictable bounce of a ball in games such as squash and handball.

Off   Off your chump (or head or rocker)   see Chump

Officer   An officer and a gentleman

A term of respect for a man of high standing, now usually used ironically. The phrase originated in the British Naval Discipline Act (1860) which mentioned conduct unbecoming the character of an officer and a gentleman . *Conduct Unbecoming* is the title of a 1969 film, and *An Officer and a Gentleman* was a 1982 film.

Oil   Oil and water

Two things that do not mix or go well together. Oil and water are immiscible.

Oil   To pour oil on troubled waters

To soothe or calm a situation with gentle words or diplomacy. A layer of oil poured on the surface of water reduces the intensity of waves. In Bede s *Ecclesiastical History* (AD791) he tells how St Aidan gave a young priest a cruse of oil with which he calmed the rough sea that he was sailing across.

Ointment   A fly in the ointment   see Fly

Old   An old fogey

A mildly derogatory term for an elderly person. The term implies that a person has all the worst qualities of old age. Fogey is a Scottish word from the 1780s applying to a person displaying all the worst attributes of old age without being old.

Old   An old wives' tale

A superstitious belief or story supposedly spread by gossiping old women.

Old   Old as the hills

Extremely old.

Old   Old habits die hard   see Habits

Old   Old hat

Boringly familiar. Old fashioned. Something that has been done many times before and is just being copied. The phrase probably alludes to the rapid change of hat fashions at the start of the twentieth century. Hats go out of fashion long before the material actually wears out.

Old   Old school

Old fashioned, maintaining old and good traditions or values, especially good manners. Very recently the term has been used to refer to music that is still loved despite being of an outdated style.

Old   Old-school tie

The mark of a high social class. The distinguishing patterns of public-school ties came to be used to refer to members of an exclusive social group, the old-school-tie brigade .

Old   Old stamping ground   see Ground

Old   The old-boy network   see **Network**

Old   The old guard

The longest serving and most faithful members of a political party or regime. Napoleon s old guard consisted of the veterans of his Imperial Guard regiment. They were said to have made the last charge at the Battle of Waterloo.

Olive   To hold out the olive branch

To make peace, to restore harmony and tranquillity. This has its origins in the biblical story of Noah who took refuge from the flood in an ark. He knew that the waters had subsided and the situation was back to normal when a dove which he had sent out returned with a fresh olive branch in its beak.

Omnibus   The man on the Clapham omnibus   see **Clapham**

On   On a downward spiral   see **Spiral**

On   On a shoestring   see **Shoestring**

On   On an even keel   see **Keel**

On   On cloud nine   see **Cloud**

On   On tenterhooks   see **Tenterhooks**

On   On the ball   see **Ball**

On   On the dot   see **Dot**

On   On the rampage   see **Rampage**

On   On the rocks   see **Rocks**

On   On the spur of the moment   see **Spur**

On   On the tip of your tongue   see **Tongue**

On   On the warpath   see **Warpath**

On   On your bike   see **Bike**

On   To jump on the bandwagon   see **Bandwagon**

On   To skate on thin ice   see **Ice**

Once   Once and for all

For the last time. The expression first appeared in William Caxton s translation of *The Foure Sonnes of Aymon* (1489): We oughte to ask it of hym ones for all.

Once   Once bitten, twice shy   see **Bitten**

Once   Once in a blue moon
Almost never. Very rarely. On rare occasions the crescent moon is said to give a pale blue glow.

Once   Once upon a time
In the past. This set phrase has been the traditional opening line of fairy tales for several centuries. It is often used ironically to complain about the current state of affairs.

One   A one-night stand   see **Night**

One   A one-track mind
An obsession with something, particularly sex. This phrase refers to the single-track railway line that only allows one direction of travel.

One   At one fell swoop   see **Fell**

One   One foot in the grave   see **Foot**

One   One for the road
One last drink before leaving. The expression seems to have originated in America after the prohibition when an alcoholic drink before setting off on a long road trip probably seemed like a good idea. Now the term is often used when there is no other good reason for another drink.

One   One good turn deserves another
Gratitude for help or kindness by way of a return of favour. This is an old proverb seen in Latin in a manuscript from the fourteenth century.

Onward   Onward and upward
Continue to improve and advance. This is a popular rallying cry of the nineteenth century, now sometimes used ironically for an amusing failure.

Open   (Someone) is an open book   see **Book**

Open   An open secret
Something supposed to be private but which is in fact known to everybody.

Open   An open-and-shut case
A straightforward matter that can be cleared up with little doubt as to the outcome. The origin of the expression is from legal cases that are

so uncomplicated that they are closed within a short time of being opened.

Open An open-ended commitment

A pledge to a project which has no definite duration or limits. This phrase was mostly used of contracts but has now been extended to many spheres.

Open Open and above board see Above

Open Open sesame see Sesame

Open With open arms

Warmly welcoming, with genuine hospitality.

Opium The opium of the people

Religion. The phrase is derived from the nineteenth-century writings of Karl Marx who considered that religion operated like a mind-numbing drug on the populace depriving them of their independence.

Order Of the highest order

The best or finest. This phrase probably stems from the notion of the hierarchy of the species (or God s creatures), according to which animals were classed into orders and humans were at the top.

Order The order of the day

The current state of things in general. Originally this was a military phrase for whatever commands were given each day. By the eighteenth century the meaning had shifted to whatever was actually happening on a particular day.

Orphan Like little orphan Annie

Looking untidy and appealingly helpless. The original orphan was the heroine of an American cartoon strip, adopted as a child by an American millionaire, Daddy Warbucks.

OTT

Overdone. Excessive. Outrageous. Theatrical. OTT stands for over the top , implying beyond the normal limit. During World War I to go over the top meant to leave the relative safety of your trench and launch an attack.

Out Out and about

Away from home or work and busy doing something.

Out   Out and out

Thorough and complete. This is an ancient phrase using a redundant meaning of out as to the finish . An example of its use from 1374 can be found in Chaucer s *Troilus and Criseyde:* For out and out he is worthiest . . .

Out   Out like a light

Instantly asleep. The image is of someone presumably so tired that they go from wakefulness to deep sleep as suddenly as a light switching off.

Out   Out of nowhere   see **Nowhere**

Out   Out of sight, out of mind

If a person is not present they will not be thought about, or if they do not make themselves seen or heard their views will not be considered. This phrase or close versions of it date back as far as the thirteenth century.

Out   Out of the blue   see **Blue**

Out   Out of the frying pan and into the fire   see **Frying**

Out   Out of the mouths of babes   see **Babes**

Out   Out of the running

No longer able to compete. The term is from sport where it is used literally, but is often used for political or other contests.

Out   Out of the woods

Clear of danger. Into safety. The expression dates back at least two hundred years in its current form.

Out   Out on a limb   see **Limb**

Out   Out the window

Suddenly gone, scrapped or rejected. The phrase often refers to plans or ideas and comes from an earlier phrase to throw the house out of the window meaning to cause a commotion or disrupt things.

Out   To out somebody

To publicise the fact that somebody is a homosexual when they themselves have chosen not to make it known. This outing is a phenomenon of the late twentieth century and part of a movement amongst some homosexuals to make their sexual orientation acceptable. See also **To come out of the closet**.

Outdoors   The great outdoors
Wild extensive natural countryside.

Over   Over a barrel   see **Barrel**

Over   Over my dead body
No chance. That will never happen.

Over   Over the hill   see **Hill**

Over   Over the moon
Delighted. Overjoyed. The wife of nineteenth-century British prime minister Gladstone is said to have invented the phrase, but probably borrowed it from the nursery rhyme: The cow jumped over the moon.

Over   Over the top   see **OTT**

Overboard   To go overboard
To do something extravagantly or to excess. The allusion is to falling from a boat into the water.

Overcome   To overcome hurdles
To succeed despite problems. The reference is to a race where a runner has to leap over hurdles round the course.

Overdrive   To go into overdrive
To force yourself to the limit of speed and efficiency. The overdrive gear in some engines is one used to reduce wear and increase efficiency when the engine is running at very high speed.

Own   To give someone a dose of their own medicine   see **Dose**

Own   To score an own goal   see **Goal**

Oxygen   The oxygen of publicity
The media coverage upon which an organisation or individual may depend heavily for existence and support. In the 1980s British prime minister Margaret Thatcher forbade TV and radio to broadcast the voices of any members of outlawed terrorist groups and their political allies in Northern Ireland. She hoped thus to deprive them, like hospital patients in need of oxygen, of the vital source of their power.

P

P Mind your Ps and Qs

Be careful what you say and do. The phrase most probably arose through teaching children how to write and spell. The teacher might warn the children of the possible confusion between the letters p and q if they are not written very carefully. Another interpretation is the distinction between the liquid measures pints and quarts, once indicated in public houses by the tags p and q . The phrase dates back at least to the eighteenth century.

Pace To put someone through their paces

To test someone s abilities. When buying a horse the prospective buyer might want to see it walk or canter to assess its speed or strength.

Pace To set the pace

To create a standard for others to achieve or compete with. Literally, to run a race at a speed that other runners can judge their speed by and attempt to beat.

Pack Pack it in

Stop it. Give it up. Quit.

Pack To be packed like sardines in a tin

To be cramped or crowded into a small space. Sardines are traditionally packaged whole into a small tin containing ten or so, with very little liquid or empty space.

Pack To pack a punch

To exert considerable power or authority, to be capable of making a strong impact; to be able to use great force.

Packing To send someone packing

To send someone away hurriedly. The idea is that you so frighten or threaten the person that they go off straight away to pack their bags.

Paddle Paddle your own canoe

To look after yourself without anyone s assistance. To be independent. *Paddle Your Own Canoe* was a popular song in the nineteenth century. The phrase probably arose from the skill of the canoeists seen by the first settlers in the West Indies.

Page A page-three girl

A nude model. A sexually attractive young woman. The *Sun* newspaper began a tradition of printing a photograph of a topless model on its page three.

Paid To put paid to something

To end something. To make sure that something is finished. The phrase comes from the counting house where paid denotes an account that has been settled.

Pain A pain in the neck

An annoyance or pest. The phrase arose in the early twentieth century and was used by P. G. Wodehouse: He got there first, damn him! Wouldn t that give you a pain in the neck! The sentiment is of course ancient and this version of the phrase is probably a euphemistic way of referring, as Charles E. Funk put it, to another part of the anatomy (*Heavens to Betsy*).

Pain No pain, no gain see No

Pains To be at pains to do something

To take great care. To go out of your way to do something properly. Pains in this context means trouble or effort.

Pains To take pains see Take

Paint To paint the town red

To go out and have a wild and boisterous time. In a 1970s Clint Eastwood western *High Plains Drifter*, a small town is literally painted red and renamed Hell . The phrase is of American origin.

Painted Not as black as you are painted see Black

Pale Beyond the pale

Outside the bounds of civilisation or the limits of civilised behaviour. The word pale comes from the Latin *palum* meaning stake or post, which in this context refers to a fencing post and thus a fence or boundary implying an area with demarcated limits. It was extended to mean the boundaries of the English settlement in Ireland in the fourteenth century. There was also an English pale round Calais (1347—1558) and a notorious Pale of Settlement for the Jews in Imperial Russia (from 1792).

Palm To palm something off on someone

To unload a burden or responsibility on to someone else by deceit. The phrase uses the analogy of juggling where a clever juggler can make an audience believe that he has thrown a ball when in fact he has it concealed in his palm.

Pan   To pan out
To happen or come to light. The expression comes from gold panning where gravel from streams is sieved in a pan to uncover pieces of gold.

Pancake   Flat as a pancake   see Flat

Pants   Ants in your pants   see Ants

Paper   A paper tiger
Something that appears more dangerous or menacing than it actually is. Chairman Mao of the People s Republic of China first used this phrase in 1946 when warding off reactionaries, implying that they may stir up trouble but they are not a threat.

Paper   Not worth the paper it's written on
Completely void, useless or meaningless. This is said of a statement, promise or agreement that is not valid.

Paper   To paper over the cracks
To cover up a problem or a potential source of embarrassment. The allusion is to wallpaper which neatly hides cracks and blemishes in a wall.

Par   On a par with someone
To be even with someone, or on the same level. The word is from the Latin *par* meaning equal .

Par   Par for the course
Average. At the desired rate. This phrase comes from golf where a course s par is a figure calculated to be the average score for the eighteen holes and is thus also an indicator of a course s level of difficulty.

Par   To be below par
Feeling unwell or unfit. In finance this means the market value of a share is below its face value.

Paradise   A fool's paradise   see Fool

Parkinson   Parkinson's law
This is the title of a 1957 book by C. Northcote Parkinson in which he claims that the amount of work done is inversely proportional to the number of people employed.

Parrot   Sick as a parrot

Heartbroken, disappointed. Amongst the suggested origins are that the phrase became popular after an outbreak of psittacosis in 1973 when humans as well as parrots were affected. In *Catwatching* Desmond Morris claims that the full expression refers to a parrot with a rubber beak, understandably sick because it cannot defend itself. In the eighteenth century the phrase melancholy as a parrot was current.

Parsnips   Fine words butter no parsnips

Well-phrased promises and eloquent declarations are useless unless they are followed by action.

Part   Part and parcel

An essential element. This phrase has been around at least since the sixteenth century when it appeared in the *Acts of Henry VIII*.

Parthian   A Parthian shot   see Parting shot

Parting   A parting shot

A last attack or scolding remark when leaving a dispute, giving the adversary no opportunity to respond. The original form of this phrase, Parthian shot (see above), comes from the horsemen of Parthia who were famous for attacking by throwing spears and arrows over their shoulders while retreating.

Parting   Parting is such sweet sorrow

It is hard to say goodbye. These are the words of Juliet in Shakespeare s *Romeo and Juliet* (Act 11, Sc. 2) as she says good-night to Romeo from her balcony.

Parting   The parting of the ways

The crucial point at which a choice has to be made between two options that will lead to different outcomes; literally to choose between two paths at a fork.

Party   A party piece

A special performance or act which is used to impress others. This comes from the habit of parents in the late nineteenth century of encouraging their children to recite or dance before the guests at a party.

Party   To toe the party line

To adhere to the policies of your political party. The line refers to the starting point of a race which you touch with your foot.

Pass   A pretty pass

A critical or strange situation.

Pass   To pass muster
To come up to the required standard. Troops in an army may be made to muster, or assemble for inspection.

Pass   To pass the buck   see Buck

Past   A past master
A person who has been the master of a guild or a brotherhood. The term is now used to mean a person who is experienced and skilled in something.

Past   A person with a past
A person who has a guilty secret.

Past   A thing of the past
Something that has become obsolete, or something that is finished.

Past   To rake up the past
To insist on reviewing previous events and situations which are better forgotten. The analogy is with gardening and turning up soil which has sunk below the surface.

Patch   A bad patch
A difficult period, usually in someone s personal life.

Patch   Not a patch on
Not nearly as good as.

Path   To cross someone's path
To meet someone or to interfere in someone s life. The path in this phrase symbolises the lifespan.

Patience   To try the patience of a saint
To be so irritating as to provoke the most holy and forbearing person.

Patter   The patter of tiny feet
The prospect of having children. When someone asks: Do I hear the patter of tiny feet? they are wondering if you are thinking of having, or are expecting, a child.

Paved   The road to hell is paved with good intentions   see Hell

Pave   To pave the way
To prepare or initiate something, making it easier for yourself or others in future. The Romans paved many roads in Britain making access easier to remote parts.

Pawn   A pawn in the game

Playing a small part in something. The pawn in chess is the least valuable and least powerful piece.

Pay   Pay as you go

To meet demands as they arise rather than building up debts. This is often used with reference to a country s economic policy. It is seen as a desirable way to run an economy but is rarely put into practice.

Pay   To pay the piper

To settle a bill or obligation. Pipers and other musicians played in taverns, giving rise to the nineteenth-century saying, He who pays the piper calls the tune , meaning that the person who pays decides what will happen.

Pay   To pay the price

To suffer all the bad consequences of something you did.

Pay   To pay through the nose   see Nose

Pay   You pay(s) your money and you take(s) your choice

If you have fulfilled your part of an agreement or negotiation the choice of what you have in return is up to you, for good or ill. The expression dates at least from the mid-nineteenth century, when in its less grammatical form it was a part of a rhyme recited at a peep show.

Pearls   To cast pearls before swine

To offer wisdom (pearls of wisdom) or good advice to those who are incapable of appreciating it. The phrase appears in the Bible: Give not that which is holy to the dogs, neither cast ye your pearls before swine (Matthew 6 : 7).

Peas   As like as two peas in a pod

So similar as to be almost identical.

Pebble   Not the only pebble on the beach

Not the most important or significant person around. This is used to bring down someone who thinks that they are important.

Pecking   Pecking order

A hierarchy in which each one dominates the one below and is dominated by the one above. Domestic fowl have a hierarchy controlled and contested by pecking with the beak.

Pedestal   To put someone on a pedestal

To hold someone in reverence or respect and set them up as an example to others.

Peg   Off the peg

Ready made.

Peg   To peg away at something

To work hard at something. To build up steadily by hard effort. The phrase comes from the card game cribbage in which pegs must be built up steadily over several rounds.

Peg   To take someone down a peg or two   see Take

Pen   The pen is mightier than the sword

The written word is more powerful and influential than crude force. The phrase first appeared in this form in Edward Bulwer-Lytton s play *Richelieu* (1839).

Penny   A penny for your thoughts

What is on your mind? What are you thinking about? The notion is explained as early as 1522 when Sir Thomas More described how a person might look so pensive that you would offer to pay them just to find out what they were thinking about.

Penny   In for a penny, in for a pound

Once you start something you cannot turn back until it is done. The phrase is usually used of a risky venture, suggesting that if you are taking a risk at all it may as well be a substantial one, presumably with greater potential rewards.

Penny   Look after the pennies and the pounds will take care of themselves

If you are careful not to waste small amounts of money frequently, you will end up saving a large amount of money. This maxim is reputed to have been invented by the secretary to the treasury, Mr Lowndes, who held office in the reigns of King William III, Queen Anne and George I.

Penny   Not to have two pennies to rub together

To be very poor. The image here is of having no more than one penny so that you cannot even jangle your money in your pocket.

Penny   Penny wise and pound foolish

Mean or pedantic with small matters but careless with bigger and more important matters.

Penny   To spend a penny

To urinate. This is a British euphemism which perhaps derives from the pun with p (pence). It may also relate to the small fee that is paid for using some public lavatories, actually one penny until the 1970s.

Penny   To turn up like a bad penny   see **Bad**

People   People who live in glass houses shouldn't throw stones
see **Glass**

Petard   Hoist with one's own petard   see **Hoist**

Peter   To rob Peter to pay Paul

To take from one person and give it to another person, or to remove something important in order to use it for something else important. Many examples of this saying have been documented, often with allusions to the Saints Peter and Paul and even to the cathedrals of the same names. The phrase is at least as old as the example used by Wyclif: How should God approve that you rob Peter, and give this robbery to Paul (c.1380).

Pick   The pick of the crop

The best of the produce, goods or even people,

Pick   To have a bone to pick with someone

To have a contention with someone. To have a matter to settle with them. Presumably the reference is to dogs that would fight if both trying to pick meat from the same bone.

Pick   To pick and choose

To be very fussy about selecting what you want.

Pick   To pick someone's brains

To quiz someone in order to extract their knowledge, wisdom or experience. The image suggests literally plucking bits of information from someone s brain.

Pick   To pick up the pieces

To start something from where it was left, usually after some disrupting event. The analogy is with having to retrieve broken elements of crockery or furniture and make something out of them, the pieces being pieces of your life.

Pickle   In a pickle

To be in a difficult plight or situation. The phrase is at least as old as Shakespeare and it is unclear why the word pickle is used in this way, though it is likely that it relates to the solution used to preserve foods by pickling . The word also refers to an acid substance used to clean metals.

Picnic   It's no picnic

It is not easy. The phrase suggests that whatever it is referring to is not going to be like a picnic which involves a pleasant and relaxing outing where the object is simply to eat and relax. This saying is of American origin.

Picnic   One sandwich short of a picnic

Crazy. The late twentieth century has seen a vogue for this way of indicatiing mental impairment.

Picture   A picture is worth a thousand words

A visual image often communicates a complex idea much more simply than a long explanation. This dictum derives from a very old Chinese proverb.

Picture   A picture of health

Looking very well. The phrase is often used as a compliment.

Picture   She was a picture

She looked beautiful. The idea is that she looked so good that the sight of her would have made a picture that people would admire.

Pie   Pie in the sky

An unrealistic or unfeasible idea. The phrase probably comes from a Socialist parody of a traditional hymn, called *The Preacher and the Slave*, by the early twentieth-century songwriter Joe Hill, in which he says: You ll get pie in the sky when you die.

Pie   To eat humble pie

To accept that you are in the wrong and face the humiliation. In this phrase, humble is a pun on umbles which are the entrails and organs of a deer which the huntsman would dine on after giving the best part, the venison, to the master of the household who would sit and dine in a higher position.

Piece   A piece of cake   see Cake

Piece   A piece of the action

A part in what is going on. The phrase implies eagerness to be involved in something. It emerged in the latter half of the twentieth century in the USA.

Piece   Pièce de résistance [pee-ess de rezistons]
Something outstanding. The best or the main part of something. The phrase is French, meaning literally resistance piece . The French is used probably because it translates so badly into English because it is a concept for which the English language has no such simple phrase.

Pieces   To go to pieces
To be suddenly unable to cope with whatever you have to face.

Pig   Pigs might fly
It will never happen. It is impossible. The origin of this phrase is uncertain, though it is one of many such phrases emphasising never . The image of a pig flying is suitably absurd to suggest impossibility.

Pill   A bitter pill
An unpleasant necessity. The full phrase clarifies the analogy: A bitter pill to swallow. The idea is that it will have a positive effect eventually but is none the less unpleasant.

Pill   To gild the pill
To make something unpleasant easier to accept. In this case gild means to put honey, jam or sugar on a tablet, which is often done to make it more palatable to a child.

Pillar   A pillar of society
Someone who is seen by others as a figure to aspire to or respect. Often it is a person of local import or just a person from whom others seek advice or guidance. The term implies a person who is morally upstanding.

Pillar   From pillar to post
From here to there without aim. Pestered or messed around. The phrase alludes to a ball being whacked around a tennis court.

Pin   Neat as a new pin   see Neat

Pinch   To feel the pinch   see Feel

Pinch   To pinch pennies
To be thrifty or mean. Penny-pincher has long been used as a term for a miserly person.

Pink   In the pink
In perfect health. This phrase uses an obscure meaning of the word pink from the sixteenth century at least that has the sense peak or pinnacle (and is possibly a corruption of these words). It appears in Shakespeare s *Romeo and Juliet* as the very pink of courtesy .

Pink   Tickled pink
Overjoyed. Delighted. The idea is that something pleases you so much that it makes you blush or laugh so that you go red.

Pinpoint   Pinpoint accuracy
Absolute precision. The clich emerged during World War II referring to bombing raids.

Pins   On pins
In a precarious situation. The thought of standing or sitting on pins suggests the uneasiness which the phrase is used to convey.

Pipe   Pipe down
Be quiet. Calm down. The term is from the navy and was originally a call for lights out .

Pipped   Pipped at the post
Defeated at the last moment. The colloquial use of the word pip to mean beat or better is an old usage that has been preserved in this phrase. The phrase alludes to horse-racing where one horse may suddenly overtake another at the finishing post.

Pitched   A pitched battle
A serious fight. The phrase is used in situations where the two sides are well matched and well prepared, hence the use of the word pitched meaning positioned or demarcated . Though the word is rarely used in this capacity it is still used when referring to fenceposts or tents for example.

Pitchers   Little pitchers have big ears   see Little

Place   A place in the sun
A position of privilege with favourable opportunities. Kaiser Wilhelm of Germany used the phrase in 1911 before World War I: No one can dispute with us the place in the sun that is our due. He was alluding to German ambitions to have African colonies to match those of France and Britain.

Plague   To avoid someone or something like the plague   see Avoid

Plain   Plain as day
Absolutely clear. Totally obvious. The idea is that at night you may not be certain what you are seeing or what you have seen, but in daylight everything is clear.

Plain   Plain sailing

Straightforward. This is often said after a more difficult stage of something is over: it s all plain sailing from here . The word plain has become distorted in being taken from the nautical term plane sailing which is a method of navigation which works on the assumption that the vessel is travelling on a flat surface when in fact it is moving around the curve of the earth.

Plate   To have a lot on your plate

To have a great deal to cope with. This can be used when someone has bad problems or has suffered some misfortune, or simply when someone has a lot of work to finish. The analogy is with having too much food to be able to eat it all.

Play   A play on words

A pun.

Play   Play it again Sam

Repeat that. These words are often used in imitation of what Humphrey Bogart is supposed to have said in the film *Casablanca* (1942). However, although he did ask the pianist to play their tune, neither he nor Ingrid Bergman used those actual words.

Play   To play a trump card

To use a clever tactic which you have reserved for the right moment. In many card games certain cards when played will automatically beat all other cards.

Play   To play cat and mouse   see Cat

Play   To play for time

To delay an action or decision in order to stave off failure or defeat. In cricketing terms this happens when the batting team sees that victory is impossible in the remaining time, but plays cautiously in order to achieve a draw instead of losing.

Play   To play (or wreak) havoc

To disrupt something, to cause serious problems. Havock was an old military command from French dating from at least the fourteenth century, meaning massacre remorselessly . The command was banned in the reign of Richard II.

Play   To play it by ear

To adapt to something by improvising or responding instinctively to the demands of the situation. The term originally only referred to playing music, implying that a musician might play without reading the music, but by listening to it or simply playing along. It has since been expanded to other contexts.

Play   To play musical chairs   see Musical

Play   To play one person off against another

To attempt to get your own way by manipulating two people This is usually done by pretending to each of them that the other has said or done certain things.

Play   To play second fiddle   see Fiddle

Play   To play to the gallery   see Gallery

Play   To play with fire

To dabble in something potentially very dangerous. To enter into something very risky. Children have long been told not to play with fire because of the danger of getting burned.

Play   To play your cards close to your chest

To keep secret what you are doing. The analogy relates to someone who perhaps has a good plan, or good cards in his hand, so they are kept hidden from others in case they give away vital information.

Play   To play your cards right

To do something the correct way to achieve success. In many card games, the sequence in which cards are put down can dramatically affect the outcome. *Play Your Cards Right* is also the name of a popular TV game show in which contestants can win money by guessing the right cards.

Pleased   Pleased as punch   see Punch

Plot   The plot thickens

It becomes more obvious that there is a secret plan or conspiracy or a hidden agenda.

Plot   To lose the plot

To become out of touch with what is going on. Literally, the phrase refers to someone watching a play or reading something and not being able to follow the story, but it has increasingly come to refer to someone who is confused.

Plum A plum job

Employment which brings a high salary and prestige. The word plum is old slang for a large sum of money perhaps because of associations with a highly prized fruit.

Plumes Borrowed plumes see Borrowed

Poach To poach on someone else's preserves

Encroaching on someone s property or infringing upon their rights. Poaching is illegal hunting of privately kept game such as grouse.

Pockets To line your pockets see Line

Point Not to put too fine a point on it

To say it frankly or bluntly. This phrase is used before you explain something truthfully and without disguising it with politeness. The analogy is with sharpening a tool very carefully, as opposed to using a more blunt instrument.

Point To miss the point

To overlook the most important thing. The point refers to the main aim of an argument or idea.

Point To stretch a point

To take something to excess or beyond the proper extent. Brewer s *Dictionary of Phrase and Fable* suggests that point in this case refers to the points or laces used to tie garments tightly before the invention of the zip, which may have been stretched to allow for extra girth after a large meal, suggesting the link with indulgence or excess.

Poisoned To hand someone the poisoned chalice see Chalice

Poke To poke fun at

To ridicule or joke about someone. This phrase has a negative tone, implying that the victim of ridicule is in some way defenceless or undeserving. The word poke suggests that the victim is made to feel the insult physically.

Poke To poke your nose into someone's business

To pry into someone s private affairs.

Poker Poker face

A blank facial expression which hides what the person may be thinking. In the card game poker the players bet for money, so if a player has a good hand he will naturally be happy. However, if his face betrays this he is open to sabotage by the other players. Similarly, if he has a poor hand but remains confident in expression he might fool his fellow players and affect their betting.

Poles   Poles apart

Very different from each other. This is often said of two people, e.g. a brother and sister, who are very different. The idea is that they are as far removed from each other as the North Pole is from the South Pole.

Polish   Spit and polish   see Spit

Politics   A week is a long time in politics

A lot of things can happen in a short space of time. When he made this remark in 1964 the newly-elected prime minister, Harold Wilson, was referring to events in the House of Commons, but the phrase has been applied to many situations.

Poor   Poor as a church mouse

Impoverished. A mouse in a church would find little to eat. The expression first appeared in Howell s collection of proverbs as hungry as a church mouse in 1659.

Pop   Pop the question

To propose marriage. The word pop suggests the sudden unexpected nature of the proposal and its effect on the bride-to-be.

Possession   Possession is nine-tenths of the law

You have more say over something when you actually have it in your hands. The idea is that the law is on your side ninety per cent of the time if you are litigating over something which you possess. The expression dates back at least to the mid-seventeenth century and also appears in the form: possession is eleven points of the law .

Possum   To play possum

To hide or feign ignorance or stay in the background. The term comes from the opossum which when confronted pretends to be unconscious or plays dead .

Posted   To keep someone posted

To give someone regular news about something or let them know what is happening. The term comes from traditional American counting houses where bills and accounts were on view and actually fixed to a wall or post.

Pot   A watched pot

Something eagerly awaited that seems to take a long time. The full proverbial expression is: A watched pot never boils , implying that if you sit and wait for something it will seem to take much longer than it would if you went away and came back.

Pot The pot calling the kettle black
Someone accusing someone of something of which they themselves are guilty.

Pot To go to pot
To deteriorate. To become dishevelled or fall into disarray. The allusion is to the pot which leftovers are put into to make a dish of scraps.

Potato A couch potato see Couch

Pound A pound of flesh
The exact terms of an agreement to the smallest detail. The phrase comes from Shakespeare s *The Merchant of Venice* in which a bargain is made literally for a pound of Antonio s flesh if Shylock s loan is not repaid. Shylock is confounded because the terms of the contract demand that exactly a pound of flesh be cut without spilling a drop of blood.

Pound In for a penny, in for a pound see Penny

Poverty Grinding poverty see Grinding

Power The power behind the throne
The people that have strong influence over a leader, but who are less in the public eye. In 1770 Pitt the Elder said: There is something behind the throne greater than the King himself.

Power The powers of darkness
The forces of evil. The realm of Satan, prince of darkness.

Power The powers that be
The people in authority. The phrase comes from the Bible: the powers that be are ordained of God (Romans 13:1).

Practice Practice makes perfect
The more you do something the better you get at doing it. This is an old proverb.

Practise Practise what you preach
Do not do what you tell others not to do. Set a good example to people to whom you give advice. This is an old proverb.

Praise   To praise someone to the skies
To honour someone with great compliments or high recommendation.

Preach   To preach to the converted
To try to persuade people who already agree with you.

Pregnant   Heavily pregnant   see **Heavily**

Pretty   A pretty penny
A large sum of money. This phrase is usually used with reference to something that appears valuable and is assumed to have cost a lot.

Prey   To prey on your mind
To worry you. To preoccupy your thoughts over a period of time. The image is of worry as a predator.

Price   The price is right
Something that is a bargain. The 1980s television game show of this name has affirmed the phrase s status as a clich .

Price   To pay a high price (for failure)
To suffer terrible consequences if you do not succeed.

Prick   To prick up your ears
To listen attentively. Animals such as horses and cats literally point their ears in the direction to which they want to pay attention.

Pride   Pride and joy
Greatest pleasure or treasure. Someone s pride and joy may be their beloved pet, their hobby, something that they have made, or another person such as a son or daughter.

Prime   In the prime of life
In the best period of your life when you are at the height of your powers.

Primrose   The primrose path
The easy route. The hedonistic way. Shakespeare refers to the primrose way to the everlasting bonfire in *Macbeth*, and the primrose path of dalliance in *Hamlet*.

Profile   To keep a low profile
To be seen as little as possible.

Promise   Off to a promising start

Beginning well. This can be used in many contexts, for example, horses or runners that come quickly off the line, or a story that has an interesting opening.

Proof   The proof of the pudding is in the eating

You can only really tell how good something is when you try it out. This saying dates back as far as the fourteenth century.

Proud   Proud as a peacock

Proud of yourself to the point of showing off. The peacock has a huge fan of stunningly patterned plumage and its mating ritual of strutting up and down to display its tail is seen as an exuberant display of pride.

Public   Public enemy number one   see Enemy

Publicity   The oxygen of publicity   see Oxygen

Pudding   The proof of the pudding   see Proof

Pull   Pull yourself together

Calm yourself and regain your nerve. This is said (often insensitively) to someone who is becoming hysterical or who is getting confused or losing control.

Pull   To pull a fast one

To trick someone. To practise a sly piece of deception quickly so that it goes unnoticed.

Pull   To pull a rabbit out of the hat

To perform a miracle or do something very cleverly. It has long been a favourite trick of magicians to produce a live rabbit from an empty top hat.

Pull   To pull it off

To manage it. To achieve something difficult or risky.

Pull   To pull no punches

To make no allowances. To use full force or verbal attack regardless. To pull punches literally means to withdraw a blow before fully hitting someone.

Pull   To pull out all the stops

To let go and use everything you have at your command. Stops refers to the controls on a church organ which allow a certain amount of air to be blown through the sound pipes. An organist can produce a louder and more intense sound by releasing more stops.

Pull   To pull someone's leg

To tease someone playfully. The allusion is probably to tripping someone up as a prank.

Pull   To pull strings

To use your influence to make things happen or get people to do things. The allusion is to the marionette puppet which is controlled by pulling strings attached to its limbs.

Pull   To pull the plug on someone

To stop someone from doing something. To withdraw support. The allusion may be to an electrical plug which is the source of power for whatever someone is doing, or a bathplug for the bathtub that they are in.

Pull   To pull the wool over someone's eyes

To deceive someone by covering something up or hiding the truth from them. The expression was in use when the wearing of wigs (in slang wool) was common.

Pull   To pull your weight

To use your full potential instead of lagging behind or not achieving as much as you could. This expression alludes to physical activities such as rowing or tug-of-war in which success depends on the combined force of all the team members.

Pump   To prime the pump

To get something ready for use or start something in motion. A pump has to be filled with liquid to start it working.

Punch   Pleased as punch

Delighted. Punch and Judy are puppet characters traditionally used to entertain children and are based on a story by the seventeenth-century Italian writer Silvio Fiorillo. Punch always has a distinctive rascally laughter and is proud of his mischief.

Punch   Punch drunk

To be weary or unsteady after a heavy ordeal. Boxers experience a state of semi-consciousness similar to being inebriated after suffering too many blows to the head.

Punishment   To be a glutton for punishment   see Glutton

Pup   To be sold a pup   see Sold

Puppy Puppy fat
The chubbiness that children have until they reach maturity.

Puppy Puppy love
A childlike infatuation. The phrase perhaps alludes to the way people love young animals. It also suggests that the love is not serious and is unlikely to last.

Pure Pure and simple
Plain and unadulterated.

Pure Pure as the driven snow see **Snow**

Purple Purple patches
Florid exaggerated language in a literary work. The colour purple is the symbol of royalty and nobility and therefore associated with splendour. Other terms for this type of language are purple prose and purple passages .

Purple Purple prose (or passages) see **Purple** above

Purse To hold the purse strings
To be in control of the money or the financial situation.

Push To push the panic button
To cause a commotion. Banks and other vulnerable buildings are fitted with panic buttons so that employees can sound the alarm in case of emergency.

Push When push comes to shove
When the struggle starts. When the situation becomes competitive. The implication of this phrase is usually that everyone involved is safe until circumstances necessitate fierce competition, at which point someone (presumably the weakest) will be ousted or lose out.

Put Put that in your pipe and smoke it
Take that! What have you got to say to that! This is usually used after a blunt rebuke to defy the adversary to reply.

Put Put up or shut up
Put forward your own plan of action if you are disatisfied or stop complaining — a favourite rebuke of British prime minister John Major.

Put Put your best foot forward see **Foot**

Put   To put a brave face on it

To try to be courageous when confronted with a terrible situation. The implication is that inwardly it is impossible to be calm or brave about the situation but you are struggling to give the appearance of courage in order to cope.

Put   To put all your eggs in one basket

To rely too heavily on one thing. The original proverb is Don t put all your eggs in one basket, that is, don t stake everything on one potentially risky venture. The idea is that if you drop one basket all your eggs will break, whereas if you had two baskets you would still be left with half your eggs.

Put   To put in a good word

To recommend someone. Someone may recommend you to an important contact, often as a personal favour, by recommending that they consider you for a job for example.

Put   To put on airs   see Airs

Put   To put out to grass

To force to retire. The phrase literally means to put an animal into pasture to graze, usually referring to an old horse that can no longer work, hence the implication that someone put out to grass has been labelled no longer useful.

Put   To put someone in the picture

To explain to someone what is going on. The picture refers to the current situation or the scene in which something is occurring.

Put   To put someone through their paces   see Paces

Put   To put the cart before the horse   see Cart

Put   To put two and two together

To draw a conclusion by putting together the evidence or information. $2 + 2 = 4$ is a simple equation often used as an analogy for basic problem solving.

Put   To put your foot down

Either to assert your authority, with the image of stamping your foot to draw people s attention and stop what they are doing, or to accelerate to full speed in a car by putting your foot on the accelerator pedal until it touches the floor, hence to go very fast.

Put   To put your foot in it   see **Foot**

Put   To put your money where your mouth is
To back something financially, or in some other practical way, and not just verbally. The phrase is often used as a sort of challenge, meaning, If you are so confident about it, put some money into it!

Put   To put your oar in   see **Oar**

Put   To put your thinking cap on   see **Cap**

QED
As demonstrated. The problem has been solved. QED stands for *quod erat demonstrandum* which means which was to be demonstrated. Euclid added this phrase after his theorems.

Qs   Mind your Ps and Qs   see P

QT   On the QT
In secrecy. QT stands for quiet.

Quack   A quack (doctor)
A doctor. The term is applied jocularly to any doctor but was originally applied to medical charlatans who sold worthless remedies. The word quack suggests that the patter of the vendor was like the insistent noise of a duck. The term is thought to have come into English by way of the Dutch word *kwakzalver* which describes a vendor of sham remedies.

Quagmire   To be in a quagmire
To be in confusion and inextricable difficulty. The image is of a person slipping and sinking in boggy land.

Quality   Quality time

A period in which valuable meaningful activity is emphasised rather than the actual quantity of time spent. It is often used with reference to time spent with the family.

Quantum   A quantum leap

A sudden great advance. The term comes from nuclear physics where it means an abrupt transition from one energy state to another.

Quarrel   It takes two to make a quarrel

One person cannot argue unless there is counter argument. This proverb is often used as a rebuke to a person who takes part in a quarrel but claims that the other person started it.

Quarters   At close quarters

Close together. From a very short distance. The quarter-deck of a ship was the portion nearest the stern usually reserved for higher ranking members of the crew. Ships fighting with cannon would be at greatest danger when they drew up so that the quarter-decks were close.

Queen   Queen Anne is dead

This is a sarcastic retort to a bringer of stale news and dates back to the death of Queen Anne (1702—14).

Queen   The Queen's English

English as it should be spoken (according to some people). The idea that the style of English spoken by the monarch is the standard to judge by dates back at least to the sixteenth century.

Queen   The Queen's highway

The term long used to refer to any public road.

Queer   A queer fish

A peculiar person. Perhaps the image refers to the various types of fish that have a very odd appearance.

Queer   To be in Queer Street

To be in financial trouble. It has been suggested that queer in this example is a distortion of query, deriving from the mark that a salesman might make on his ledger to denote a street where people are not likely to be able to afford his wares.

Queer   To queer the pitch

To outdo someone or forestall them by underhand methods. The reference to pitch possibly refers to a market trader s stall which could be sabotaged by a rival.

Question   A leading question

A question that leads its audience to a particular answer. This type of question is often used in courtroom cross-examinations by prosecution lawyers to try to trap defendants into giving certain information.

Question   A question mark hangs over that

It is doubtful or uncertain.

Question   It is only a question of time

It is sure to happen sooner or later.

Question   Out of the question

Impossible. There is no chance of that. The idea is that it is not even a point of discussion.

Question   The burning question

The question that we are desperate to know the answer to. The idea is that if you do not ask the question soon it will burn your tongue because the desire to know is so intense.

Question   To beg the question

To assume as fact what is in doubt, to adopt as true a matter which you are supposed to be trying to prove. The usual motive for doing this is to avoid an issue.

Question   To pop the question   see Pop

Qui   To be on the *qui vive*

To be on the alert. *Qui vive* , meaning Who lives? , is the French equivalent of Who goes there? the traditional watchman s cry.

Quick   Quick as a flash

At great speed. The image is of the speed of a bolt of lightning.

Quick   Quick on the draw

To be fast in reacting to something. The allusion is to drawing your gun from your holster or your sword from its sheath.

Quick   Quick on the uptake   see Uptake

Quick   The quick and the dead

The living and the deceased. Quick meant alive in Old English though this meaning is now obsolete except for this example.

Quick   To be cut to the quick   see Cut

Quickie   Just a quickie
A brief question. A simple inquiry. This phrase is also sometimes used to mean a hurried bout of sexual intercourse.

Quiet   Quiet as a mouse
Silent. Without commotion.

Quite   Quite something
Something impressive or special.

Quits   To call it quits
To declare an even result. Ultimately this is from the French *quitter* meaning to leave or quit . Here it has the sense of leave off or discharge so that the result of a game or contest can be declared a draw.

Quote   Quote chapter and verse   see Chapter

Quote   Quote unquote
A citation of someone s actual words. The phrase is used to indicate precisely where another s reported words begin and end in your speech. Many speakers accompany this phrase with a gesture to signify inverted commas, usually by raising their hands to the level of each ear and curling their forefingers.

R

Rack   To go to rack and ruin
To fall into disrepair, to become destitute. The word rack is a variant of wrack or wreck .

Rack   To rack your brains
To strain hard to think of something or work something out. The rack was an instrument of torture upon which people s bodies were stretched. Its use was banned in 1640.

Rag   Ragtag and bobtail
Lowly people. This old expression has evolved out of two separate terms. Rag and tag was long used to mean inconsequential people and bobtail referred to the grooming of a horse s tail and was used to mean a contemptible person. Thus in effect the full phrase means something like the scum .

Rage   All the rage
In fashion. The latest. The implication of the word rage is that everybody is wildly excited about the new thing which is spreading so quickly.

Rage   Road rage   see Road

Rags   From rags to riches
From poverty to prosperity. A person like Cinderella who starts out at a disadvantage and rises to greatness is a rags-to-riches success .

Rags   Glad rags   see Glad

Rags   Rags and tatters
Shredded or scruffy clothing. A dishevelled state.

Rain   Come rain or shine
Whatever the weather, no matter what happens, good or bad.

Rain   It never rains but it pours
When things go wrong, they go badly wrong. Things seem to go wrong all at once rather than bit by bit.

Rain   Right as rain

Fit, feeling well or healthy. The suggestions as to why rain is regarded as right according to this expression include the possibility that people simply like the alliteration; another possibility is that rain can be regarded as normal and sound as it is necessary to life.

Rain   To rain cats and dogs

To rain heavily. The most probable derivation of this phrase connects it with northern mythology and the symbolic significance of the cat as a signal of rain and storms, and the dog or the wolf (which were connected with Odin the storm god) as a signal of the wind.

Rain   To take a rain check

To cancel and defer to a later date. The phrase originated in America where a rain check was a ticket for a baseball game given to people attending a game that was postponed due to bad weather, entitling them to see another game. It has since taken on a broader meaning and is even used in countries where the term is not used with reference to sport.

Rainy   To save for a rainy day

To put something aside for later. To save something up for an unspecified occasion. To reserve for a time of greater need. The idea is that rain represents bad circumstances under which the thing to be saved (often money) might be more useful.

Raise   To raise Cain   see Cain

Raise   To raise the roof

To vent anger. To burst with rage. To applaud with great enthusiasm. The image is of blowing the roof off a building with the force of your outburst.

Rake   To rake up the past   see Past

Rally   To rally round

To come together in support. To rush to help a person in need or a national cause. The original phrase to rally round the flag comes from a song written during the American Civil War called *Battle Cry of Freedom*.

Rampage   On the rampage

In an enraged state. In a frenzy, wild and on the loose. The word rampage probably comes from the word ramp meaning to show aggression, especially of a wild animal.

Ramrod   As straight as a ramrod

Perfectly straight. A ramrod is a stick used to tamp explosives into a bore-hole for mining or into a long-barrelled gun. Because the barrel is very narrow the rod must be completely straight.

Ran   An also ran   see Also

Rank   The rank and file

The ordinary people. This is a military term for a company of soldiers standing in lines and rows. When in this formation the ordinary soldiers are together, while the officers are separate from the group.

Rap   A rap on the knuckles   see Knuckles

Rap   Not to care a rap

To be completely unconcerned. A rap was the name given to a coin of very low value in circulation in the eighteenth century in Ireland.

Rare   A rare bird

Something extraordinary, a prodigy. The Latin, *rara avis*, was used by Juvenal to describe the black swan. It has since come to be used to refer to something that is marvelled at because it is so rare.

Raring   Raring to go

All ready to begin; eager to start. The term raring comes from a colloquial version of roar or rear like an animal charged with energy making noises or standing on its hind legs. The word is obsolete except for its use in this expression.

Raspberry   To blow a raspberry   see Blow

Rat   The rat race

The constant struggle of competition and the pressure of work. The image is of an unpleasant and chaotic race to get ahead involving a large number of competitors.

Rat   To smell a rat

To suspect that something is wrong. The image suggests a cat sniffing the scent of the rodents which it is hunting. This expression was current in the sixteenth century and appears in John Skelton s *The Image of Hypocrisy* (1550): Yf they smell a ratt they grisely chide and chant.

Rations   Iron rations   see Iron

Rats   Rats abandon a sinking ship

Selfish and cowardly people flee from a disastrous situation leaving thers to face it. This expression derives from an old superstition that if rats actually deserted a ship it was doomed to sink. It also plays on the image of the rat as a low and despicable creature in view of the old naval tradition that it is noble to go down with your ship.

Raw   A raw deal
An unfair exchange, a harsh fate. It has been suggested that the word raw is used here to imply injury; the result of the deal makes you feel hurt or raw .

Razor   To be on a razor's edge
To be in a highly precarious or dangerous situation. The image suggests that one small slip could be fatal.

Read   Read my lips
Listen very carefully, concentrate This was the title of a song by Joe Greene in 1957, but the expression became popular after George Bush used it in 1988 on accepting the Republican nomination in the US presidential elections. He asked his audience to hear and remember that he would not increase taxes.

Read   To read between the lines
To make inferences and deductions from something written or spoken, or from an entire situation. The idea is that the real meaning of a passage is hidden within the text.

Read   To read someone like a book
To infer effortlessly what someone is thinking or know their intentions from what they say or even from their expression.

Read   To read the riot act
To give a severe warning to people misbehaving or offending. King George I instituted the Riot Act in 1716, which was to be read aloud to riotous crowds warning that they should return to their homes by order of the king.

Real   The real McCoy   see McCoy

Reap   To reap the whirlwind   see Whirlwind

Reckoning   The day of reckoning   see Day

Recommendation   Self-praise is no recommendation   see Self-praise

Record   Off the record
Unofficial, in confidence or unattributable. This was originally a legal

term for evidence which a judge orders to be struck from the records of the court proceedings. It was later used by government officials giving news to the press but unwilling to be cited as the source of the information.

Recovery   Green shoots of recovery   see Green

Recovery   On the road to recovery

Getting better. This is often said of someone who has been ill.

Red   A red herring   see Herring

Red   A red-letter day

A special day. A day to remember. In traditional diaries and ecclesiastical manuscripts feast days and saints days were always marked in red.

Red   A red rag to a bull

A blatant provocation. It has long been thought that bulls respond to the colour red in an angry charge. There is no scientific evidence for this belief which seems to stem from the Spanish tradition of bull fighting in which the matador waves a red cloth to provoke the bull.

Red   Red-carpet treatment

To treat with high respect. To receive like royalty. It is an old tradition for red carpets to be laid down for monarchs and dignitaries to walk on.

Red   Red tape

Bureaucracy. Legal or official obstacles to doing something. Lawyers and bureaucrats traditionally bound their papers together with red ties.

Red   To see red

To give way to extreme anger. This image probably comes from the colour of blood which has always been associated with passion, but it may also be connected with the fury of the bull when provoked by the matador waving a red cloth, although the movement, not the colour is what excites the bull.

Red   To see the red light

To become aware of impending danger. To take something as a warning that it is time to stop. The red light refers to the railway signal which indicates danger.

Red-handed   To catch someone red-handed

To find someone trying to do something in secret. The image is of someone found with blood still on their hands fresh from a murder.

Redbrick   A redbrick university
Any British university except Oxford and Cambridge but not including those that were previously polytechnics.

Rein   Free rein
Open opportunity, liberty to do anything. The phrase refers to the reins used to control a horse.

Reinvent   To reinvent the wheel
To do something that has already been done and could be done in an easier way.

Respect   With all due respect
I don t mean to be rude, but . . . This is often said when you want to disagree or make a strong criticism without causing offence.

Rest   No rest for the wicked
You cannot relax. Literally this phrase means that sinners must endure eternal torment in Hell after death, but is now used humorously to imply that you are so busy you must have been wicked to deserve such hardship.

Rest   To rest on your laurels   see Laurels

Return   To return to the fold
To go back to your social group or place where you once lived or worked and probably left in haste or on bad terms. The fold is a kind of pen where animals are kept.

Revenge   Revenge is sweet
It is satisfying to get your own back on someone.

Rhyme   Neither rhyme nor reason   see Neither

Rich   Rich as Croesus   see Croesus

Rich   Rich beyond the dreams of avarice
Richer than you could ever imagine. The idea is that there is a state of wealth even beyond the desires of someone very greedy.

Ride   To go along for the ride
To be present without taking part in the action, to be uninvolved. The expression dates from the mid-twentieth century.

Ride   To ride for a fall
To go about things in such a reckless way that you almost invite trouble. The image is of riding a horse in such a way that you are bound to fall off.

Ride   To ride hell for leather   see **Hell**

Ride   To ride off into the sunset
To effect a romantic departure. This clich comes directly from film in which a classic romantic ending is for the hero to ride on horseback towards the setting sun.

Ride   To ride roughshod over someone
To crush someone s ideas. To treat someone with no consideration; with complete disdain. When a horse is rough-shod its shoes have been attached with the nails sticking out slightly to prevent it from slipping. To ride over someone sounds bad enough, but the idea of having the horse rough-shod to cause extra damage gives a powerful image. The strength of the image has declined as most people are no longer familiar with the terminology of horseshoes.

Ride   To ride your hobby horse   see **Hobby horse**

Ride   To take someone for a ride   see **Take**

Ridiculous   From the sublime to the ridiculous   see **Sublime**

Right   Mr Right
The perfect man or male partner.

Right   Right as rain   see **Rain**

Right   Right on
Politically correct, addressing issues that are in fashion. The phrase originated amongst black Americans in the 1920s and was a cheer of support or approval, perhaps meaning right on target . It has recently been expanded to refer to political correctness .

Right   The right-hand man
The chief aide, assistant or sidekick. The term derives from the cavalry in which the man that rides at the right of the line bears heavy responsibility for the safe progress of the troops.

Right   To be on the right side of someone
To be in someone s favour. This expression is more often used in the negative. See also **Wrong   To be on the wrong side of someone.**

Riley   The life of Riley   see **Life**

Ring   That rings a bell
That sounds familiar to me.

Ring   To ring down the curtain
To bring an end to something, to close matters. This phrase refers to the custom of ringing a bell as a signal for the lowering of the curtain in the theatre.

Ring   To ring the changes
To go through all the possibilities or combinations. The reference here is to the British tradition of church bell-ringing, where all the possible sequences of peals from the (usually four) bells are run through.

Rise   Rise and shine!
Wake up and get up! This is an extremely common wake-up call that urges you to be bright and cheery rather than slothful and yawning. It most probably originated in military circles in America.

Rise   To feel your hackles rise   see **Hackles**

Rise   To rise from the ashes   see **Ashes**

Rise   To rise from the ranks
To achieve success by working up from a lowly position. A soldier may work his way up to being an officer or general. The term is often now used for self-made people.

Rising   A rising tide
An increasing trend. This phrase often has a negative connotation, perhaps suggesting that the rising tide threatens to flood or engulf something.

Risk   To risk life and limb
To put yourself in great danger in order to do something. This phrase dates back at least to the seventeenth century. The image of not only risking the loss of limbs but risking death as well is a powerful one and is made all the more emphatic by the use of alliteration.

River   To sell someone down the river   see **Sell**

Road   Road Rage
A fit of uncharacteristic or unwarranted anger whilst driving a motor car. This term has caught on in the 1990s to the extent that it has been accepted as a behavioural phenomenon in some court cases.

Rob   To rob Peter to pay Paul   see **Peter**

Robbery   Highway robbery   see **Highway**

Rock   The rock of ages
Jesus Christ. The phrase comes from a hymn of the same name written by Augustus Montague Toplady in 1775.

Rock   To rock the boat   see **Boat**

Rocker   Off your rocker   see **Chump**

Rocket   To give someone a rocket
To give someone a severe scolding. The image of a rocket implies that your reprimand is so powerful as to blow them sky high.

Rocks   On the rocks
With ice. A spirit poured into a glass over ice is said to be on the rocks .

Rocks   To be on the rocks
In crisis, in a precarious position. A boat will very quickly get badly damaged if it gets stuck on the rocks. When not referring to someone s financial position the phrase is often said of a project or relationship that is facing problems.

Rod   To make a rod for your own back
Do something that will cause you trouble later on.

Rod   to spare the rod and spoil the child   see **Spare**

Rogue   A rogue trader
A dealer or salesman who uses dishonest tactics. The phrase was assured of its status as a clich in 1995 when a bank trader called Nick Leeson was jailed for causing the collapse of an international bank in Singapore. The word rogue was originally used of a certain type of strong healthy beggar who chose not to work.

Rolling   A rolling stone
A person who never stays for long in one place or situation. The original proverb was: A rolling stone gathers no moss , implying that restlessness and constant change were inevitably harmful and would end in an absence of any kind of security, emotional or material.

Rome   All roads lead to Rome
All thoughts lead to the same conclusion. In the Roman Empire all roads were laid radiating from the centre of Rome.

Rome   Rome was not built in a day
Great achievements require perseverance. Be patient. This saying was documented in the sixteenth century and is probably older.

Rome   When in Rome
Follow the local custom. Do as others around you do. The full expression is, When in Rome, do as the Romans do.

Roof   To go through the roof
To have a fit of rage. To be furious. See also **Raise the roof**

Roof   To raise the roof   see **Raise**

Root   Money is the root of all evil   see **Money**

Root   The root of the matter
The main point of something. The original notion.

Root   To take root
To become established (as does a plant when its roots develop).

Rope   Enough rope to hang him (or her) self
To allow someone to continue on a misguided course of action to the point where their actions lead to their downfall. The idea is that you are in a position to stop them but calculate that they will learn better by finding out for themselves. This proverb appeared in John Ray s *English Proverbs* (1678).

Ropes   To know the ropes
To be familiar with something, to know how to handle certain situations. The allusion is to the rigging of sailing ships which sailors had to be conversant with.

Rose   A rose by any other name
Names are not important. The phrase comes from Shakespeare s *Romeo and Juliet* in which Juliet says, What s in a name? . . . a rose by any other name would smell as sweet.

Rose-coloured   Rose-coloured spectacles
A flowery and idealistic view of the world. A person who sees the world through rose-coloured spectacles is someone who has an unrealistic outlook.

Rot   Tommy rot   see **Tommy**

Rotten   A rotten apple
A malicious person who spoils things for others. The image is of a basket of good apples marred by one bad one.

Rough   A rough diamond   see Diamond

Rough   Rough and ready
Unpolished but quick to act. President (General) Taylor of America (1784—1860) was nicknamed Old Rough and Ready for his methods of combat.

Rough   Rough and tumble
Hard play. Friendly fighting.

Rough   To take the rough with the smooth
To accept and deal with adverse, as well as good, circumstances.

Round   A round peg in a square hole
A misfit.

Round   A round robin
A petition signed in a circular pattern so that there is no name appearing at the top of the list. The idea is French in origin, and the word robin is a corruption of the French word *ruban* meaning ribbon .

Round   To go round in circles
To become locked in the same argument by continually covering the same points without sight of a resolution.

Roving   To have a roving eye
To be an inveterate ogler of members of the opposite sex (usually when you already have a partner).

Royal   A battle royal   see Battle

Rub   To rub salt in a wound
To make amusement of a sensitive subject, to cause further offence. Another version of the phrase is simply to rub it in which means to pick up on a sore point and continually make reference to it. In the past salt was sometimes used as a reasonably effective but painful disinfectant.

Rub   To rub shoulders with
To be in close company with.

Rub   To rub someone up the wrong way
To anger or offend someone. The image is of a cat or similar animal that may scratch or bite if its fur is stroked in the wrong direction.

Rubber   To rubber stamp something
To authorise something or give it automatic approval.

Rubicon   To cross the Rubicon
To take a step when you know you cannot turn back. The Rubicon is a river which Julius Caesar crossed to enter Italy in 49 BC thus stepping out of his own territory of Cisalpine Gaul and challenging the authority of the Roman senate.

Rue   To rue the day
To deeply regret doing something which you only realise as being a mistake in retrospect.

Rug   Snug as a bug in a rug   see Snug

Ruin   Ruin stares someone in the face
Someone is in a situation where financial collapse (or loss of reputation) is imminent.

Rule   The golden rule
The key element. The essential thing to remember.

Rule   To do something by rule of thumb
To do something by using a rough guide or measure, or by experience. The phrase alludes to the use of the thumb as a rough measure by holding it against something or at arm s length with one eye closed.

Rule   To rule the roost
To assert yourself as the boss, to take charge of important decisions. In a chicken coop the cock or rooster will dictate which hen he is to nest with. This phrase also appears with the word roast instead of roost, suggesting an analogy with cooking, or control in the kitchen.

Rule   To rule with a rod of iron   see Iron

Run   A dry run   see Dry

Run   In the long run
Eventually. The final result or consequences. The phrase refers to a long race in which a runner may be overtaken at the start but will eventually have saved enough energy to overtake and win.

Run   Run of the mill
Average, unremarkable. This is a term used for the average output of corn ground in a mill before it is graded for quality or different uses.

Run   Something runs in the family
It is an inherited characteristic of the family members.

Run   Something runs its course
Something follows its allotted path or timespan. The allusion is to a river that follows a set course from source to sea.

Run   To give someone a run for their money
To put someone to the test or give them a strong challenge. To make sure that someone does not have or achieve something without opposition or obstacle.

Run   To run amok
To be in a violent frenzy. To run wild dangerously. The word amok (sometimes amuck) comes from the Malay word *amog* meaning frenzy.

Run   To run round in circles
To chase about wildly looking for something or trying to do something with little success.

Run   To run like clockwork
To go exactly as planned or to work absolutely smoothly. Clock mechanisms have to be made to work with great precision so that no time is lost or gained.

Run   To run out of steam
To lose enthusiasm or the will to continue. This probably refers to a steam engine which runs out of fuel that creates steam and slowly comes to a stop.

Run   To run rings round someone
To beat someone by a large margin. The image here suggests that you are so much faster than someone else in a race that you are able to run right round them and still win.

Run   To run riot
To go wild. To go out of control. This phrase was originally used of hunting dogs that had lost the scent of the quarry.

Run   To run the gamut   see **Gamut**

Run   To run the gauntlet   see **Gauntlet**

Run   To run the show
To direct events. To be the main organiser of something and stand out as such.

Run   To run to earth

To uncover something, to track something down. In this phrase earth refers to a fox or rabbit s underground burrow. Thus the phrase originally meant to hunt down an animal to its burrow where the hounds would be encouraged to dig it out.

Run   To run to seed

To go past the best point. To become slightly too old or degenerate. The allusion is to vegetables which are inedible once they start to seed.

Run   To run with the hare and hunt with the hounds

To try to stay on both sides of a debate. To show sympathy for both parties involved. This phrase dates back as far as the fifteenth century.

Running   In the running

Viable. Still in the contest. See also Out of the running.

Running   Out of the running   see Out

Russian   Russian roulette

Extreme risk or danger, usually self-inflicted. The game of Russian roulette supposedly came from a sport invented by soldiers in the Russian army during World War I and involved putting one bullet in a gun with six chambers, spinning the rotating chamber and then firing it at your head with a one in six chance of shooting yourself.

Rut   To be stuck in a rut

To be unable to get out of an adverse or boring situation. When road surfaces were muddy and poorly maintained, horse-drawn coaches would often become stuck in the fissures created by other coach wheels.

S

Sack   To get the sack
To be dismissed. To lose your job. This phrase comes from a similar French saying current in the seventeenth century and refers to the bag in which the tools of your trade are kept, so that when you are given notice to leave your job you must take your bag and go.

Sackcloth   To be in sackcloth and ashes
To be penitent. To humble yourself in regret at something you have done. This expression comes from the Bible: And I set my face unto the Lord God, to seek by prayer and supplications, with fasting, and sackcloth and ashes (Daniel 9 : 3). The allusion is to an ancient Hebrew custom of wearing coarse cloth (the crudest material) daubed with ashes as a sign of penance.

Sacred   A sacred cow   see Cow

Sadder   Sadder but wiser
Having learnt something useful from an unpleasant or difficult experience. This phrase has been in use since the sixteenth century and a good example appears in *The Rhyme of the Ancient Mariner* by Samuel Taylor Coleridge (1798): He went like one that hath been stunned, And is of sense forlorn: A sadder and a wiser man, He rose the morrow morn.

Safe   Safe and sound
Out of danger. Both words in this context have roughly the same meaning but have been used together for the appeal of the alliteration since at least the sixteenth century.

Saga   Aga saga   see Aga

Sail   To sail close to the wind
To stay just within the limits (e.g., of decency, of propriety or danger). Literally, the phrase means to sail with the head of the boat as close in to the direction of the wind as possible while still keeping the sails filled.

Sailing   Plain sailing   see Plain

Salad   Salad days

Youth. The time of youthful inexperience. The term salad is a metaphor for being green or na ve.

Sally   An Aunt Sally   see Aunt

Salt   The salt of the earth

The good, valuable or reliable people. The best of the human race. This is what Jesus called his disciples, implying that they formed a simple but vital section of all the people (Matthew 5 : 13).

Salt   To rub salt in a wound   see Rub

Salt   To salt something away

To store something for later use (usually money). Before refrigerating machinery existed many foods (especially meats) were preserved in salt and stored away for use in winter.

Salt   To take something with a pinch of salt

To accept something only with strong reservations and not take great notice of it. This is a translation of the Latin phrase *cum grano salis* used by Pliny in his account of how Pompey was supposed to have discovered an antidote to poison which, however, had to be taken with a grain or pinch of salt.

Sam   Play it again Sam   see Play

Samaritan   A good Samaritan   see Good

Sanctity   The odour of sanctity   see Odour

Sardines   To be packed like sardines in a tin   see Packed

Sauce   What is sauce for the goose is sauce for the gander

The principle is the same for man or woman or for whichever situation. The idea is that male and female geese taste the same and therefore the same sauce can be used for either. The phrase is an old proverb dating at least to the sixteenth century.

Save   Save your breath

Don t say it. It does not need to be said. When something is obvious or when whatever you say will do no good someone may use this expression to tell you not to bother.

Save   To save face

To avoid or redeem yourself from embarrassment or loss of reputation. Face here means figuratively your public aspect, your reputation.

Save   To save for a rainy day   see **Rain**

Save   To save your bacon   see **Bacon**

Save   To save your skin
Narrowly to avoid danger. This phrase is often used with the negative connotation of saving your own life, job, position or reputation without thinking about anyone else s plight.

Saved   Saved by the bell
Conveniently interrupted. When in the middle of something you do not want to do or in an awkward situation you might be unexpectedly relieved by an interruption. The bell probably refers to the bell that is rung between rounds in a boxing contest.

Saving   Saving grace
The good aspect that redeems something which is otherwise poor.

Saying   It goes without saying
It is obvious. It does not need to be said (but I will say it anyway).

Scared   Scared to death
Frightened. What literally would be a very powerful image has been reduced to an everyday expression of normal feelings of fear.

Scene   Change of scene
Different surroundings.

Scent   A false scent   see **False**

School   Old school   see **Old**

School   Old school tie   see **Old**

School   School of hard knocks   see **Knocks**

Schoolgirl   Schoolgirl complexion
Youthful appearance. An older woman showing no outward sign of ageing.

Score   To know the score
To know what is going on. To know what to do in a given situation. The phrase perhaps alludes to a musical score.

Score   To score an own goal   see **Goal**

Scot-free   To go scot-free
To be freed or to get away with something. Scot comes from Old

Norse *skot* meaning a contribution and has been used in the past to refer to taxes and other such payments. Thus the phrase implies getting away without paying your due, undeservedly.

Scrape   To scrape the barrel   see Barrel

Scrape   To scrape through
To pass by a very small margin.

Scratch   To come up to scratch
To meet the required standard. To pass the test. The origin of this phrase lies in the early rules of boxing. The scratch was a line scratched into the centre of the ring which a knocked-down fighter had to crawl to in order to be declared still in the game. If he failed to come up to the scratch he was declared beaten.

Scratch   To scratch the surface
To perform or investigate something in a superficial or inadequate way. The reference is to farming or gardening where digging must be deep to be productive.

Scratchcard   Scratchcard solutions
Glib easy answers or offered solutions to serious problems. This is a phrase of the 1990s alluding to the increased popularity of gambling by buying a card which may have a prize-winning symbol hidden under its surface which has to be scraped. No skill is required to win.

Screw   To have a screw loose
To be slightly mad or eccentric. The idea is that you are in need of some adjustment like a machine.

Sea   A sea change   see Change

Sea   To get your sea legs
To get accustomed to travelling on a boat in rough weather without feeling sick.

Seamy   The seamy side of life
The degenerate side. The reverse side of a fine carpet or tapestry shows all the threads and seams, hence it is the seamy side.

Seat   To fly by the seat of your pants
By instinctive judgement. Early pilots did not have sophisticated instruments to tell them whether the plane was lifting or dropping so the only way to judge was by the physical impact on the pilot in his seat.

Second   Second nature
Natural ability. If something is second nature to someone it means that they can do it almost without thinking about it.

Second   Second sight
The power to predict things or see the future.

Second   Second to none
The best. Something that cannot be bettered.

Second   Second wind   see **Wind**

Second   To play second fiddle   see **Fiddle**

Second   To second-guess
To anticipate what someone is going to do. To be one step ahead, with the benefit of hindsight.

Secret   An open secret   see **Open**

See   To see light at the end of the tunnel   see **Light**

See   To see red   see **Red**

See   To see the light
To become enlightened, to realise, to see sense. The phrase refers to the light of reason .

See   To see through someone or something
To see someone s true character or intentions or realise what is really going on.

Seed   To run to seed   see **Run**

Seeing   Seeing is believing
You can believe what you see. This is an old proverb.

Seek   Seek and ye shall find
If you try hard enough to get what you want, you will find it. In the Bible these are the words of Jesus in Matthew 7 : 7.

Seen   To have seen better days   see **Better**

Seen   When you've seen one, you've seen them all
They are all roughly the same, or one is no more interesting than any other.

Self-made   A self-made man

A highly successful and wealthy businessman who started out with very little. The phrase is often proudly used by the man himself.

Self-praise   Self-praise is no recommendation

What someone tells you about themselves is not necessarily good grounds to judge them by. This is an old proverb.

Sell   To sell someone down the river

To betray someone or let them down badly. This phrase alludes to the days of the slave trade in America. If a slave owner sold a man to a land-owner further down the Mississippi the slave knew that he faced much harsher conditions and more oppressive treatment.

Send   To send someone packing   see Packing

Separate   To separate the sheep from the goats   see Sheep

Separate   To separate the wheat from the chaff   see Wheat

Sesame   An open sesame

A way of getting what you want. This magical command comes from *Ali Baba and the Forty Thieves* from *The Arabian Nights* in which it opened the great door to the robbers cave.

Set   To set someone's teeth on edge   see Teeth

Settle   To settle old scores

To resolve an old conflict. To get revenge after a long time. A score is a debt or a bill owed to a shopkeeper or someone providing a service.

Settle   To settle someone's hash   see Hash

Seventh   To be in seventh heaven   see Heaven

Sex   Sex rears its ugly head

Sex seems to be made responsible for all human motivation. After the psychological research of Sigmund Freud it became a twentieth-century preoccupation to assume that sex pervaded all human activity and this saying is a cynical comment on that fashion.

Sex   The gentle sex   see Gentle

Shadow   To be a shadow of your former self

To have somehow lost your strength or character or courage or other attributes or to have lost weight. This very visual image has become less forceful through over-use.

Shadow   To be afraid of your own shadow   see **Afraid**

Shake   To shake the dust from your feet

To show contempt for a place, to leave it behind you and show no intention of returning. This saying comes from an Eastern custom which is alluded to in the Bible (Matthew 10 : 14) and means that just as a person might treasure the very soil of a beloved country, so all trace of a hated place must be symbolically removed from your feet.

Shake   To shake with laughter

To convulse with laughter.

Shakes   No great shakes   see **No**

Share   The lion's share   see **Lion**

Share   To share and share alike

To reciprocate other people s altruism or hospitality. To play an equal part. This saying was documented in the sixteenth century and is probably older still.

Shave   A close shave

A near disaster. A narrow escape. Literally a close shave is the work of a good barber or a sharp razor. The closer to the skin the beard is cut the greater the danger of slicing the skin.

Shebang   The whole shebang

The lot, everything. A shebang was originally American slang for a hut and, from that, a humorous term for your own place or your home or all your possessions.

Shed   To shed light on something

To uncover clues to a mystery. To inform.

Sheep   The black sheep of the family

The one who does not follow the rest of the family in temperament or profession or character or, often with children, the naughty one. This phrase comes from the older saying, There s a black sheep in every flock. Even today a black sheep may be worth less than a white one.

Sheep   To separate the sheep from the goats

To group two different things, or distinguish between them. This is an old practice of shepherds who graze both animals together. It is mentioned in the Bible (Matthew 25 : 31). There is an implication that sheep are more desirable than goats.

Shell   To come out of your shell

To lose your shyness or reserve and converse more or interact more with others. The image is of a snail or tortoise which retires into its shell at the sight of people.

Shift   Shift the goal posts   see Goal

Shilly-shally   To shilly-shally
To dither or be indecisive. This is a corruption of Will I? Shall I?

Shine   To take a shine to someone
To start to like someone.

Ship   The ship of state
The nation. This is an old metaphor which sees the country as a vessel and the population as a ranked crew.

Ships   Ships that pass in the night
Casual acquaintances. People who often greet but do not know each other well. This image comes from *Tales of a Wayside Inn* by Henry Wadsworth Longfellow (1863). Ships passing each other in fog or at night would shine a light as a signal and call to each other but could not see each other.

Shirt   To give the shirt off your back
To give everything you have got. The last thing to give after everything else would be the clothes that you are wearing.

Shoestring   On a shoestring
Using very little money. With a very low income or budget. This phrase perhaps alludes to the tiny earnings of people who used to sell shoelaces in the street.

Shoot   Don't shoot the messenger   see Kill

Shoot   To shoot down in flames
To bring someone down harshly and effectively. Strongly to refute someone s argument. The image is of a battle between fighter planes.

Shoot   To shoot your bolt   see Bolt

Shop   To talk shop
To talk about your trade, usually with someone of a similar trade.

Short   To give someone short shrift   see Shrift

Shot   A shot in the arm
A boost, something invigorating. The phrase refers to an injection of morphine or cocaine.

Shot   A shot in the dark
A wild guess. This phrase probably arose during World War I and refers to a gunshot fired without the soldier being able to see the target.

Shot   Shot to hell
Badly damaged. Wrecked.

Shot   Shot to pieces
Destroyed or disintegrated. Shattered with tiredness or stress. From the image of a mutilated soldier, though the image no longer has its strength.

Shoulder   To give someone the cold shoulder   see **Cold**

Shoulder   To put your shoulder to the wheel   see **Wheel**

Shoulders   To have broad shoulders
To be strong enough morally or physically to bear burdens and hardship.

Shout   To shout something from the rooftops
To announce something previously private so that it becomes public knowledge.

Shout   To shout the odds   see **Odds**

Shouting   It's all over bar the shouting
The results (of a competition, argument or election) are certain, although the official announcement or decision has not yet been declared. The term is from competitive sports where, in the past, the final result was shouted or called.

Show   Get the show on the road
Get started. Put something into action. Side-shows often toured around the country roads in trailers.

Show   The show must go on
Things have to continue despite disaster. The phrase comes from the performing arts and probably arose in the circus in the nineteenth century, where it was the responsibility of the band and the ringmaster to keep the audience entertained if anything went wrong during any of the dangerous acts.

Show   To show your hand

To reveal your intentions or your part in something. In card games showing your hand tells the other players what you have secretly been trying to do.

Shown   To be shown up in your true colours   see Colours

Shrift   To give someone short shrift

To give someone little chance to repent. To deal with someone bluntly. Short shrift, or brief confession, was the name of the few moments in which a criminal was allowed to confess and receive forgiveness before execution.

Shy   Once bitten twice shy   see Bitten

Sick   Sick as a dog

Feeling downcast and miserable (not necessarily physically ill). The original connection between sickness and a dog is in the Bible: As a dog returneth to his vomit, so a fool returneth to his folly (Proverbs 26 : 11).

Sick   Sick as a parrot   see Parrot

Side   To sidetrack

To divert or digress. Sidetracking is a railroading term from America meaning to build a siding or parallel extension to the main track, hence its extended meaning.

Sigh   To heave a sigh of relief

To show a strong feeling of alleviation.

Sight   A sight for sore eyes

A greatly welcomed appearance. Usually this is said to someone whom you have missed during an ordeal or about something you have longed for.

Sight   Sight unseen

Without having been looked at, under cover. This phrase dates back at least to the seventeenth century.

Sign   A sign of the times

Evidence of the current predicaments in society. This phrase is often used negatively to refer, for example, to social problems. It was the title of a 1980s film by American pop star Prince. The phrase comes from the Bible where Jesus says to the Pharisees: . . . ye can discern the face of the sky; but can ye not discern the signs of the times.

Sign   Sign on the dotted line
Agree, show your consent; make something official.

Signed   Signed, sealed and delivered
Done. Completely finished including every detail. This was originally a legal term for a completed and despatched act or order or writ. It has probably lasted because of its attractive rhythm and alliteration.

Silence   Silence is golden
It is often better to think than to speak. This phrase comes from an old proverb: Speech is silver, silence is golden. The proverb is thought to be of oriental origin.

Silver   Every cloud has a silver lining   see Every

Silver   Sold for thirty pieces of silver   see Sold

Sin   To live in sin   see Live

Sin   Ugly as sin   see Ugly

Sin   Wages of sin   see Wages

Sink   Sink or swim
Fail or succeed. This phrase is used in situations where the onus is on the person in question to achieve something or fail to do it. The phrase is extremely old. An earlier version of it, seen as early as the fourteenth century, was float or sink which hints at a connection with the medieval practice of ducking. This was done to assess whether a person was a witch or not. If the person sank they were innocent. If they floated they were considered possessed.

Sink   To sink your teeth into something
To tackle something with vigour or enthusiasm. The image is of biting hard into something with relish.

Sinking   A sinking feeling
A strong sense of uneasiness. On a boat there may be a few moments of terrible uncertainty when you are not sure whether the vessel is going down or not.

Sit   To sit on the fence
To take a neutral stance, to abstain. The idea is that you stand on neither territory, but stay on the neutral division between the two.

Sit   To sit tight

To hold on to your position. To sit and wait until something is resolved. In the card game poker a player may sit tight by neither continuing to bet nor dropping out of the round.

Sit   To sit up and take notice

Pay attention to someone s plight or demands. Recover from illness or some other indisposition.

Sitting   A sitting duck   see Duck

Sitting   Sitting pretty

Taking advantage of a favourable situation. The phrase is often used cynically by people in a less fortunate position. It was the name of a musical in the 1920s.

Six   Six feet under

Dead. The phrase alludes to the depth at which coffins are buried under the ground.

Six   Six of one and half a dozen of the other

The same, two identical things described differently. The expression is often used to attribute equal blame when something has gone wrong.

Sixes   To be at sixes and sevens

In a state of confusion or disarray. The phrase comes from an old dice game that has since become obsolete.

Sixth   A sixth sense

A mysterious ability to predict things or be aware of things that others cannot detect. The normal five senses are sight, taste, smell, touch and hearing.

Sixty-four-thousand dollar   The sixty-four-thousand-dollar question

The crucial point. The question whose answer everything hinges on. This phrase comes from the prize given for answering the final star question in an American quiz.

Skeleton   A skeleton in the cupboard

A closely kept secret from someone s past, a shocking revelation about someone s personal life.

Skid   To be on Skid Row

To have a low status. To be a social reject. The phrase is American in origin and refers to people who have supposedly skidded or slipped from the path of virtue.

Skin   By the skin of your teeth   see **Teeth**

Skin   No skin off my nose   see **Nose**

Skin   To be all skin and bones
To be very thin. To be undernourished. The idea is that you have no flesh on you.

Skin   To get under someone's skin
To irritate or pester someone. This phrase suggests that someone is almost a physical irritant like a parasite that enters the skin.

Skin   To have a thick skin   see **Thick**

Sky   The sky's the limit
There is no restriction. Do what you want to do. There are endless possibilities. This phrase dates back at least three centuries.

Sledgehammer   To use a sledgehammer to crack a nut
To apply excessive force. To take drastic measures to resolve a small problem.

Sleep   Beauty sleep
Eight hours of restorative sleep which makes you look healthy and attractive. The idea of adequate sleep promoting beauty became strong in the twentieth century, but old sayings also confirm the importance of sleep.

Sleep   To sleep on something
To go to bed and get some rest rather than trying to resolve a problem when you are tired. To take time to consider something, or delay a decision until morning.

Sleeve   To have something up your sleeve
To have a surprise solution or an unexpected idea. Magicians hide things up their sleeves and produce them unexpectedly.

Sleeve   To laugh up your sleeve   see **Laugh**

Slim   Slim pickings
Poor choice. Meagre takings. This phrase comes from the result of a poor harvest in farming.

Slip   A Freudian slip
Accidentally letting out something that you are thinking about, when intending to say something else. Dr Sigmund Freud (1856—1939) was a highly influential psychoanalyst who studied the subconscious. To him

a slip such as that described would have been evidence of subconscious desires at work.

Slip   To slip through your fingers

To miss an opportunity that you very nearly had. The allusion here is to a small animal which you had caught but accidentally allowed to escape — or indeed to anything of value that has eluded your grasp.

Slippery   A slippery customer

A devious and untrustworthy person. Someone who you would not like to have dealings with.

Slippery   Slippery as an eel

Elusive, hard to find or keep track of. Eels are extremely difficult to hold because not only are they very slimy, but they also wriggle with great force.

Sloane   A Sloane ranger

A member of the rich and fashionable set who seek to flaunt their wealth and status. Sloane Square in London was popular with the young and wealthy yuppies during the 1980s. The term Sloane arose from people (and the satirical magazine *Private Eye*) mocking a certain stereotypical young rich person flaunting expensive cars and horse-riding equipment. *Harpers and Queen* invented the term Sloane Ranger in 1975.

Small   Small beer

A trivial or insignificant matter. Small beer traditionally meant beer low in alcohol, so it was of no consequence to people used to stronger ale.

Small   Small fry

Minions, insignificant people or children. This derives from the word fry meaning young fish.

Smart   Smart Alec

A show-off or know-all. The phrase originated in America in the 1860s but the identity of the original Alec has become obscure.

Smart   The smart set

Fashion-conscious people.

Smell   To smell a rat   see Rat

Smokescreen To put up a smokescreen

To try to hide your motives or intentions from your opponents. The device of a smokescreen is used in warfare to obscure the enemy s view of an attack or an escape.

Snail To go at a snail's pace

To go extremely slowly.

Snake To be a snake in the grass

To be a devious or hidden critic. To be hypocritical. This phrase comes from the writings of the Latin poet Virgil.

Snow Pure as the driven snow

Untainted. Fresh and unsullied. White symbolises purity and innocence. Snow in a drift is also a fitting image of softness and fragility.

Snug Snug as a bug in a rug

In perfect comfort. The origin of the word snug is obscure, though it may be related to the snuggery which is an eighteenth-century word for the lounge-bar of an inn. This amusing image is attractive for its rhyme and rhythm.

So So far, so good

All has gone well up to now. This phrase has been in use since at least the seventeenth century.

So So near and yet so far

Failing at the point of being close to success.

Sob A sob story

An excuse designed to evoke sympathy, especially when you have done something wrong or let someone down.

Sober Sober as a judge

Very serious. Sedate and rational. Not drunk. A judge is seen as a serious and clear-thinking person. The phrase is now widely used to mean the opposite of completely drunk.

Society The affluent society   see Affluent

Soft A soft touch

Someone who is easy to influence, or is lenient or tolerant. To touch someone for something means to ask for a loan or favour.

Soft To soft soap

To manipulate someone with skilful blandishments.

Sold   Sold for thirty pieces of silver

Betrayed for a meagre reward. In the Bible Judas betrayed Christ and was rewarded with thirty pieces of silver.

Sold   To be sold a pup

To be swindled. This is an old phrase referring to an old trick where a market trader might sell someone a pig concealed in a bag, which on arriving home the buyer would find to be a puppy or sometimes a cat.

Soldier   To soldier on

To continue bravely. To struggle courageously like a good soldier.

Something   Something is rotten in the state of Denmark

see **Denmark**

Son   Son of a gun

Damn! This is a euphemism for son of a bitch which is a much stronger expression, usually used simply as an exclamation rather than an insult. As with many euphemistic phrases it uses rhyme.

Song   To make a song and a dance about something

To cause an unnecessary fuss about something. This colourful idea suggests that you do not simply take a suggestion but you write a song about it and even a special dance to go with it.

Soul   To call your soul your own

To be independent, to be private. This expression, current from the sixteenth century, is more often negative, so that people who resent the feeling of being dominated by others may say they can t call their soul their own .

Sound   Sound as a pound

Perfectly well, trustworthy. The phrase has stuck because of its rhyme.

Soup   Alphabet soup   see **Alphabet**

Sow   To sow your wild oats   see **Oats**

Spade   To call a spade a spade

To speak plainly or literally.

Spanner   To throw a spanner in the works

To disrupt badly. To put a spanner into machinery literally might stop everything and cause extensive damage. The phrase has been expanded to refer to any process which is vulnerable to disruption.

Spare   Spare the rod and spoil the child
To treat children too softly, to leave faults uncorrected. This comes from the Bible: He that spareth his rod hateth his son; But he that loveth him chasteneth him betimes (Proverbs 13 : 24).

Speak   Speak for yourself
Don t include me.

Speak   Speak of the devil
Here comes the person we were just talking about. It was once thought that if you spoke about the Devil he would appear.

Speak   To speak the same language
To form an understanding, to make a breakthrough in a negotiation.

Spectacles   Rose-coloured spectacles   see Rose-coloured

Spill   To spill the beans   see Beans

Spiral   On a downward spiral
Deteriorating constantly. This term is often applied to financial trouble.

Spirit   The spirit is willing but the flesh is weak
I would like to do it but I am not physically capable. This comes from the Bible where Jesus warns his disciples against temptation (Matthew 26 : 41).

Spit   Spit and polish
Smart appearance. Perfect presentation. This term derives from the military where superiors tell their men to clean and polish their boots and their shoes for inspection. Traditionally this was done with spittle and rubbing.

Spitting   The spitting image of someone
A strong likeness of someone. The word spit meant likeness , though this meaning is now redundant. The phrase was for a long time spit and image but has become distorted in speech to its present form.

Split   To split hairs   see Hairs

Split   To split your sides
To laugh uncontrollably. It is an old amusing idea that you might laugh so much that your sides burst.

Spot   A blind spot   see Blind

Spot   To put someone on the spot
To interrogate someone. To get someone in a vulnerable position where they must confess.

Spots   To knock spots off someone   see Knock

Spout   Up the spout
Ruined, gone. The allusion is to the tube in a pawnbroker s shop through which items are sent from the shop to the store. The phrase is also commonly used as a crude term for pregnant .

Spread   To spread like wildfire   see Wildfire

Spring   No spring chicken   see Chicken

Spur   On the spur of the moment
Suddenly, without deliberation. A spur is a protrusion of rock.

Squad   The awkward squad   see Awkward

Square   A square deal
A fair and honest business. Square in this case means level or fitting.

Square   A square meal
A good, satisfying meal. In the eighteenth century ships crews were fed on square wooden trays so that they could be easily stored and stacked.

Square   A square peg in a round hole
A mis-match, particularly a person in the wrong job or social group. The image is obvious.

Square   Back to square one
Back to the start. We ll have to start all over again. Square one is the starting point of many traditional board games in which a wrong move might send you back to the beginning.

Stab   A stab in the back
A cruel attack or betrayal. It has long been thought cowardly in combat to attack from behind.

Staff   The staff of life
Bread. The thing that supports us, like a walking stick or crutch. This idea has been developed from the Bible: . . . the stay and the staff, the whole stay of bread and the whole stay of water (Isaiah 3 : 1).

Stage   A stage whisper

A whisper that is really intended for everyone to hear, just as actors pretending to whisper must make sure that the audience hears.

Stalking   A stalking horse

A person put forward to mislead. The term is now often used in politics, where people insist on a challenge to the prime minister so a candidate is put forward (usually by the prime minister s own party) who has little chance of success, in order to test the chances of a more popular candidate. The term comes from hunting, where a hunter would get off his horse on seeing his prey and approach it by using his horse as a cover in order to get close enough to shoot.

Stamping   Someone's old stamping ground   see Ground

Stand   To stand on ceremony   see Ceremony

Stand   To stand up and be counted

To reveal publicly your opinions or allegiances and accept the consequences. Being counted implies voting. Votes have not always been secret. Voters of one persuasion might be asked to stand or raise their hands so that the number of votes could be counted.

Stand   To stand your ground

To maintain your stance. To refuse to give in. The idea is that you defend your territory.

Stark   Stark naked

Completely or unmistakably nude. The word stark in this case serves to intensify the image, meaning utterly or totally . A more recent and cruder version of the phrase that has become popular is: Stark bollock naked .

Stark   Stark raving mad

Insane. Making a ludicrous suggestion. This phrase doubly emphasises the madness by saying not only raving (frenzied) mad, but stark (utterly) raving mad.

Start   To start from scratch

To go back to the beginning. To build up from nothing at all. The scratch is the starting line in races.

Start   To start off on the wrong foot

To make an initial mistake. To go about something the wrong way. This phrase probably comes from the military, where each step must be co-ordinated in a troop of marching soldiers. If you start the march with the wrong step you will remain out of time with the others.

Steal   To steal someone's thunder
To deprive someone of the glory or praise for something.

Steam   To let off steam   see Let

Steer   To steer clear of someone or something
To avoid. The analogy in this phrase is to driving a car or boat and circling around something or someone to avoid danger. The phrase has doubtless stuck not only due to its attractive rhyme but also its usefulness in expressing avoidance with a hint of fear or trepidation.

Sterling   Sterling qualities
Good, reliable or trustworthy character. The term sterling was given to the British currency and also to valued gold and silver, so when used figuratively to refer to a person it implies that they are approved or reliable.

Stew   To stew in your own juice
To take the consequences of your own actions. This phrase is based on a very old idea. Chaucer used a phrase that translates as: I made him fry in his own grease in *The Wife of Bath s Tale* (*c*.1350).

Stick   A stick-in-the-mud
Someone content with their situation and not willing to be changed. Stubborn but content. Horse-drawn coaches were extremely hard to move if their wheels became stuck. Versions of this phrase have persisted since at least the fourteenth century.

Stick   The stick and the carrot
A combination of bullying and gentle persuasion or bribery. The phrase refers to the notorious difficulty of moving a stubborn donkey. The two methods that you might try are to hit it with a stick or to coax it with a carrot.

Stick   To stick out like a sore thumb
To be painfully out of place, to be embarrassingly visible.

Stick   To stick your neck out   see Neck

Stick   To wave the big stick
To threaten force. The big stick represents force or oppression.

Sticking The sticking place
The point at which an attack, like the thrust of a dagger or sharp weapon, begins to hurt. The verb to stick means to stab . Shakespeare uses the words literally in *Macbeth* when Macbeth and his wife are planning to murder Duncan: But screw your courage to the sticking place, and we ll not fail. However, the expression is increasingly used to mean the place where an obstacle is encountered, a stumbling block. This has arisen because of the association of stick with the idea of getting stuck or unable to proceed.

Stickler A stickler for detail
A pedant. Someone who is particular about small matters. This phrase can be used both as a criticism and a compliment depending on the context. Stickler is a now obsolete word for an umpire or referee in sporting games. The term was used at least as early as the sixteenth century.

Sticks To be in the sticks
To be far from the town. To be in the countryside. This is an American colloquialism.

Still Still waters run deep
Quiet people may be profoundly knowledgeable or philosophical. This assertion was noted as early as the fifteenth century.

Still The still small voice see Voice

Sting To have a sting in the tail
To have a vicious or dangerous aspect as well as a superficial pleasantness. The reference is to a bee or a scorpion.

Stink To stink to high heaven
To smell terrible or to be extremely suspect. The idea is that the awful smell is so strong that it will drift right up into the heavens.

Stir To stir up a hornet's nest see Hornet

Stone A heart of stone
A cold and unfeeling character. The image suggests cold and impenetrability.

Stone A rolling stone see Rolling

Storm A storm in a teacup
A big fuss about something very trivial.

Story But that's another story see Another

Straight   As straight as a ramrod   see **Ramrod**

Straight   Straight from the horse's mouth   see **Horse**

Straight   To go straight
To become honest. To give up criminal ways. Bent or crooked has long referred to criminality so straight is naturally the opposite.

Strange   Strange bedfellows
An unlikely partnership. People working or living together in unlikely circumstances.

Stranger   A little stranger
A new-born child.

Straw   The last straw   see **Last**

Straw   To draw the short straw
To be the unlucky one. To take the worst consequences. Drawing straws is an age-old method of deciding who has to do something. One straw is shorter than the others but all are concealed so that someone picks the short one and loses.

Straws   Straws in the wind
To make a feeble and futile effort to resist something. This is an old saying in which straws refers to pieces of straw.

Straws   To clutch at straws
To try vainly to hang on to something when there is no hope. The idea is that a drowning person clutches at anything that floats, like straw, even though it will not help them.

Street   Up my street
My favourite. My kind of thing.

Streets   Streets ahead
Far in advance. The image conveys distance by picturing the length of several streets put together.

Stride   To take something in your stride
To cope with something easily or casually as if you could do it while walking along without breaking your stride.

Strike   To strike the right note   see **Note**

Strike   To strike while the iron is hot   see **Iron**

Strings   To have two strings to your bow   see **Bow**

Strings   To pull strings   see **Pull**

Strip   To tear a strip off someone   see **Tear**

Strong   The strong silent type
A gentle but robust individual. This is a stereotyped idea of a man put about principally by films and magazines.

Stuffed   A stuffed shirt
An overbearing man with an inflated sense of power or position. The image suggests that he is actually less important than the shirt he is wearing.

Stumbling   A stumbling block
An obstacle or hindrance to understanding or progress. The phrase is from Leviticus (19 : 13): Thou shalt not curse the deaf nor put a stumbling block before the blind. The biblical phrase meant a physical block which someone might trip over.

Stump   To stump up
To pay up. To pay what you owe. This is an American term, probably from the logging trade where stumps meant cash, or that which was laid down on a tree stump as wages.

Stung   Stung to the quick   see **Cut**

Stymie   To stymie someone
To put someone in a frustrating and difficult position. To hinder someone. This was originally a golfing term, now obsolete, meaning to block someone s path to the hole with your ball.

Sublime   From the sublime to the ridiculous
From normal things to absurdity. This is a quote from *Age of Reason* by Tom Paine (1794). Napoleon also took it as a favourite saying as he was an admirer of Paine s work.

Sugar   Sugar daddy
A father figure as a protector. This is a term often used when a woman takes a much older (and especially wealthy) man. This term is of American origin.

Sun   A place in the sun   see **Place**

Sunday   Sunday best
Your smartest clothes. It is an old Christian tradition to wear your best clothes on Sunday, especially for going to church.

Sundays   Not in a month of Sundays   see **Month**

Sundry   All and sundry   see **All**

Surf   To surf the internet   see **Internet**

Survival   Survival of the fittest   see **Fittest**

Swallow   To swallow your pride
To be humble. To allow yourself to face something potentially humiliating.

Swan   A swan song
The final poetic or artistic work before death. According to legend the swan utters a plaintive beautiful song just before it dies. The phrase is used in retrospect to refer to any final work of a deceased person.

Swan   To swan around
To meander about aimlessly. Swans appear to swim around a lake with no direction or effort. This term was used by troops during World War II to describe a tank roaming aimlessly across the battlefield.

Swear   To swear like a trooper
To use the strongest language or to swear in a continuous blast. This was something that soldiers were known for and perhaps to a certain extent excused for.

Sweep   To sweep someone off their feet
To overwhelm someone and surprise them pleasantly. The most common use of this phrase is in a romantic context.

Sweep   To sweep something under the carpet
To ignore something due to laziness or unwillingness to face up to facts, as you might sweep dirt under the carpet because it is easier than picking it up.

Sweet   Sweet Fanny Adams
Nothing, having no useful content. Fanny Adams was an eight-year-old girl who was murdered in the late nineteenth century at about the time that tinned meats were introduced into the navy. Naval officers joked about the poor quality of the meat and suggested that it might contain remains of Fanny Adams. The term was then extended to mean useless and then abbreviated to sweet FA which conveniently served as an abbreviation for the cruder phrase sweet f**k all .

Sweet   To have a sweet tooth
To have a taste for sweet or rich foods.

Sweetness Sweetness and light
All that is good. This phrase is usually used sarcastically for something which is excessively pure, pious or sentimental. The phrase comes from *Battle of the Books* by Jonathan Swift (1697) in which he says that the bees give us sweetness (honey) and light (wax that can be made into candles).

Swelled A swelled (or swollen) head
An over-inflated sense of self-worth or ego. Pride is said to swell your head.

Swing To get into the swing
To get accustomed to something or feel more at ease or part of something, to develop a rhythm in doing something. The term comes from the swing of a pendulum and was in use in the nineteenth century.

Swings Swings and roundabouts
Things even themselves out eventually. The original phrase was: What you lose on the swings, you gain on the roundabouts.

Swoop One fell swoop see **Fell**

Sword A double-edged sword see **Double-edged**

Sword The sword of Damocles see **Damocles**

Sword To live by the sword
To live dangerously or fight constantly. This saying comes from the Bible: All they that take the sword shall perish with the sword (Matthew 26 : 52).

Swords To cross swords with someone
To get into physical or verbal conflict with someone.

Systems All systems go
Start! Everything ready! This term comes from the American space research agency NASA and is used primarily in launching rockets but has been extended to general use when getting something organised or ready to run.

T

T To a T

Exactly. Perfectly or precisely. In this phrase T refers to a T-square which is used to draw and measure right angles accurately.

Tables To turn the tables

To reverse a situation, to switch roles or positions, to get revenge. This expression comes from the old tactic of turning the board round in a game such as chess or draughts to alter the players standings and change the game.

Tabs To keep tabs on someone

To monitor or control someone s behaviour or progress. A tab is a tag or mark for identifying something. Probably in this phrase the allusion is to an army officer s tab on his collar which denotes his rank.

Tack To be on the right tack

To be doing something the right way. To be following the best course of action. Tacking is a nautical term referring to the zig-zagging of a sailing vessel when it has to sail into the wind.

Tail To have a sting in the tail   see Sting

Tail To turn tail

To flee. To turn and leave. The allusion is to an animal. You see its tail when it is facing away from you.

Tail With his tail between his legs

Dejected, downcast. A dog is seen to show its mood with its tail. It wags in the air when it is happy and hangs limply when it is not.

Take Take care!

Look after yourself, goodbye! This phrase is now so commonly used as a final word on departing that the only real meaning it has left is goodbye .

Take Take it from me

Believe me. I know what I am talking about. It presumably refers to the advice or information given when the phrase is used to convince someone.

Take   Take it or leave it
You decide. The offer is there for you to accept or decline.

Take   To take a back seat   see Back

Take   To take a dim view of something
To disapprove of something. The phrase suggests that you look at something in a negative light, or as you would look at something uninteresting or dull.

Take   To take a leaf out of someone's book
To follow someone s example. The idea is that you take instruction from someone who shows expertise in what you are trying to do.

Take   To take a place by storm
To gain great popularity or support suddenly. This is especially used of public figures and entertainers to describe a successful appearance. This was a military term in use in the seventeenth century meaning to attack a city or fortification with great force.

Take   To take a rain check   see Rain

Take   To take a shine to someone
To like someone immediately. To get on with someone instantly. The origin of this phrase is somewhat obscure but it most likely uses shine to suggest a smile or the radiance of a happy face.

Take   To take heart
To muster courage. This phrase is sometimes expressed as an exhortation, Take heart of grace. The heart has long been thought of as the centre of courage as well as emotion.

Take   To take it on the chin   see Chin

Take   To take matters into your own hands
To deal personally with things that others are normally responsible for. The phrase has come to imply taking on something serious or important, perhaps because you are dissatisfied with the way that others are tackling it.

Take   To take off your hat to someone
To show someone admiration or respect, particularly for a great achievement. Until recently it was long the custom to take off your hat as a sign of respect or reverence, for example to the dead or when entering a church or simply to show courtesy when meeting someone.

Take   To take pains

To be extremely careful in doing something.   See also **Pains**

Take   To take root   see **Root**

Take   To take someone at their word
To believe someone. Someone s word is their pledge or promise.

Take   To take someone down a peg or two
To lower someone s self-esteem. To deflate someone s boastfulness
with a rebuff. The phrase refers to a ship s colours (flags bearing the
vessel s allegiance) which were raised using pegs to show honour or
glory. The higher the colours, the greater the glory.

Take   To take someone for a ride
To lead someone astray, to play a trick on someone. The idea is
probably that you lead someone away from the truth.

Take   To take someone to task
To call someone to account for their actions,

Take   To take someone to the cleaners   see **Cleaners**

Take   To take someone under your wing   see **Wing**

Take   To take someone's name in vain   see **Name**

Take   To take something in your stride   see **Stride**

Take   To take something lying down
To submit to something without resistance. This phrase is more often
used in the negative indicating that you are prepared to fight or resist.

Take   To take the bit between your teeth
To tackle something resolutely. When a horse bites the bit (the metal
mouthpiece holding the reins) instead of leaving it in the natural gap in
its teeth where it should go, it cannot easily be controlled.

Take   To take the bull by the horns   see **Bull**

Take   To take the flak
To be the object of someone s anger or disapproval. Flak was originally
an abbreviation for the German word for an anti-aircraft gun.

Take   To take the law into your own hands   see **Law**

Take   To take the rough with the smooth   see **Rough**

Take   To take the wind out of someone's sails   see **Wind**

Take   To take to something like a duck to water
To undertake a new activity effortlessly. Ducklings are completely at home in water.

Take   To take to your heels
To run away.

Take   To take umbrage   see **Umbrage**

Take   To take your breath away
To astonish or amaze you. The idea is that something is so surprising that you are momentarily breathless or speechless.

Taken   To be taken aback
To be surprised or shocked. When a ship s sails are blown the wrong way until they touch the mast they are said to be aback with the impact of the blast of wind.

Tale   An old wives' tale
A false and highly superstitious story or rumour. *The Old Wives Tale* is the title of a 1595 play by George Peele and also a novel by Arnold Bennet (1908).

Talk   The talk of the town
The subject of envy, gossip or ridicule. If you are the talk of the town , the idea is that everybody is talking about what you have done or what you have got.

Talk   To talk through your hat   see **Hat**

Talk   To talk turkey   see **Turkey**

Talk   To talk your head off
To talk incessantly.

Tall   A tall story
A unbelievable tale. A complex lie or fiction.

Tall   Tall, dark and handsome
The ideal man, perhaps not always so in reality but the common use of this phrase suggests that this description is a stereotyped fantasy .

Tall   To walk tall   see **Walk**

Tan   To tan someone's hide
To scold someone severely. To spank a child. Leather or hide is tanned by curing it in tannin. For at least two hundred years hide has been comically used to refer to your bottom.

Tarbrush   A touch of the tarbrush
Having black racial characteristics. This is a racist description, a derogatory remark about someone whose parents may be of mixed race.

Tarred   To be tarred with the same brush
To be treated the same as someone else when your situation is different. Sheep were once treated for infections and sores using tar.

Tatters   Rags and tatters   see Rags

Tea   Not for all the tea in China   see China

Tea   Not my cup of tea   see Cup

Teach   You can't teach an old dog new tricks
You cannot change the attitude of someone who is set in their ways. This is an old proverb alluding to the way in which many animals (including humans to a certain extent) are more open to learning when they are young.

Teacup   A storm in a teacup   see Storm

Tear   A tear-jerker
A sad story or film with an emotional ending.

Tear   To tear a strip off someone
To scold someone in a humiliating fashion. This comes from the military custom of publicly depriving a disgraced soldier of his status by ripping off the fabric bands which indicate his rank from his uniform.

Tear   To tear your hair
To show extreme frustration or anger. The image suggests a frenzy.

Tears   A vale of tears   see Vale

Teeth   Armed to the teeth   see Armed

Teeth   By the skin of your teeth
Only just. By a tiny margin. The original phrase from the Bible (Job 19 : 20) means a narrow escape suggesting that you escape injury, say, by such a narrow measure that it is as thin as the skin on your teeth, that is, non-existent.

Teeth   To grit your teeth   see Grit

Teeth   To set your teeth on edge
To jar your nerves. To feel a sudden aversion to something. This useful phrase describes the sensation we feel when someone scrapes

their nails across a hard surface making an almost unbearable noise and making us clench our teeth. The phrase appears in the Bible: In those days they shall say no more, the fathers have eaten a sour grape and the children s teeth are set on edge (Jeremiah 31 : 29).

Tell   Tell it to the marines   see Marines

Tell   To tell tales
To reveal confidences. The full form of this phrase is To tell tales out of school alluding to children who tell their parents what another child did or said. Parents and teachers often tell children not to do this.

Tenterhooks   To be on tenterhooks
Kept in suspense or great expectation. Tenter-hooks were used to stretch cloth in a wooden frame.

Test   The acid test   see Acid

Test   To stand the test of time   see Time

Tether   To be at the end of your tether   see End

That   That is that
That is the end of it. That is all there is to it. That is the final word. This is a very common and useful phrase which used in context can effectively replace what would be much longer explanations.

There   To be all there   see All

Thereby   Thereby hangs a tale
That is the basis of a good story. This is an old expression which was frequently used in this form by Shakespeare and has since been preserved even though the word thereby is almost obsolete.

Thick   In the thick of it
In the middle of something. In trouble. At the centre of a situation. The thick probably alludes to dense undergrowth; the middle of a wood or forest.

Thick   Thick and fast
In dense numbers, coming in rapid succession. The clumsiness of any definition of this phrase demonstrates its usefulness. The phrase has been in use since at least the sixteenth century.

Thick   Thick as thieves

Intimate. In close confidence. This old phrase alludes to the close plans and secrets that crooks might share. It has persisted for the appeal of both the image and the alliteration.

Thick   Through thick and thin

No matter what happens. Under any circumstances. There are many ways to interpret thick and thin in this phrase. Thick may allude to dense undergrowth which makes proceeding difficult. Thin , however, suggests that the phrase refers to times of plenty compared with times of poverty and hunger.

Thick   To have a thick skin

To be impervious to insult or criticism. The idea here is that the thicker your skin is the less sensitive it will be to minor irritation or injury. A rhinoceros for example cannot easily be injured even by bullets.

Thick   To lay it on thick

To flatter excessively or make excuses or punish. The phrase suggests that rather than just one layer of flattery, etc., we get extra doses. Perhaps this clich was originally an extension of the image of buttering up (flattering excessively).

Thin   The thin end of the wedge

The seemingly inconsequential beginning of something which will prove to be much more significant. A wedge used for splitting wood is a tapered piece of metal with a sharp point broadening to a thick head.

Thing   Just the thing

Perfect. Ideal. Exactly what is needed.

Thing   To have too much of a good thing

If you have something you like to excess you will spoil yourself or the pleasure will diminish. An older proverbial version of this phrase is: Enough is as good as a feast.

Thinking   Put your thinking cap on   see Cap

Third   The third degree

A thorough interrogation. An intense questioning, usually by the police. The Masons have a thorough examination of a member s qualifications if he seeks to become Master Mason, which means that he advances to the third degree. This is the most likely source of the term.

Thirty   Thirty pieces of silver   see Sold

Thorn   A thorn in your side
A grave nuisance or an annoying person. This appears in the Bible as a thorn in the flesh (Corinthians 12 : 7) which is a form sometimes still used.

Thrash   To thrash something out
To debate an issue in order to resolve or clarify it. This term comes from the process of thrashing or beating wheat to separate the useful part from the unwanted husks.

Threads   To pick up the threads
To resume where you left off or gradually to take up a line of argument or conversation. The allusion is to weaving, where you might have to stop to change the thread and then start where you left off.

Three   Three sheets to the wind
Drunk. In nautical terminology a sheet is the name given to a rope which holds a sail in place. If it is allowed to go slack the sail is said to go to the wind which renders it ineffective. So if three sails are left in this state the vessel will sail erratically like the stagger of a drunkard.

Throat   To cut your own throat
To ruin your own chances by making a bad mistake.

Throat   To jump down someone's throat
To confront someone suddenly and criticise what they have just said. The image is of attacking someone opportunistically when their mouth is open to say something, and suffocating their argument.

Through   Through and through
Completely.

Through   Through the mill   see Mill

Throw   To throw down the gauntlet
To challenge someone. The term is from the Middle Ages when a knight would challenge another to combat by throwing his chainmail glove to the ground.

Throw   To throw good money after bad   see Money

Throw   To throw out the baby with the bathwater   see Baby

Throw   To throw someone to the wolves   see Wolves

Throw   To throw your weight around   see Weight

Thumb   All thumbs

Clumsy with your hands. This is said when you have trouble using your fingers for picking something up.

Thumb   To be under someone's thumb

To be oppressed or dominated. This phrase has come to be used as a taunt to someone who is badgered by their partner. The idea is that you could be squashed at their whim.

Tick   To tick someone off

To tell someone off. The allusion is to ticking a list of misdemeanours or a list of those that misbehave as a teacher might do with unruly pupils.

Tick   What makes him or her tick?

What makes people do what they do or think the way they do, or what keeps them going? This is said when someone s motives are puzzling or when their stamina or enthusiasm is surprising. The image compares the person s mind with a clockwork motor.

Ticked   Tickled pink   see Pink

Ticket   That's the ticket

That s the way to do it! That s right. This phrase comes from the custom of issuing tickets to the needy which they could exchange for meals.

Tickle   To tickle someone's fancy

To attract someone.

Tide   To tide someone over a difficulty

To help someone (usually financially) throughout a period until their position improves. Tide is now obsolete as a verb, but it denotes a time period when seen as a noun in words such as Yuletide .

Tie   Old-school tie   see Old

Tie   To tie the knot

To get married. This has long been a term describing the contract of marriage. It may relate to the gypsy wedding tradition of tying a lock of the bride s hair together with a lock of the groom s as a symbol of matrimony.

Tiger   A paper tiger   see Paper

Tight   Tight as a drum

Very close fitting. Taut. The skin of a drum has to be stretched as tight as possible to get the greatest resonance.

Tight Tight as a tick

Mean and miserly, or drunk. Ticks are bloodsucking insects which are notoriously hard to remove from an animal s skin. The first meaning of the phrase makes the analogy with a miser and his money. The second meaning alludes to the capacity of a flea to gorge itself on blood like a drinker on alcohol.

Tighten To tighten your belt

To prepare for a period of economic hardship.

Till Till hell freezes over see Hell

Till Till the cows come home see Cows

Tilt Tilt at windmills

To take on impossible challenges. This is the favourite pastime of Cervantes *Don Quixote*, protagonist of the seventeenth-century classic. In one episode Quixote decides to do battle with thirty windmills which he sees as monstrous giants . Tilt is another term for duel or joust.

Tilt To ride or go at full tilt

At full speed, with strong determination. The term is from medieval jousting where a knight might charge his opponent at top speed, his weapon poised to strike.

Time A time warp

A situation or place which seems to have remained unchanged or backward for a long time. In the twentieth century the expression has become fashionable through fantasy and science-fiction tales which centre round characters in a time warp, or magical transfer from one period to another.

Time From time immemorial see Immemorial

Time In the nick of time see Nick

Time On borrowed time

Beyond a deadline. With dangerously little time left.

Time The time is ripe

This is the right point to do something. The analogy comparing maturing fruit or crops with the passage of time is an old one, often mentioned in Shakespeare s works.

Time The time of your life

A wonderful time, a high point in your memory.

Time   Time and again
Repeatedly. Over and over. The older version of this phrase is times and again , meaning several times and then again which more clearly suggests continuity.

Time   Time and tide wait for no man
Do not hesitate. You cannot halt the passage of time. Tide originally meant the same as time as it does in a few remaining forms such as Yuletide meaning Christmas time. Since the fifteenth century the form of the phrase has changed and tide has come to refer to the sea tide.

Time   Time flies
Time seems to move very quickly in retrospect. This proverbial expression often continues when you re having fun .

Time   Time will tell
Wait and see. The results will emerge eventually.

Time   To have time on your hands
To have spare time. To have little to do or to have some time to yourself.

Time   To kill time
To do something simply to allay boredom or fill in time before the next appointment or activity.

Time   To stand the test of time
To endure; to survive change. Time often represents both changes and challenges so it is easy to see why this phrase calls it a test .

Tip   The tip of the iceberg
Merely the very beginning of something much more significant. A tiny part of a much bigger phenomenon. Floating icebergs often protrude only a fraction above the water due to their weight, so all that we can see is the part above the surface. Thus the phrase is usually used in situations where the full extent of what is there is not at first apparent.

Tip   To tip the scales
To upset the balance, to sway the outcome in one direction.

Tit   Tit for tat
A blow for a blow. You get what you give. Both words in this phrase are obsolete terms meaning tug, jerk and tap . An older version of the phrase dating back to the fifteenth century is tip for tap .

To To the manner born   see **Manner**

Today Here today and gone tomorrow
Fleeting, transient.

Toe To toe the line   see **Party**

Tom Tom, Dick and Harry
Anyone. Nobody specific. Ordinary people. These names were all extremely common two centuries ago when the expression arose.

Tom Uncle Tom   see **Uncle**

Tommy Tommy rot
Nonsense, rubbish. The tommy shop was the company-owned store where workers in nineteenth-century workshops were forced to obtain goods as part of their wages. Such goods were often poor quality and expensive.

Tomorrow Tomorrow is another day
Things may change tomorrow. Let s wait and see what happens.

Tongue On the tip of your tongue
Something that you feel that you can remember but just cannot quite bring to mind. This is an example of a clich which is actually a very useful term for describing a phenomenon of human memory recall. Its usefulness is highlighted by the fact that psychologists studying memory use the term, sometimes abbreviating it to TOT, as there is no more concise description.

Tongue To bite your tongue
To restrain yourself from saying something.

Tongue To lose your tongue
To be rendered speechless or not know what to say. An adjunct to this phrase is the question asked of a child who will not speak: What s the matter? Has the cat got your tongue?

Tongue Tongue in cheek
Insincerely. With sarcasm. This expression comes from a facial gesture sometimes made to denote that you are not serious in the same way that you might use a wink.

Too Too good to be true   see **True**

Too Too little, too late   see **Little**

Too   Too many cooks   see Cooks

Too   Too many irons   see Irons

Too   Too much of a good thing   see Thing

Too   Too near the bone   see Near

Tooth   A sweet tooth   see Sweet

Tooth   Fight tooth and nail   see Fight

Tooth   Long in the tooth   see Long

Top   Over the top   see Over

Top   To be on top of the world
To be elated. To be at your happiest.

Top   To go over the top   see OTT

Top   Top brass   see Brass

Top   Top drawer   see Drawer

Topsy   Topsy-turvy
Upside down. The wrong way round. It is possible that topsy derives from top and so and turvy comes from the obsolete Old English word tearflian meaning to roll over. The phrase was already in use in its current form in Shakespeare s time.

Touch   A soft touch   see Soft

Touch   Touch and go
Uncertain. Close to disaster. This phrase may come from seafarers who would use it to describe situations of great potential danger such as when the keel of the boat touches the bottom or rocks but continues on its course.

Tough   A tough nut
A difficult and determined person.   See also Nut

Tour   To do the grand tour
To make a ceremonious visit or viewing of a place or country. In the seventeenth and eighteenth centuries it was fashionable among the wealthy to send their older sons on an educational tour of France, Switzerland, Italy and Germany for up to two years.

Towel   To throw in the towel

To concede or surrender. This expression comes from boxing where a towel or sponge was sometimes thrown into the ring by the loser s side to signify surrender.

Tower   A tower of strength

A person who supports others in time of need. This image comes from Tennyson s *Ode on the Death of the Duke of Wellington* (1852) in which he describes the duke as that tower of strength which stood four-square to all the winds that blew .

Town   To go out on the town

To go out drinking or dining or to see a show. The phrase is often said with a cynical tone when someone is seen to be out enjoying themselves.

Town   To go to town on something

To do something to the full. To overdo something. This expression is of American origin and probably alludes to the fact that rural settlers often lived at great distances from the nearest town, so that when they did go there it was necessary to stock up extensively with what would seem like an excess of supplies.

Town   To paint the town red   see Paint

Track   A good (or bad) track record

A person or a company s achievements or lack of them. In horse-racing a horse s track record is an important factor in predicting the odds. The phrase has only relatively recently come to be used about people, and even more recently about business. If a company has a good track record it is to be recommended.

Track   A one-track mind   see One

Track   Off the beaten track   see Beaten

Tracks   To make tracks

To depart, to leave hurriedly. This expression arose in America in the nineteenth century and alludes to the tracks or footprints left by an animal which a hunter might follow.

Trader   A rogue trader   see Rogue

Train   A train of thought

The mental flow of an idea or series of connected ideas. Thomas Hobbes most probably invented this term. It appears in his *Leviathan* (1651) and he defines it there as mental discourse . It is such a descriptive and useful phrase that it has not only stuck but has few rivals as succinct. This is another example of a clich usefully describing a hard-to-define mental phenomenon.

Tread   To tread on someone's corns   see Corns

Triangle   The eternal triangle   see Eternal

Trick   That will do the trick
That s just what is needed. That will serve the purpose.

Tricks   A bag of tricks   see Bag

Tried   Tried and true
Repeatedly tested and reliable. This phrase arose in the 1950s in *A Fable* by William Faulkner.

Trip   To trip the light fantastic
To dance. This expression comes from John Milton s *L Allegro* (1632): Come, and trip it as ye go, on the light fantastick toe.

Trojan   To work like a Trojan
To work very hard. The Trojans were made out to be patriotic and industrious people by Homer in the *Iliad* and Virgil in the *Aeneid*.

Trooper   To swear like a trooper   see Swear

Trousers   To wear the trousers
To be the person in charge, usually within a couple. The implication is that this ought to be the man, but the expression is mainly used when it is the woman who rules.

True   Too good to be true
Amazingly fortunate or suspiciously good. This phrase is often used when a result is unexpectedly good and you suspect that there is a hidden catch.

True   True blue
Strongly loyal, or a loyal person. This was originally the name given to a deep blue cloth dye which did not lose its colour, hence the link with constancy. The Presbyterians of Scotland used the term in the seventeenth century, then the Whigs did so and then the Tories (blue being the official colour of the Conservative Party).

Trumpet   To blow your own trumpet
To give yourself praise, to boast. This is a very old phrase stemming from Roman times.

Trumps   To turn up trumps

To produce something good when it matters most. To bring good fortune. Trump cards in many card games are ones which win over other cards.

Truth   The gospel truth   see **Gospel**

Truth   The naked truth   see **Naked**

Truth   The truth will out

The secret will be revealed eventually. This phrase was in common use by the sixteenth century.

Truth   To be economical with the truth   see **Economical**

Truth   To tell you the truth

Honestly. This is such an over-used phrase that it no longer has any relevance to the truth, but simply allows someone to offer an opinion.

Tune   To change your tune

To change your behaviour for the better. To humble yourself. An alternative version of the phrase is: To sing a different tune.

Tunnel   Light at the end of the tunnel   see **Light**

Turkey   Cold turkey   see **Cold**

Turkey   To talk turkey

To come to the essential point. This comes from the story of a Red Indian and a white man sharing the spoils after a day s hunting: three crows and two wild turkeys. The white man cunningly allotted himself two birds, the turkeys, and offered the Red Indian three birds, the crows. The resentful Indian advised the other to stop talking about the number of birds and to talk turkey instead.

Turn   Done to a turn

Thoroughly cooked. This is reminiscent of the days when roasting meat had to be revolved on a spit over an open fire. When it no longer needed turning, it was cooked.

Turn   Not to turn a hair

To fail to react to something in any way. To take absolutely no notice. The implication of the phrase is that you are so unmoved or unimpressed that not only do you not turn round but not even a single hair moves.

Turn   One good turn deserves another   see **One**

Turn   Something turns you on
Something excites you, perhaps sexually. The image is of an electric switch.

Turn   To turn someone's head
To give someone false ideas of their potential, to seduce by flattery.

Turn   To turn the corner
To overcome a crisis or an illness and be close to a solution or to full recovery.

Turn   To turn the other cheek   see **Cheek**

Turn-up   A turn-up for the books   see **Book**

Turtle   To turn turtle
To capsize or end up in a position of helplessness. When a turtle or tortoise is turned on its back it cannot easily right itself and remains stuck.

Twain   And never the twain shall meet   see **Never**

Twiddle   To twiddle your thumbs
To be bored. To fidget while you have nothing to do or while you are waiting for something.

Twilight   A twilight zone   see **Zone**

Twinkling   In the twinkling of an eye
Very quickly. In an instant. This phrase comes from the Bible: We shall not all sleep, but we shall all be changed, In a moment, in the twinkling of an eye (Corinthians 15 : 51—2).

Two   To put two and two together   see **Put**

U

U U and non-U

Acceptable and unacceptable. This term represents a distinction between what was seen to be upper class and not upper class in speech and social etiquette. It was popularised by the writer Nancy Mitford in an article she wrote in 1955.

U U turn

A sudden complete reversal of intentions, plans or opinions. Though this term is still primarily used in its literal sense of a 180¡ turn, it is often used in politics to refer to a sudden radical change in policy.

Ugly Ugly as sin

Repulsive, highly unattractive. It dates back at least to the seventeenth century.

Ugly Ugly duckling see Duckling

Umbrage To take umbrage

To be offended at something. The word umbrage comes from the Latin *umbra* meaning shade . The phrase originally meant to feel overshadowed.

Unalloyed Unalloyed bliss

Pure pleasure. Unspoilt enjoyment. Alloyed metal is any metal composed of two or more base metals. For example brass is an alloy of copper and zinc.

Uncle A Dutch uncle see Dutch

Uncle Uncle Tom

A black person who is seen by black rights activists as betraying the cause by being subservient to white people. The name comes from that of a character in Harriet Beecher Stowe s *Uncle Tom s Cabin* (1852). The character was based on a slave who was later ordained and presented to Queen Victoria.

Uncrowned The uncrowned king (or queen)

Someone whose prowess or popularity is undoubted though perhaps not officially recognised.

Under   To take someone under your wing   see **Wing**

Under   Under a cloud   see **Cloud**

Under   Under someone's thumb   see **Thumb**

Under   Under the weather   see **Weather**

Under   Under your belt   see **Belt**

Underbelly   The soft underbelly
The vulnerable or weak part. This phrase comes from animals that can only easily be wounded by attacking the relatively soft skin on the belly. In folklore dragons are said to have only one weak point and this lies on the underbelly. The phrase has been extended to refer to people, and in particular plans or arguments or policies.

Unguarded   In an unguarded moment
Suddenly or unexpectedly.

Unhinged   To be unhinged
To be mentally disturbed. To lose your normal balance of mind. The image is of a door becoming unstable after a hinge comes loose.

University   Redbrick university   see **Redbrick**

University   The university of life
Experience. This is often said jokingly, referring to the fact that people often acquire valuable knowledge through experience and not through formal education.

Unsung   Unsung heroes   see **Heroes**

Untold   Untold riches
Enormous wealth.

Unturned   To leave no stone unturned   see **Leave**

Unvarnished   The unvarnished truth
The simple facts, without attempts to make them sound better.

Unwashed   The great unwashed   see **Great**

Up   On the up and up
Improving.

Up   Up a gum tree   see **Gum**

Up Up and about
Out of bed and moving around, particularly after an illness.

Up Up for grabs see **Grabs**

Up Up in arms see **Arms**

Up Up the spout see **Spout**

Up Up to scratch see **Scratch**

Up Up to the hilt see **Hilt**

Up Up to your eyes (or ears) see **Eyes**

Up Up your sleeve see **Sleeve**

Uphill Uphill struggle
A task or problem which seems to get increasingly difficult or demoralising.

Uppermost What is uppermost in your mind
The main thing that you are thinking or worrying about.

Uppers To be on your uppers
To be extremely poor, to be driven to poverty. Uppers refers to the top part of your shoes as opposed to the soles which, it is suggested, have completely worn through and you cannot afford to mend them.

Ups Ups and downs
High points and low points. Happy moments and sad moments. This is a useful phrase for graphically describing the familiar fluctuations of fortune.

Upset To upset the apple cart see **Apple cart**

Uptake To be quick on the uptake
Working something out quickly. Fast to react or take an opportunity. Though the compound verb to take up is still in use with more or less the same meaning, the word uptake is obsolete other than in this set phrase.

V

V   To give the V sign
To indicate scornful dismissal by holding up the first two fingers of the right hand in a V shape. One explanation attested by contemporary accounts is that it comes from events at the Battle of Agincourt where the French, confident of victory, threatened to cut off the bow-fingers of all the English archers. When the English won their archers held up their bow-fingers in a V sign of triumph. However the writer Germaine Greer suggests that the sign is meant to represent part of the female anatomy.

Vain   To take someone's name in vain   see Name

Vale   Vale of tears
The world. Life seen as full of sorrow and pain. The image of the world as a vale or valley is old and suggested in several psalms. In *Confessions* (1864), Robert Browning uses the phrase vale of tears to describe one way of seeing the world.

Van   To be in the van
To be leading the way, in fashion for example. The vanguard was the leading platoon of soldiers in an army, so the term came to be used to refer to leaders in anything.

Variety   Variety is the spice of life
Greater choice or diversity makes life interesting. Spices are used to make bland foods more interesting, so variety is said to have the same effect on life.

Veil   To take the veil
To become a nun. This phrase refers to the traditional headdress which nuns have to assume on taking their vows.

Velvet   An iron hand in a velvet glove   see Iron

Vengeance   With a vengeance
With a grudge. Determined to get revenge. This phrase is often used when someone does something with furious determination.

Vent Vent your spleen
To let out your anger. To shout angrily. The spleen was long thought to be the seat of anger.

Venture To venture an opinion
To offer your thoughts tentatively on a subject or problem.

Verse To quote chapter and verse see **Chapter**

Version Watered-down version see **Watered**

Vested Vested interest see **Interest**

Vicious A vicious circle
A situation in which one action will cause a difficulty which in turn will cause another problem and so on. The term comes from formal logic where it means a failure to make a connection between premise and conclusion.

View A bird's eye view see **Bird**

View To take a dim view of something see **Take**

Violet A shrinking violet
A modest or shy person with hidden qualities. Violets are known for their beauty and symbolise modesty because they grow in sheltered and hidden places.

Viper To nourish a viper in your bosom
To trust and befriend someone who will later betray you.

Virgin Virgin soil / territory / ground
Land that has never been cultivated.

Virtue To make a virtue of necessity see **Necessity**

Vital Vital statistics
A woman s bust, waist and hip measurements. The true meaning of this term relates to population statistics — births, marriages and deaths — but the more recent meaning has progressed from being a joke about the ideal figure for a woman to a common way of referring to the measurements.

Voice The still small voice
Conscience, a message from God as to how to act. This is a biblical quotation from Kings (19: 11) which speaks of how Elijah was given a message from the Lord by a voice: . . . and after the earthquake a fire; but the Lord was not in the fire; and after the fire, a still small voice .

Voice   To voice an opinion

To say either what you think about something or to say what others might think.

Void   Null and void

Not valid. Not legally binding. Useless.

Volumes   To speak volumes

To be highly informative or telling, like a thick book on the subject. This is often said of a person s habits or clothing when plenty can be gleaned from their appearance.

Vote   To vote with your feet

To show strong disapproval by leaving. To walk out on something as a sign of your feelings.

W

Wages   The wages of sin
The consequences of doing wrong. The Bible says the wages of sin is
death (Romans 6 : 23).

Wagon   To hitch your wagon to a star   see **Hitch**

Wait   To wait on someone hand and foot   see **Hand**

Walk   To walk on air   see **Air**

Walk   To walk over someone
To show complete disregard or disrespect for someone.

Walk   To walk tall
To be proud and bold or courageous. The phrase alludes to the
straight-backed posture which we assume with the neck outstretched
and head held high.

Walk   To walk the plank
To be cast out or fired or to go to some terrible fate. Pirates in the
seventeenth century used this as a form of execution. The captive or
traitor was made to walk off the deck along a plank over the sea with his
hands bound.

Walking   A walking encyclopaedia (or dictionary)
A person with a wide general knowledge.

Walkover   A walkover
An easy victory. The image suggests that the victors in a game or a
battle simply walk across their flattened opponents.

Wall   Off the wall   see **Off**

Wall   To have your back against (or to) the wall   see **Back**

Wallflower   To be a wallflower
To be unadventurous or overcautious or unwanted. This term refers to
a plant which grows on or near old walls. It then came to be used as a
term for a woman who sat out instead of dancing.

War   All-out war
Total warfare. A battle using all resources to their full extent. All-out signifies that all the troops are on the battlefield and out of the trenches. The term has lost much of its strength and might now be used even with reference to a domestic dispute.

War   An old war horse
A veteran soldier. The allusion is to the charger used in warfare.

Warm   A warm welcome
A friendly greeting. This phrase is very often used in television by chat-show hosts, for example, to introduce their guests.

Warm   To warm the cockles of your heart   see Cockles

Warp   Time warp   see Time

Warpath   To be on the warpath
To be ready to fight or in an aggressive mood. American Red Indians called their route to a battle the path of war.

Warts   Warts and all
Giving all details truthfully including the smallest defects. These words come from the instructions given by Oliver Cromwell (1599—1658) to Sir Peter Lely who painted his portrait. Cromwell refused to pay for a flattering picture of himself and demanded roughnesses, pimples, warts and everything as you see me .

Wash   It'll all come out in the wash
It will all turn out well in the end. The problems will all be removed like dirt in a laundry.

Wash   The story won't wash
It will not be believed. That isn t a good enough excuse or alibi.

Wash   To wash your dirty linen in public   see Dirty

Wash   To wash your hands of something
To remove or distance yourself from a matter completely. To leave it to other people to do. In the Bible (Matthew 27 : 24) Pontius Pilate washed his hands before the multitude to demonstrate his unwillingness to be involved in the trial of Jesus.

Wash-out   To be a wash-out
A failure. A fiasco. The term comes from ships on which naval signals were given on a slate which was washed when the message had been sent.

Washed   To be all washed up
To be exhausted. To have no energy left. Washed out has the same meaning but is more commonly used in America.

Waste   To waste your breath   see **Breath**

Waste   Waste not, want not
If you are careful with your resources you might save yourself from going without. This is an old proverb.

Watched   A watched pot never boils   see **Pot**

Water   Head above water
Solvent, out of trouble. The analogy is with bathing when you are not in danger if you keep your head out of the water.

Water   It won't hold water
It will not bear close examination. It is not well thought out.

Water   Of the first water   see **First**

Water   To be in deep water
In trouble, having trouble coping. The allusion is to swimming in waters that are too deep with regard to your swimming ability.

Water   To get into hot water
To get yourself into trouble and bring blame upon yourself. The allusion is presumably to the hot water in a cooking pot.

Water   To throw cold water on something   see **Cold**

Water   Water under the bridge
Something that is in the past. It has long since finished or ceased to have importance. An older version of this phrase with a very similar meaning clarifies the analogy: much water has flowed under the bridges means that a long time has elapsed. The phrase is often used for situations where nothing was done in response to something important at the time it happened, but it is too far in the past to do anything now.

Watered   A watered-down version
A less intense or dramatic version, like a drink that is less potent after it has been diluted.

Waterloo   To meet your Waterloo
To be finally defeated as was Napoleon at the Battle of Waterloo (1815).

Way   The way of all flesh   see Flesh

Way   To have ways and means
To have resources or methods to do what needs to be done. The Committee of Ways and Means is a group of MPs which deals with taxation and the upkeep of public services.

We   We are not amused   see Amused

We   We shall not look upon his like again
We will never know another person like him. He was unique. This is said in admiration of a dead person and is taken from *Hamlet* (Act 1, Sc. 2) where the prince speaks of his dead father.

Weak   As weak as a kitten   see Kitten

Wear   To wear out your welcome   see Welcome

Wear   To wear the trousers   see Trousers

Wear   To wear two hats   see Hats

Weasel   Weasel words
Words used to mislead or conceal the truth deliberately. Stewart Chaplin defines the term in his article of 1900: Weasel words are words , that is, all words can be misinterpreted.

Weather   To keep a weather eye open
To watch out for trouble. The phrase was used by sailors and coast guards for being alert to changing weather conditions and is so defined in the *Sailor s Word Book* (1867).

Weather   To weather a storm
To stand up to a particularly bad situation or period.

Weather   Under the weather
In a time of difficulties, unwell.

Wedge   The thin end of the wedge   see Thin

Week   A week is a long time in politics   see Politics

Weigh   To weigh in the balance
To test something out. To scrutinise something to see if it is fair or correct. The balance refers to scales for weighing, which are also a symbol of justice.

Weigh   To weigh your words

To speak cautiously, to assess the impact of what you say. The expression has been in use for centuries and appears in the fourteenth-century *Ayenbite of Inwyt*.

Weight   To throw your weight around

To use or abuse the strength of your influence or position of power.

Welcome   To wear out (or outstay) your welcome

To stay longer than your hosts would like. To do something to make yourself unwelcome.

Well   All well and good

Fine. This is often used in the context of a reproof, such as: That s all well and good, but what about . . . ?

Well   Well he (or she) would, wouldn't he (or she)!

Naturally he (or she) would react like that! These were the words of Mandy Rice-Davies in 1963. As a prostitute involved in the Profumo scandal she was told in court that Lord Astor denied involvement with her. With this rejoinder she made it clear that in her opinion he was not to be believed.

Well-heeled   To be well-heeled

To be wealthy or prosperous. The allusion is to the state of repair of your shoes. Compare this with the opposites down at heel and on your uppers .

Well-nigh   To be well-nigh impossible

To be impossible or nearly impossible. The word nigh comes from Old English and means near , and well in this context means very .

Wend   To wend your way

To go, to venture towards. Wend in Old English is of the same origin as wind (turn).

West   To go west

To die or become lost. More recently the phrase has come to imply going mad or losing your senses. The allusion is to the sun which travels west throughout the day and then sets.

Wet   A wet blanket   see **Blanket**

Wet   To wet your whistle   see **Whistle**

Wet   Wet behind the ears   see **Ears**

Wham   Wham bam, thank you, ma'am

A short and purely sexual encounter with a woman. This phrase is used to condemn the indifference shown by a man to a woman after they have had sex.

Whammy   A double whammy   see **Double**

Wheat   To separate the wheat from the chaff

To distinguish what is valuable from what is worthless. The expression is from traditional farming in which winnowing, separating the husk from the grain, was done by hand.

Wheel   To put your shoulder to the wheel

To apply yourself to hard work. The expression arose in the seventeenth century when carts stuck in rutted roads had to be pushed out by men putting their shoulders hard against the embedded wheel.

Wheel   To reinvent the wheel   see **Reinvent**

Wheel   To wheel and deal   see **Deal**

Wheels   Wheels within wheels

Different levels of (increasing) complexity. The term appears in the Bible in a tale of four creatures whose appearance and their work was . . . a wheel within a wheel (Ezekiel 1 : 16), meaning that they acted as one under God, but each had their own complex lives.

When   When all's said and done

After all, in the end, in conclusion. When all is considered.

When   When in Rome do as the Romans do   see **Rome**

When   When my ship comes in

When I make my fortune. The allusion is to a merchant who sends out a ship to bring back a cargo of valuable and exotic goods.

When   When push comes to shove   see **Push**

When   When the cat's away   see **Cat**

When   When the chips are down   see **Chips**

Whip   The whip hand

Control over someone. To have hold of the hand in which someone has a whip means that they are unable to strike back at you.

Whip   To have a whip round

A quick collection of money from people as donations to a cause.

Whipping   A whipping boy

A scapegoat. At one time if a prince had done wrong he had to have a whipping boy to take physical punishment in his place.

Whirlwind   To reap the whirlwind

To face worse consequences for your actions than they deserve. The full saying clarifies the analogy: Sow the wind [like a seed] and reap the whirlwind [like a harvest].

Whistle   A whistle-stop tour

A quick visit to several locations *en route*. In America it was common for a politician to visit many small towns on a campaign tour. Many of the towns were too small to be regular train stops so a signal (whistle) was given to stop at the station and the politician would speak from the back of the train.

Whistle   To blow the whistle on someone   see Blow

Whistle   To wet your whistle

To have a drink. This phrase has been used since at least the fourteenth century and probably refers to the lips pursed like a whistle.

Whistle   To whistle for it

Not to get something. To try in vain for something. It was an old superstition among sailors that if the wind died it could be brought back by whistling. The current meaning of the phrase reflects the futility of this custom.

Whistle   To whistle in the dark

To be optimistic or cheerful in a bad situation. When someone is alone on a dark night they might whistle to allay fear.

White   A white elephant   see Elephant

White   A white lie   see Lie

White   To show the white feather

To show signs of cowardice. In cockfighting a bird with a white feather in its tail was seen as inferior.

White   To show the white flag

To surrender. The white flag is an internationally recognised signal of surrender.

White   White as a sheet

Terrified, pale with fright.

Whitewash   To whitewash a story
To cover up a damaging story. Whitewash is the thin paint used to cover dirty or marred brick or stone surfaces.

Who   Who he?
Who is this? I do not know this person. The question has become a ritual joke in papers and magazines, especially *Private Eye*. The founder editor of *The New Yorker*, H. W. Ross, used to scribble these words at the end of any articles containing names he did not recognise.

Whodunit   A whodunit
A story from the genre of detective or murder-mystery thrillers, especially of the type written by Agatha Christie, in which the tale begins with a murder and continues as a guessing game to determine the culprit until the truth is revealed at the end. The term comes from the colloquial expression: Who done [did] it?

Whole   To go the whole hog   see Hog

Why   The whys and the wherefores
The details. The explanation. Wherefore is an archaic term meaning why .

Wicked   No rest for the wicked   see Rest

Wicket   On a sticky wicket
In a weak or tricky situation that requires skill or judgement to overcome. The allusion is to cricket in which a wet or sticky playing surface causes the batsman problems when the ball bounces off it towards him.

Wild   Call of the wild   see Call

Wild   To sow your wild oats   see Oats

Wild   Wild horses could not make me
Nothing could force me to do it.

Wildcat   A wildcat strike
An unofficial or impromptu strike. The term wildcat usually refers to a person s reckless or unrestrained behaviour.

Wildfire   To spread like wildfire
To become rapidly and widely known or successful. The term wildfire is from Old English and originally referred to fast-spreading and erratic fire in a forest, usually started during a clearing operation and a constant source of anxiety in Anglo-Saxon times. It is now

almost exclusively used to refer to anything that spreads rapidly among people.

Willy-nilly   To do something willy-nilly

Commonly thought to mean to do something chaotically, carelessly or anyhow. More correctly, to be forced to do something whether one likes it or not. This term arose as a distortion of the Latin *nolens volens* meaning willing or not, which was translated as will-he nill-he to preserve the rhyme. It is now somewhat antiquated, but was common in the nineteenth century.

Wind   It's an ill wind   see Ill

Wind   Second wind

To proceed with new vigour after a difficult start. It is a common experience in physical activity to find sudden strength after warming up initially.

Wind   The wind of change

A new tide of opinion. A trend towards a new view. This phrase was used by Harold Macmillan in a speech to the South African parliament in 1960 to refer to changes in political thinking in and about Africa.

Wind   There is something in the wind

Something is about to happen. Something is being plotted or prepared.

Wind   Three sheets to the wind   see Three

Wind   To get the wind up

To get scared or nervous about something.

Wind   To get wind of something

To hear of something. To learn some news of something that is going to happen. This phrase alludes to a dog s ability to track things that it cannot see from their scent in the air.

Wind   To know which way the wind blows

To know what is going on. To be aware. This phrase probably comes from sailors for whom it was essential to know the direction of the wind.

Wind   To sail close to the wind   see Sail

Wind   To take the wind out of someone's sails

To discourage someone or reduce their pride or enthusiasm. The sails of a windmill can be immobilised when the miller wishes to stop grinding.

Windfall   To have a windfall

To get an unexpected bonus without any effort, like a piece of fruit which is blown from the tree by the wind and so does not have to be picked.

Window   Out the window   see Out

Window   Window dressing

Putting on an act or being dramatic in order to present yourself in a favourable light. The true meaning of this phrase is to create a display in a shop window to attract customers.

Wine   Wine, women and song

Merriment. Hedonistic pleasures.

Wing   To take someone under your wing

To protect someone, or to adopt someone as your apprentice or dependant. The allusion is to a bird protecting its young and keeping them warm by nestling them into its feathers.

Wings   To clip someone's wings   see Clip

Wink   To tip someone the wink

To give someone a subtle or secret hint.

Winkle   To winkle something out

To extract something or find something out. This term comes from the way in which winkles (a type of shellfish) are eaten by picking the flesh out of the shell with a pin.

Winks   Forty winks   see Forty

Winter   A winter of discontent   see Discontent

Wipe   To wipe the floor with someone

To treat someone with complete disregard or to defeat someone outright.

Wishful   Wishful thinking

Unwarranted optimism or vain hope.

Witch   A witch hunt

Victimisation and persecution of people of different views from your own. For long periods of history many people including church figures believed that witches lived among normal people, and several episodes have been well documented of systematic victimisation of single women who were tried in such a way that they could not survive no matter what the outcome. In politics the term is used to describe the searching out and exposing of opponents supposed misdemeanours.

With To be with it
To be aware of what is going on; to be alert. This is often used in the negative to describe a senile person or anyone in a state of drowsiness or confusion.

With With a vengeance see Vengeance

With With all due respect see Respect

Within To be within an ace of see Ace

Without Without a leg to stand on see Leg

Wits To be at your wits' end
To be driven mad. To be intensely annoyed or frustrated. Wits refers to sanity or wisdom. The phrase suggests that you are on the point of losing your sanity.

Wits To have your wits about you
To be shrewd, alert or cautious. Here wits refers to your intelligence or wisdom.

Wits To live by your wits
To live by your ingenuity and presence of mind.

Wives An old wives' tale see Tale

Woe Woe betide
Be warned. Watch out. This was originally a curse to warn that calamity would happen. Betide is Old English meaning occur or befall . It is now used as a warning, but usually in jest as it has lost its strength of meaning through abundant use in fairy tales.

Wolf A wolf in sheep's clothing
A person who turns out to be a danger or a menace after seeming harmless or appearing innocent.

Wolf A wolf whistle
A whistle made by a man in admiration of a woman, usually one he does not know.

Wolf   To cry wolf   see Cry

Wolves   To throw someone to the wolves
To make a scapegoat of someone to avoid harm or criticism. To sacrifice someone to save yourself.

Wonders   Wonders will never cease
How amazing. What a surprise. This is nearly always said sarcastically when something predictable happens.

Wood   Not to see the wood for the trees
To miss the obvious by looking for something more complicated than necessary.

Woods   Out of the woods   see Out

Wool   Dyed in the wool   see Dyed

Wool   To pull the wool over someone's eyes   see Pull

Wool-gathering   To be wool-gathering
To let your mind wander from what you are doing. It was once common in rural communities to send children out to collect scraps of wool for weaving from hedges where sheep had scratched; so the analogy is with the children wandering along hedgerows seemingly aimlessly.

Word   A buzz-word
A catchword or slogan.

Word   By word of mouth
Information passed from person to person rather than written or broadcast.

Word   In a word
To summarise. In brief, the answer is . . .

Word   To put in a good word for someone   see Put

Words   Actions speak louder than words   see Actions

Words   To eat your words
To take back what you said. To be forced to retract a statement by something that embarrassingly proves you wrong.

Words   To take the words out of someone's mouth
To say exactly what someone else was about to say.

Work   All in a day's work   see All

Work   To have your work cut out
To have a lot of work to do. To have difficulty in getting everything done. Originally, cut out implied outlined or detailed but the meaning of the phrase has shifted over time.

Work   To work your fingers to the bone
To work extremely hard. To toil or struggle for long periods of time. This powerful image has lost much of its strength through over-use.

Works   To give someone the works
To attack someone verbally or physically, or to entertain someone lavishly with no expense spared. This phrase is of American origin.

World   On top of the world   see Top

World   Out of this world
Amazing. Fantastic or extraordinary. Originally this meant something completely foreign or unknown, but has come to refer to anything similarly striking.

World   The world and his wife
Just everybody. An enormous number and variety of people, or a way of sarcastically saying too many people .

World   To do someone the world of good
To be extremely beneficial. The world is used as a measure of power and extent.

World   To think the world owes one a living
To have the attitude that you do not have to work and that you should be looked after.

Worm   The worm has turned
The passive or coy one has decided to resist or attack.

Worm   To worm your way out of something
To get out of an obligation or duty by sly methods. The allusion is to a slippery worm wriggling free from something.

Worms   To open up a can of worms   see Can

Worn   Worn to a frazzle   see Frazzle

Worship   To worship the ground someone walks on
To have such strong admiration or love for someone that you think they cannot do wrong. The allusion is to followers of saints or popes who might literally kiss or bless the ground where their mentor stood.

Worst   If the worst comes to the worst
Assuming that everything goes wrong. In the worst possible circumstances.

Wrack   To go to wrack and ruin   see **Rack**

Wreak   To wreak havoc   see **Play**

Write   Nothing to write home about   see **Nothing**

Writing   The writing on the wall
A sign of impending disaster or danger. In the Bible, the night before Belshazzar s death a mysterious hand appears and writes his fate on the wall (Daniel 5 : 5—31).

Wrong   A wrong 'un
A cheat or a swindler.

X   Mr X
A person with a mysterious identity. An unnamed person. The use of the letter X to denote an undisclosed identity perhaps stems from the days of widespread illiteracy when a person signing an official document might simply mark it with an X.

X   Triple X
Highly censored. Top strength. This term was initially just a rating for the most sexually explicit or violent films, but the term has come to be used to label anything that is extreme or *risqu* .

X   X amount
An unknown quantity. An unspecified amount.

X-Ray   X-Ray specs
Supernatural vision. Uncanny perceptiveness. The idea of spectacles with which you can see through solid objects probably emerged from comic books. The idea is an attractive one, made more so by the rhyme of the phrase.

Y

Yarn   To spin a yarn
To tell a story or an elaborate lie. A yarn is a length of thread which used to be spun by hand. The phrase suggests that the story is hand-made rather than true. This phrase dates back at least to the seventeenth century.

Yawning   A yawning gap or gulf
An enormous obstacle or difference of opinion. The use of the word gulf to refer to any difficulty is at least as old as the Bible. The image of a yawn adds the comparison of a wide-open mouth, though the phrase has lost its strength through over-use.

Year   A year and a day
A long time. A test period. This is an old legal time measurement which was used by the Crown either in penalty (a felon s property might be withheld for this period) or in deciding a verdict (if an injured person died within this time then the assailant might be guilty of murder).

Year   From the year dot
Right from the beginning. For a very long time.

Year   Year in year out
Every year. Always, without fail.

Years   It puts years on me
It makes me look or feel older. This might be said about a hairstyle or an unflattering item of clothing or a trying ordeal.

Yen   To have a yen for something
To have an urge or a strong desire for something. Yen is from Chinese and relates to opium which is a highly addictive drug.

Yeoman   Yeoman service
Loyal and diligent work or assistance. The yeomen gained this reputation for their service to the English army. The phrase dates back to the sixteenth century.

Yes   Yes and no
Partially. Not entirely. There is an advantage and a disadvantage.

Yesterday   I was not born yesterday   see **Born**

Yoke   To shake off the yoke
To relieve yourself of a burden.

Yorick   Alas poor Yorick   see **Alas**

Young   A young fogey
A precocious youth. A young person who acts like an elderly person. See **Old fogey**.

Yours   Yours truly
Me. Myself. This is a traditional term for signing off a letter and has become a way of referring to yourself.

Yourself   To keep yourself to yourself
To be careful not to confide too much in others, nor to interfere in other people s affairs.

Yuppie   A yuppie
A young fashionable ambitious person. The word was invented as a noun in the 1980s from the initials YUP standing for young upwardly mobile person . It quickly became an adjective to describe the values and habits of such people. As the 1980s and 1990s began to be dubbed greedy and selfish years yuppie acquired an increasingly negative connotation.

Z

Zero   Zero hour
The crucial moment. The point when your fate will be determined. In World War I this was a military term for the point at which an attack or operation would be launched so that all subsequent stages of the plan could easily be time-co-ordinated from zero.

Zone   A twilight zone
An indistinct boundary area, either physical or abstract. The term has been in use since the start of the twentieth century but became popular when used with reference to US politics in the 1980s. Bureaucrats with an ill-defined role were said to occupy a twilight zone.